Pathways to God 2

Junior Certificate

KEVIN MULLALLY

Theological advisor: Dr Anthony Draper, All Hallows College, Dublin

GILL & MACMILLAN

Dedicated to the students and staff of Kylemore College, Ballyfermot

Gill & Macmillan Ltd
Hume Avenue
Park West
Dublin 12
with associated companies throughout the world
www.gillmacmillan.ie

ISBN-13: 978 07171 4019 0
ISBN-10: 0 7171 4019 9

Design, typesetting and print origination by Anú Design, Tara
Colour reproduction by Typeform Repro

*The paper used in this book is made from the wood pulp of managed forests.
For every tree felled, at least one tree is planted,
thereby renewing natural resources.*

Contents

Section 1

Section 2

Section 3

Section 4

Section 5

Acknowledgments

Special words of thanks to all those who supported and encouraged me over the time of writing these two books, especially my family; Mam, Dad, Niall and Conor, Cathy, Robbie, Fran, Tom, Sinead, Emma, Diarmuid, Siobhan, Amanda, Paul K., Therese, Paul T., Fiona, Joe, Piaras, Sean and Gottfried, and Fr Tony Draper.

Photo Credits

For permission to reproduce photographs and other material the author and publisher gratefully acknowledge the following:

38, 41BL, 89, 145, 165TL, 196C, 208T, 208B, 230, 231 © Alamy Images; 255T © The Allen Library; THE ART ARCHIVE: 15 © Private Collection/Dagli Orti, 36C © Bibliotheque Universitaire Geneva/Dagli Orti, 41BR © City Mission London/Eileen Tweedy; BRIDGEMAN ART LIBRARY: 5 © Staatliche Kunstsammlungen Dresden, 29 © Museo Capitolino, Rome, Italy, 182 © Santa Maria della Grazie, Milan, Italy, 245 © Museum of Fine Arts, Houston, Texas, USA, Robert Lee Memorial Collection, gift of Sarah C. Blaffer; 98, 148T, 188T, 214C, 216T, 248L, 267, 270, 289 © Camera Press Ireland; CORBIS: 127L © Ricki Rosen, 127R © Marc Asnin, 148B © Danny Lehman, 208CB © Peter Turnley, 214B © Hans Georg Roth; 258T © Empics; 196T courtesy of the Garda Press Office; 36R, 41TR © Getty Images; 43, 137 © Imagefile Ireland; 196B courtesy of The Campaign for Nuclear Disarmament (www.cnduk.org); 167 courtesy of Irish Capuchin Archives; 212T © Irish Image Collection; 39L © Doug McKinlay/Lonely Planet Images; 41TL © Mary Evans Picture Library; 33T, 105, 127C, 158, 165BL, 258B, 297 © Reuters; 143, 188B, 212B, 248R © Rex Features; 33B, 36L, 39R, 41B, 118, 165R, 168, 170, 208CT, 209, 214T, 215, 216B, 244, 255B, 266, 272 © Topfoto

The author and publisher have made every effort to trace all copyright holders, but if any has been inadvertently overlooked we would be pleased to make the necessary arrangement at the first opportunity.

Section 1

The Spread of Christianity

- Recap on the Events of Jesus' Life
- The Ascension of Jesus into Heaven
- Pentecost

The Christian Community in Jerusalem

- Paul
- Paul's Conversion
- Paul's Journeys
- Paul's Letters

Christianity Grows and Splits

- The Split begins
- The Great Schism
- The Eastern Orthodox Church
- Protestants
- John Calvin / Martin Luther
- The Anglican Church today
- Protestant Churches

The Titles of Jesus

- Christ / Messiah
- Our Lord
- Son of God
- Son of Man

The Christian Community You Are In

- Time to Think and Pray

The Spread of Christianity

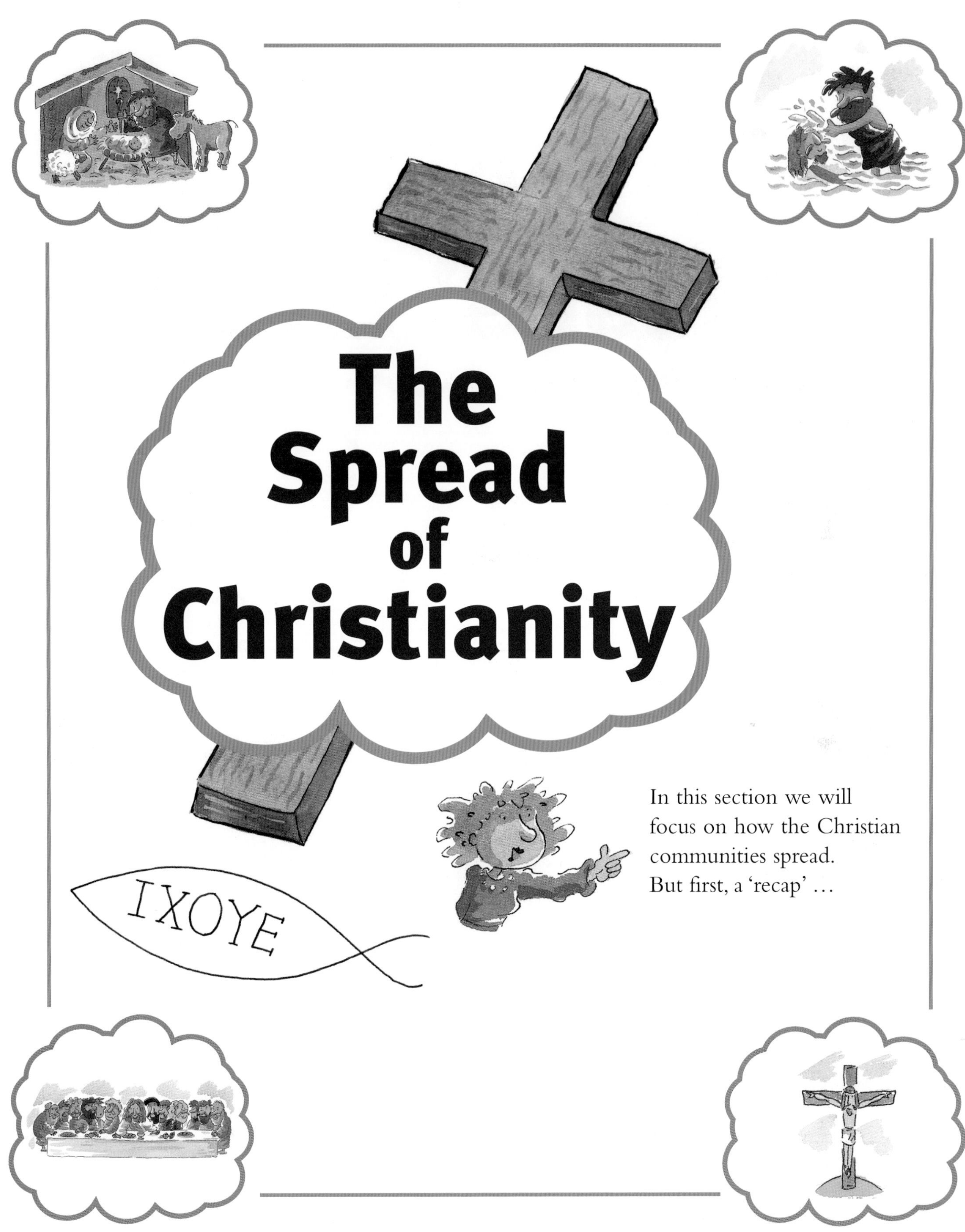

In this section we will focus on how the Christian communities spread. But first, a 'recap' …

Recap on the Events of Jesus' Life!

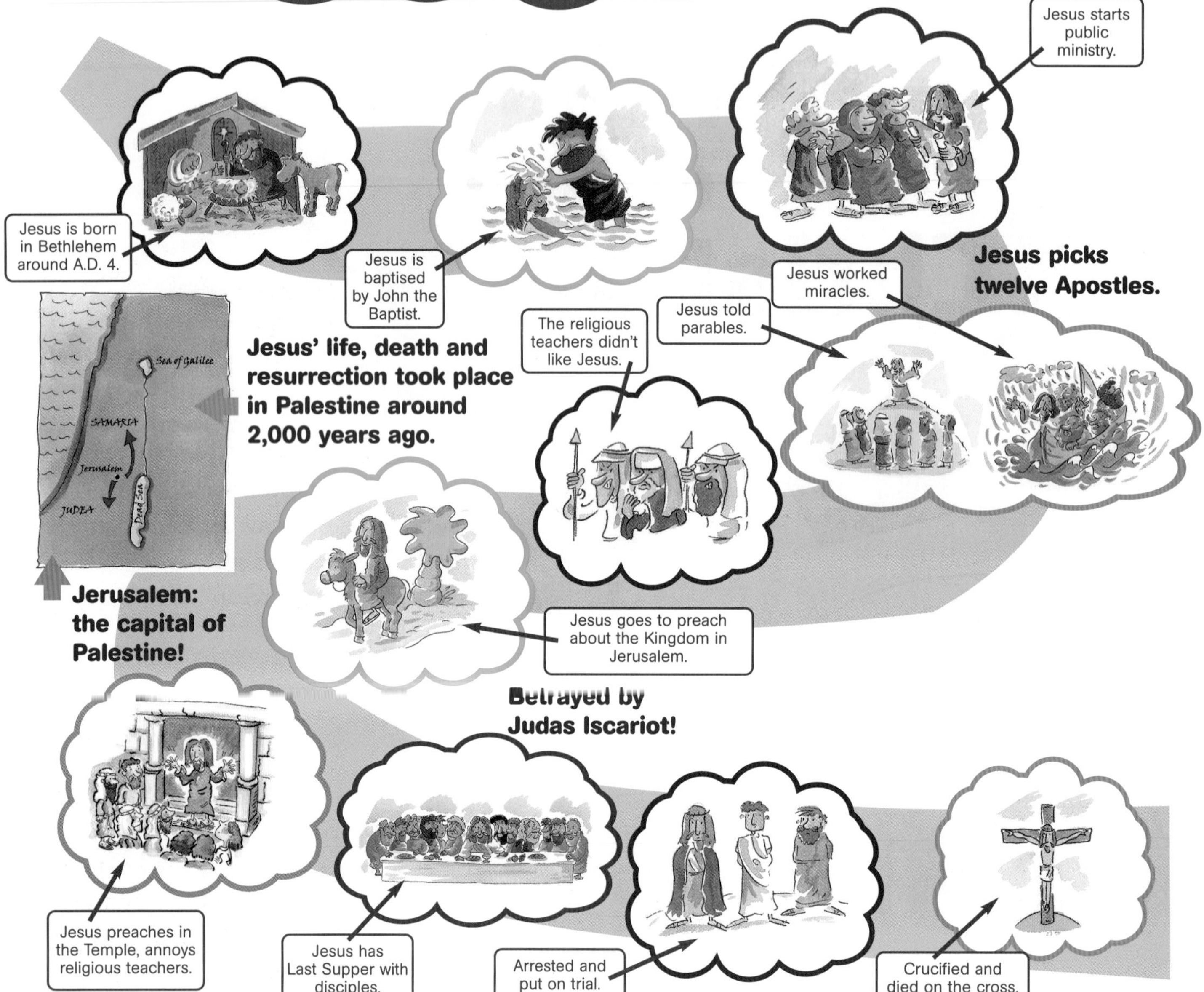

Jesus is born in Bethlehem around A.D. 4.

Jesus is baptised by John the Baptist.

Jesus starts public ministry.

Jesus picks twelve Apostles.

Jesus worked miracles.

Jesus told parables.

The religious teachers didn't like Jesus.

Sea of Galilee

SAMARIA

Jerusalem

JUDEA

Dead Sea

Jesus' life, death and resurrection took place in Palestine around 2,000 years ago.

Jerusalem: the capital of Palestine!

Jesus goes to preach about the Kingdom in Jerusalem.

Betrayed by Judas Iscariot!

Jesus preaches in the Temple, annoys religious teachers.

Jesus has Last Supper with disciples.

Arrested and put on trial.

Crucified and died on the cross.

The Resurrection: Jesus rises from the dead!

The Resurrection is the core belief of Christianity and its denominations. God, the loving Father, raised Jesus, His Son, from the dead.

. . . It is written in the Gospels that after the Resurrection Jesus appeared to the **disciples** and the **Apostles**!

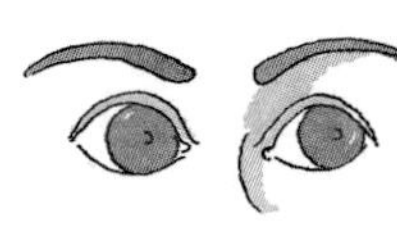

Look up John 20:26 in the Gospels.

After the Resurrection, when Jesus appeared to them, the Apostles were truly delighted and happy, so much so that they were **transformed**!

The Apostles were changed forever as people, and given new strength to go out onto the streets and say, 'Jesus has risen', 'He is with us', 'God has raised his son from the grave!' and to proclaim this Good News to all people!

Make sentences for each word

- Nativity • Bethlehem
- Baptism • Palestine
- Miracle • Preach
- Pharisee • Temple
- Supper • Trial
- Crucifixion • Resurrection
- Belief • Apostles

Qqs

Qqs means Quick Questions

Q1. Around what year was Jesus born?
Q2. What was the name of the town where Jesus was born?
Q3. Who baptised Jesus?
Q4. What did Jesus do as part of his 'public ministry'?
Q5. Name one miracle Jesus performed.
Q6. Which city did Jesus enter on a donkey?
Q7. Name the capital of Palestine.
Q8. Name one thing that annoyed the Jewish religious authorities.
Q9. Who betrayed Jesus?
Q10. Who asked Jesus questions during his trial?

Complete each sentence:

Jesus was born in ______.
John the ______ baptised ______.
Jesus preached during his public ______.
Jesus' miracle was calming the ______.
The ______ and ______ didn't like Jesus.
Jesus travelled to ______, the capital of ______.
Jesus preached in the ______.
______ ______ betrayed Jesus.
______ ______ questioned Jesus when he was on trial.

More Qs to do . . .

A What is the core belief of Christianity?
B What does 'Resurrection' mean?
C What made the Apostles delighted and happy?
D Why did this make them delighted and happy?
E What happened to them after they realised Jesus had risen?
F What was the 'Good News' they went out to proclaim?

To Do

Pick any one of the recap scenes and draw a big poster describing what it is!

. . . the next important moment in Jesus' life is

'The Ascension! of Jesus into Heaven'

TO KNOW

Bethany =
2 miles (3km) east of Jerusalem, on the way to Jericho and across the Mount of Olives.

TO KNOW

Ascension =
the ascent of Jesus into Heaven (rising to Heaven).
Pentecost =
celebration of the gift of the Holy Spirit to the disciples (birthday of the Church).

Ascension... from the word **ASCEND**, meaning 'to go up', 'to rise up'!

. . . If you look up **Luke 24:50-53** and **Acts of the Apostles 1:3-14**, you will see what happened . . .

Forty days after the Resurrection the disciples were gathered together in a room in Jerusalem when Jesus suddenly appeared to them. He said to them, **'Peace be with you!'** Then He opened their hearts and minds to the message of the Scriptures. He said to them, **'Stay in the city until you are clothed with the power from on high!'**

Luke's Gospel tells us that after this Jesus and the Apostles went to Bethany. There, **'He blessed them . . . and was carried up to Heaven' (Luke 24:51). 'THE ASCENSION'**

Acts of the Apostles adds: 'Jesus promised, **'You will receive power when the Holy Spirit has come upon you.'** Then a cloud took him from their sight' (Acts 1:9-11). The Apostles knew Jesus was the Son of God and now they waited for the coming of the Holy Spirit.

What did **the Ascension** really mean ??

Good question!
Let's have a look!

... **the Ascension** of Jesus is important because...

- Jesus had now passed fully into the **Presence of God**.

- Jesus had come from God, the Father, and was now **returning fully to God**.

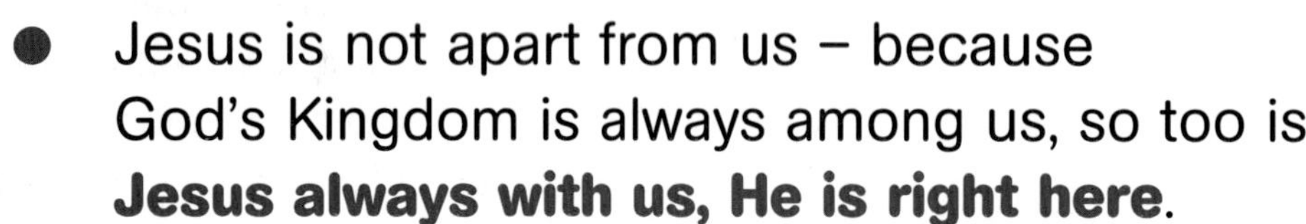

- Jesus is not apart from us – because God's Kingdom is always among us, so too is **Jesus always with us, He is right here**.

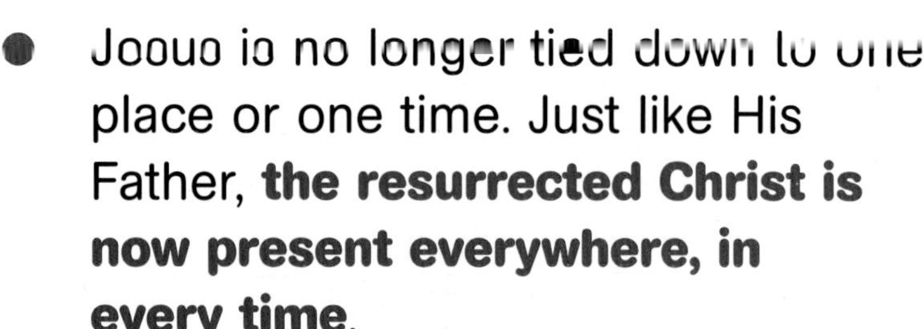

- Jesus is no longer tied down to one place or one time. Just like His Father, **the resurrected Christ is now present everywhere, in every time**.

Over to you!

Fill in the blanks:

The next _____ event in Jesus' life is the _____. Ascension means going _____. When you read _____ 24:50-53 and the Acts _____ _____ _____ you will see what happened. While the disciples were _____ in a room in _____ forty days after the _____, Jesus appeared to them. Jesus said to them, '_____________________!' He then opened their _____ and _____ to the message of the _____. He also said to them, 'Stay in the _____ until you are clothed with the _____ from on _____.' Luke's _____ goes on to say that Jesus and the _____ went to _____. While there, Jesus _____ them and was carried to _____. The Acts of the _____ adds that Jesus promised, 'You will receive _____ when the _____ _____ has come upon you.' Then a cloud took him from their _____.

Find words from this Word Wheel

When you find each word, use it in a sentence!

BETHANYKTUVKTUVPOWERIXYASCENSIONCEGHIHEAVENLORTVHOLYSPIRITXVBCPEACEPOSTAPOSTLESLSRB

Questions to Do

Q1. What does the word 'Ascension' mean?
Q2. What books do we read to find out about the Ascension?
Q3. Where were the disciples gathered together?
Q4. What did Jesus say to them when he appeared?
Q5. According to Luke's Gospel, what did Jesus also say?
Q6. Where is Bethany?

A. What happened at the Ascension?
B. Why did Jesus tell the disciples to wait for power from on high?
C. What did the Apostles realise?
D. Explain why Jesus' Ascension was important.
E. What does the Ascension tell us about the presence of Jesus on Earth?

COPY AND COLOUR

. . . so the delighted disciples returned to Jerusalem and waited for the Holy Spirit to come.

PENTECOST

TO KNOW

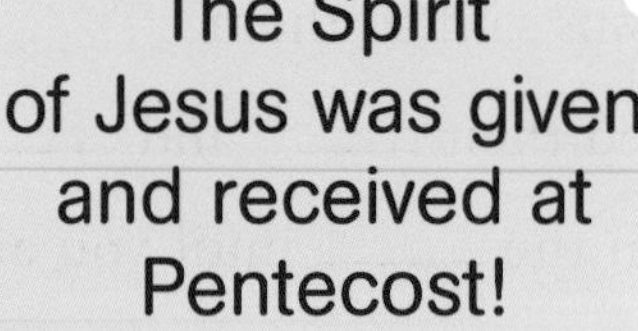
The Spirit of Jesus was given and received at Pentecost!

Pentecost = originally this was the Jewish feast of Sharuot. It takes place fifty days after Passover to celebrate the grain harvest. The word 'Pentecost' means 'greet for the fiftieth time'.

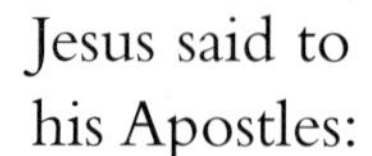
Jesus said to his Apostles:

'But you will receive power when the Holy Spirit has come upon you; and you will be my witnesses in Jerusalem, in all Judea and Samaria and to the ends of the Earth.'
(Acts 1:8)

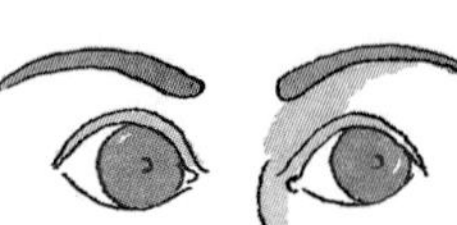

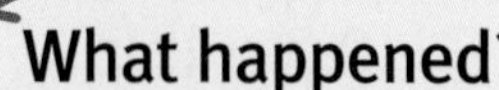

Let's have a look

Read the Acts of the Apostles (2:1-13).

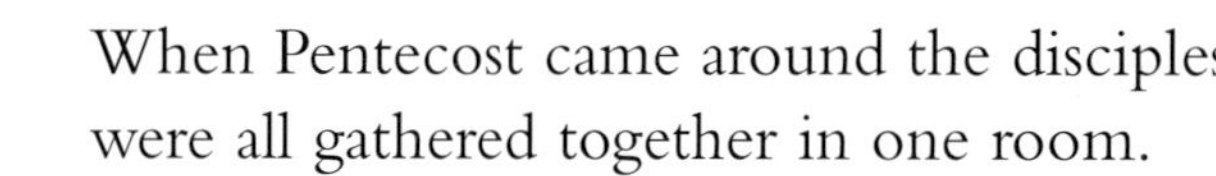

- When Pentecost came around the disciples were all gathered together in one room.

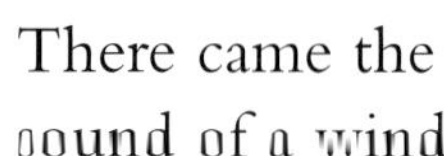

- There came the sound of a wind.

- Divided tongues, as of fire, rested on each one of them.
- They were filled with the Holy Spirit.

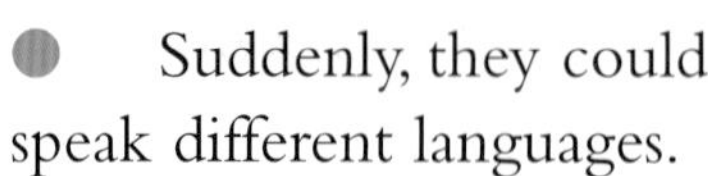

- Suddenly, they could speak different languages.

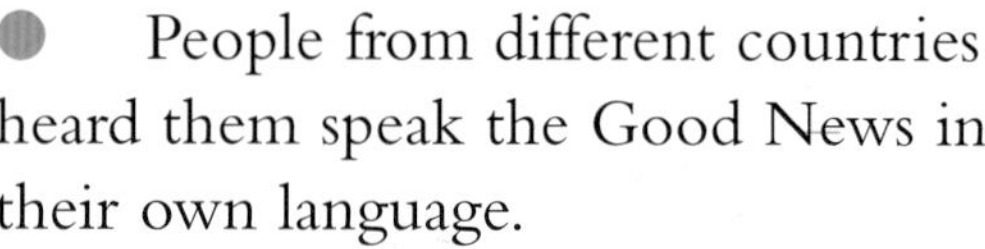

- People from different countries heard them speak the Good News in their own language.

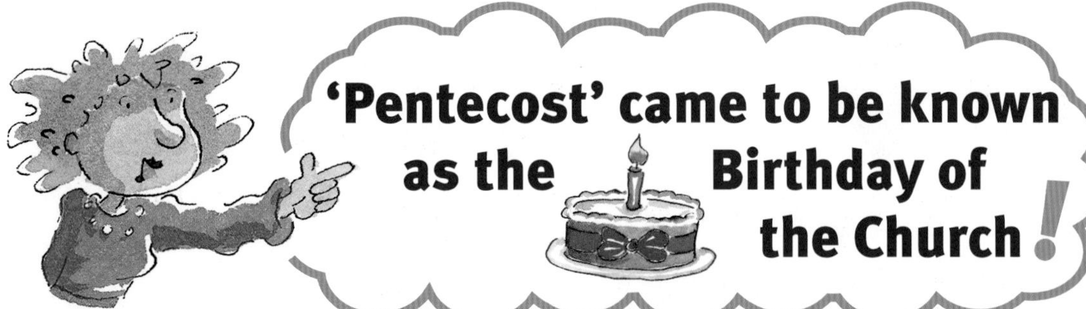
'Pentecost' came to be known as the Birthday of the Church!

For this was the beginning of the spreading of Jesus' message

It was a moment of transformation for the Apostles!

The twelve Apostles, who had been scared and nervous following Jesus' death, were now out in the streets shouting about Jesus, his message and his life! They had been transformed by the power of the Holy Spirit.

In the Old Testament Book of Exodus (19) the Jewish people received the Ten Commandments from Moses fifty days after the Passover. This marked the beginning of the Jewish people being God's chosen people.

The Spirit was with Jesus as He preached His message. The same Spirit was now with the Apostles to help them spread the message.

In the New Testament we see that fifty days after the Resurrection the Apostles received the gift of the Holy Spirit! This marked the beginning of the Church of Jesus Christ!

Over to you!

Unmuddle each of these and put them into a sentence . . .

TECSTPNEO
PSTALESO
TISPIR
GUESTON
GUNGESLAA
MTOTASFRAINRINO
RVOPSEAS
GNINBGEIN

Some art to do!
Draw a poster showing that Pentecost is the Birthday of the Church.

or Design a giant birthday card.

Using 6–8 boxes, draw a cartoon strip that tells the story of Pentecost. Label each picture and use speech bubbles.

Qs

Q1. What was 'Pentecost' originally?

Q2. When does Sharuot take place?

Q3. Reading Acts 1:8, what did Jesus say to the Apostles?

Q4. On Pentecost day, what happened to the Apostles?

Q5. Why were other people amazed?

Q6. What did Pentecost come to be known as?

Figure out these muddled word tiles

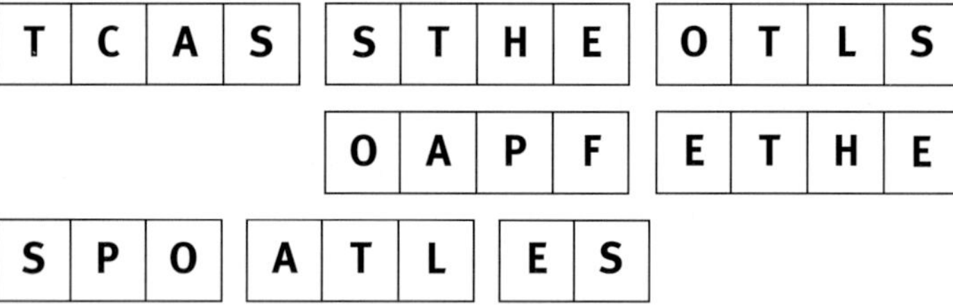

Use each word in a sentence

Research to do

Read over the Acts of the Apostles 2:1-13 in the New Testament. People from different countries and towns are named. Find these different countries and towns on a map.

More Qs to do . . .

A. What did Jesus mean when he said the Apostles would be his witnesses?

B. How did the Spirit change the Apostles, and why?

C. What does transformation mean?

D. What marked the beginning of the Jewish people as God's chosen people?

E. What marked the beginning of the Church of Jesus Christ?

F. What strengthened the Apostles to spread Jesus' message?

G. The Holy Spirit gave them power; write down what you think this power is.

The Christian COMMUNITY IN Jerusalem

After the four Gospels, the next book of the Bible is the Acts of the Apostles. In this book, written by **Luke, the Evangelist**, we read about how the Christian community **(Church)** grew and developed.

- The Apostle **Peter** was the most prominent person in the early Christian community. James was important also.
- Throughout Jerusalem, Peter and the other disciples preached the Word of God and showed **Jesus' love** in all they did and said.

'The power that had been in Jesus as He proclaimed God's kingdom … was now present in the Apostles.' (Acts 4:10)

Jerusalem

NB

This early Christian community was a community of Jewish people only. They saw Jesus as the Messiah. They shared everything and celebrated the Breaking of Bread in their homes.

TO KNOW

Breaking of Bread = remembering the Last Supper of Jesus.

Church = the Christian community of all those who believe in and worship Jesus.
Acts = an abbreviation for the book, 'Acts of the Apostles'.

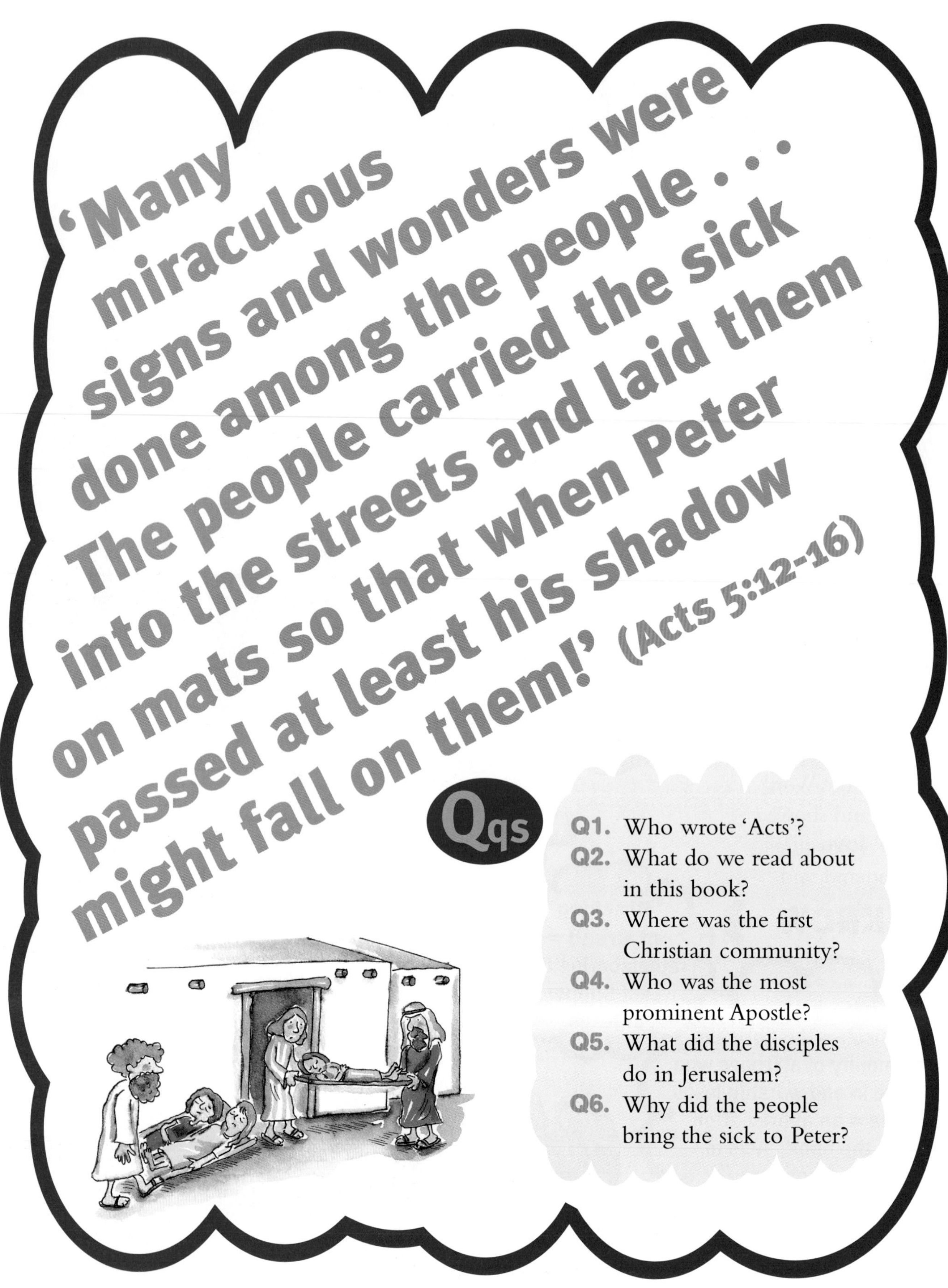

'Many miraculous signs and wonders were done among the people . . . The people carried the sick into the streets and laid them on mats so that when Peter passed at least his shadow might fall on them!' (Acts 5:12-16)
Qqs

Q1. Who wrote 'Acts'?
Q2. What do we read about in this book?
Q3. Where was the first Christian community?
Q4. Who was the most prominent Apostle?
Q5. What did the disciples do in Jerusalem?
Q6. Why did the people bring the sick to Peter?

. . . As we continue to read the **Acts of the Apostles** we see that life wasn't easy and the Apostles often got into trouble with the Jewish leaders because they were preaching Jesus the Christ!

- The ruling religious council, the **Sanhedrin**, kept a very close eye on the Apostles.

The Sanhedrin became unhappy with the Apostles' preaching.

- The Sanhedrin had the Apostles arrested and ordered them to stop preaching in Jesus' name (Acts 5:40).

'But they went on ceaselessly teaching and proclaiming the Good News of God's Kingdom.'

- It got so bad that one of the Jerusalem community's members, **Stephen**, was charged with **blasphemy** and stoned to death.

After Stephen's death there was widespread persecution of the Christian community in Jerusalem.

- Many of Jesus' followers fled to the areas of Judea and Samaria, away from the persecution, but the Apostles stayed in Jerusalem, spreading Jesus' word.

TO KNOW →

Stephen became the first Christian **martyr**, which means a person who gives witness to his or her belief and dies for it.

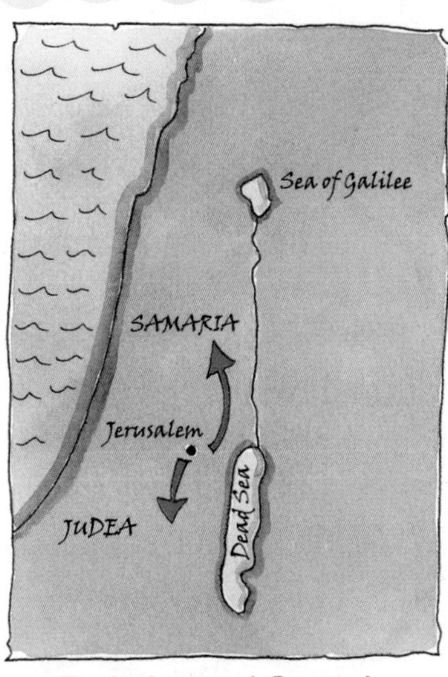

To Judea and Samaria

. . . it so happened that because many followers were forced to flee to Judea and Samaria, the message of Jesus started to spread even further!

. . . one member of the Jerusalem Church who fled was a man called **Philip**. He went to Samaria and started preaching the **Good News** there!

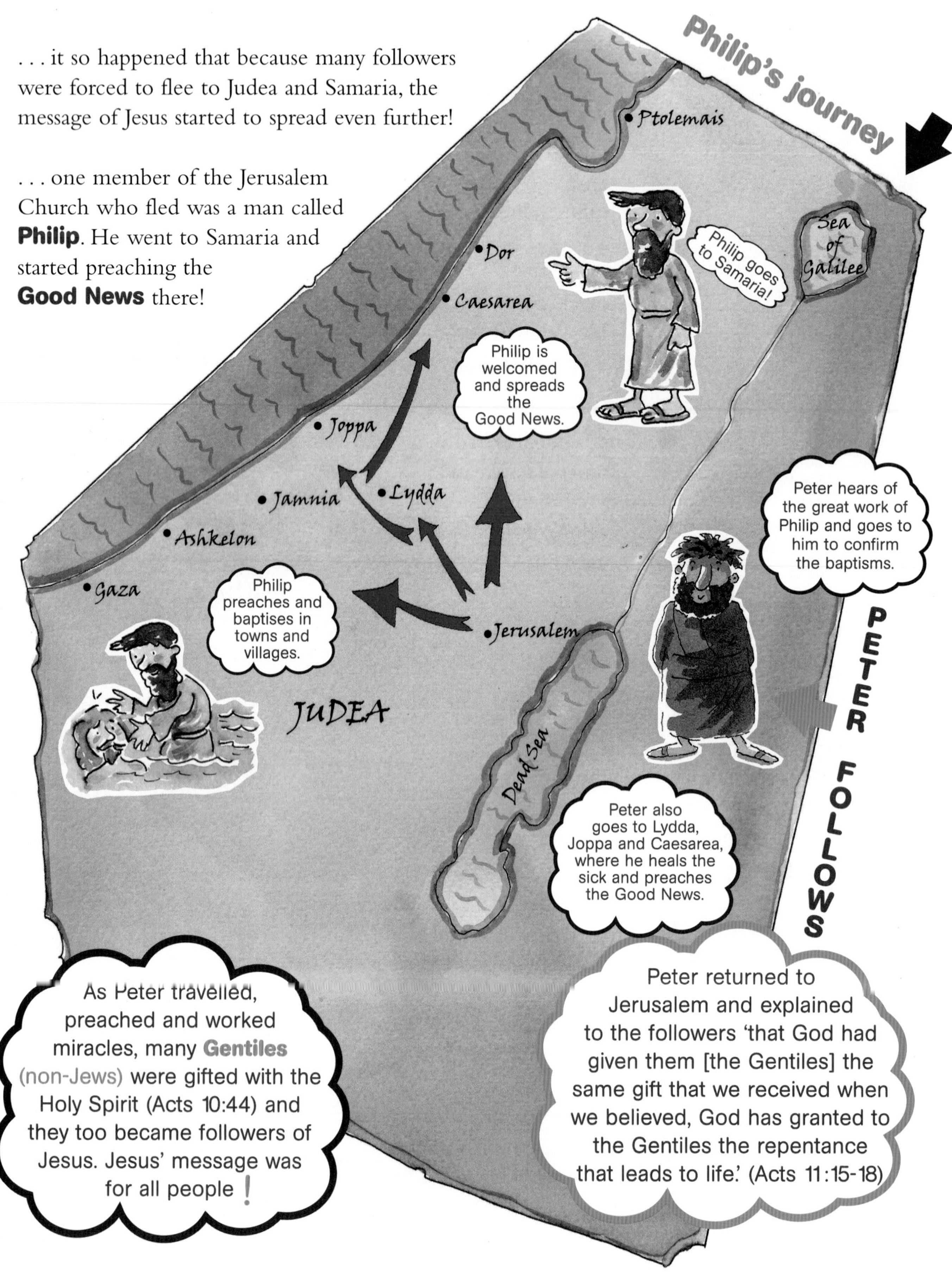

Philip's journey
Ptolemais
Sea of Galilee
Dor
Caesarea
Philip goes to Samaria!
Philip is welcomed and spreads the Good News.
Joppa
Jamnia
Lydda
Ashkelon
Gaza
Philip preaches and baptises in towns and villages.
Jerusalem
JUDEA
Dead Sea
Peter hears of the great work of Philip and goes to him to confirm the baptisms.
PETER FOLLOWS
Peter also goes to Lydda, Joppa and Caesarea, where he heals the sick and preaches the Good News.
As Peter travelled, preached and worked miracles, many Gentiles (non-Jews) were gifted with the Holy Spirit (Acts 10:44) and they too became followers of Jesus. Jesus' message was for all people !
Peter returned to Jerusalem and explained to the followers 'that God had given them [the Gentiles] the same gift that we received when we believed, God has granted to the Gentiles the repentance that leads to life.' (Acts 11:15-18)

Fill in the blanks:

LET'S TRY THESE

As we read the _____ _____ _____ -_____ we see that _____ wasn't _____ for the Apostles and they got into trouble with the _____ leaders. The ruling _____ council, _____ _____, kept a very close _____ on the Apostles. They became _____ with the _____ preaching. They had the Apostles _____ and _____ them to stop _____ in Jesus' name. But they went on _____ teaching and _____ the _____ News!

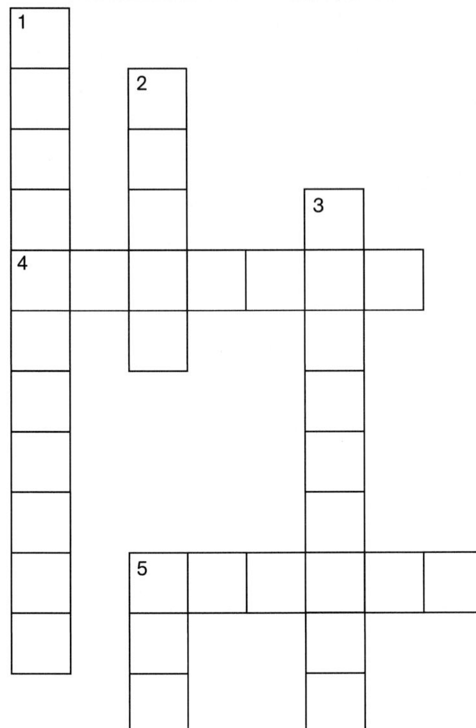

Across

4. The first martyr.
5. Went to Samaria.

Down

1. This happened to the Apostles.
2. Fled to this area.
3. Apostles stayed here.
5. What the Apostles did.

Qqs

Q1. Why was life not easy for the Apostles?

Q2. What was the name of the religious council?

Q3. What did the Sanhedrin order the Apostles not to do?

Q4. What happened to the disciple, Stephen?

Q5. What does 'martyr' mean?

Q6. Why did some of Jesus' followers flee to Judea and Samaria?

Q7. Who stayed in Jerusalem?

To Do

Draw a map of Palestine, showing Samaria and Judea. Show the place to which Philip travelled and the place to which Peter travelled!

Design a poster that reads (in bubble writing) 'Jesus' message is for **all** people!' and show all the people around it!

Give these Questions a go . . .

A. Explain why the Sanhedrin were unhappy with the Apostles' teachings.

B. Why did the Apostles continue to preach unceasingly?

C. Do you think the Apostles were brave to stay in Jerusalem? Why?

D. What was a good result of some disciples being forced to flee Jerusalem?

E. Where did Philip go, and why, and what did he do there?

F. Why did Peter follow Philip?

G. Why was it important for Gentiles to hear Jesus' message?

The Message of the **Life, Death and Resurrection** of Jesus spread not only to Jews but to **Gentiles** as well. This marked the formation of a new religion of followers of Jesus.

Another very important person who helped to bring the Message of Jesus to the Gentiles was

NB We know all about Paul from the Acts of the Apostles and from all the letters he wrote to spread the Good News, which are in the New Testament.

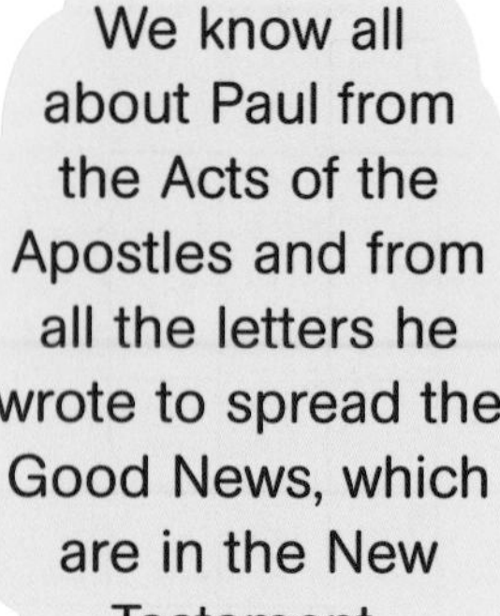

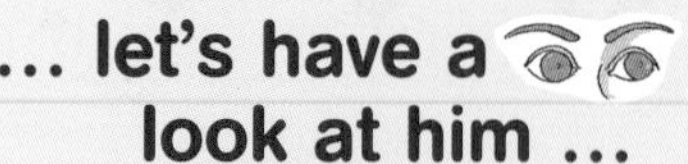

PAUL

- Paul was born a Jew in Tarsus.

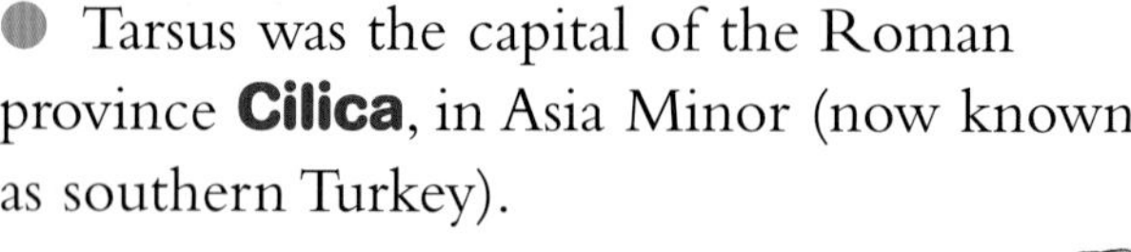

- Tarsus was the capital of the Roman province **Cilica**, in Asia Minor (now known as southern Turkey).

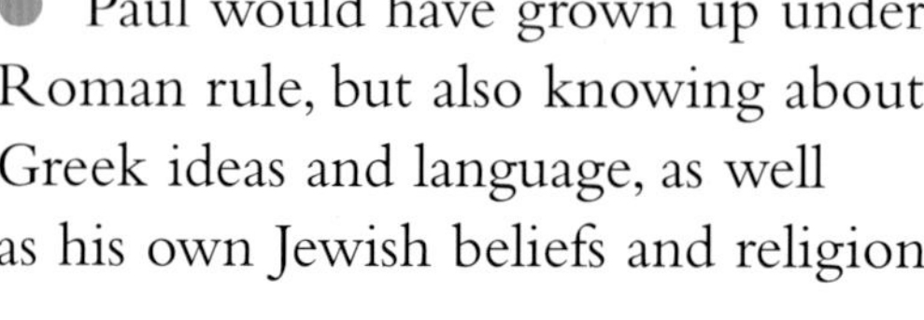

- Paul would have grown up under Roman rule, but also knowing about Greek ideas and language, as well as his own Jewish beliefs and religion.

Paul Fact File

Name: Paul (Saul).
Religion: Jew.
Home: Tarsus.
Job: Pharisee (tentmaker, learned in Tarsus).
Education: Greek philosophy, Jewish religion, Roman traditions.

TO KNOW

Saul was Paul's Jewish name and Paul was his Roman name.

- Like his father, Paul became a **Pharisee** and went to Jerusalem to study the law!

- As a strict Pharisee, Paul was involved in the persecution of the followers of Jesus (Acts 22:3-5).

. . . so, up to this point, Paul – acting out of his strict Pharisee obligation – was involved in persecuting the followers of Jesus in Jerusalem . . .

But then something happened . . .

'Paul's Conversion'

TO KNOW

Conversion = to change from one thing to another!
Damascus = capital of Syria.

Paul asked the high priest's permission to go to Damascus to hunt down followers of Jesus and bring them back for trial.

On his way to Damascus, a light from Heaven suddenly flashed before him, blinding him instantly. He fell to the ground. Then he heard a voice!

'Saul, Saul, why do you persecute me?'

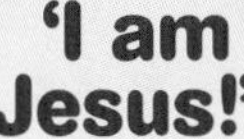

The voice told him to go to the city. Two men travelling with him helped the blind Saul to get to the city of Damascus.

A disciple called Ananias lived in Damascus. In a vision, Jesus had told him to go and find Saul, 'who is praying and had a vision of you!'

'The Lord Jesus has sent me, so that you may regain your sight and be filled with the Holy Spirit.'

Ananias finds Saul and puts his hands on him.

'Immediately something like scales fell from Saul's eyes. Saul can see again – he is no longer blind.'

After that Saul got up and was baptised as a follower of Jesus Christ!

For many days Saul preached the Good News in Damascus.

'Jesus, he is the Son of God ... the Messiah!'

Those who saw Paul were amazed!

Over to you!

Find the special words in the word wheel and make a sentence with each one in your copy!

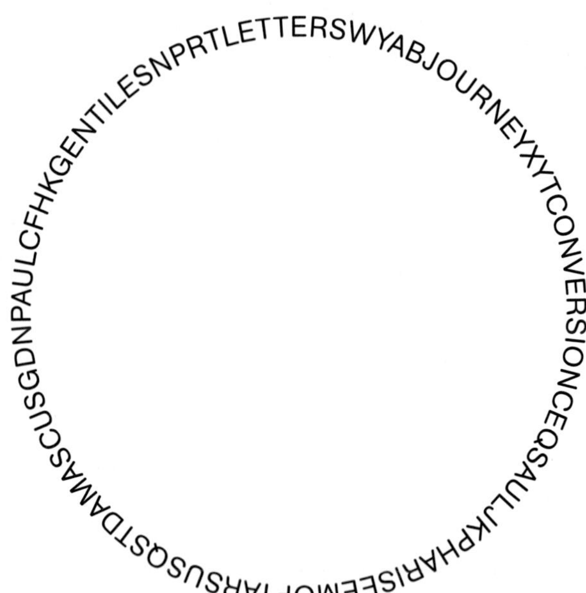

Qqs

Q1. Where can we find out about Paul?
Q2. What religion did Paul belong to originally?
Q3. What was his educational background?
Q4. Name his profession and his skills.
Q5. Where was Paul born?
Q6. Where is Tarsus?
Q7. Where did he go to study the law?
Q8. Why was he called Paul and Saul?

True / False ?

- Paul was a Greek from Rome. **T / F**
- He became a carpenter. **T / F**
- Saul was his Greek name. **T / F**
- Tarsus is in Cilica. **T / F**
- His father was a Pharisee. **T / F**
- He didn't persecute Christians. **T / F**
- He had a conversion. **T / F**
- His conversion occurred on the way to Bethlehem. **T / F**
- He heard the voice of Moses. **T / F**
- Ananias healed his blindness. **T / F**

Unmuddle each of these words:

LPAU • STRSUA • WJE • SPHIEARE

KEREG • LCIACI • WAL • LSAU

NCVRIOESN • EJSUS

SAMDCSUA • AAIASNN

Write an explanation for each word in your copy.

More Qs

A. As a Pharisee, what was Paul involved in?
B. What was it that changed Paul?
C. What does 'conversion' mean?
D. What did Jesus say to Paul?
E. What did Ananias do?
F. After he could see again, what did Paul do?
G. How important was this conversion for Paul?
H. In your opinion, why was Paul converted?
I. Why was it that the people who saw Paul preach were amazed?

Some art to do

- Draw 8–10 boxes and use them to make a cartoon strip that tells the story of Paul's conversion!
- Draw a big poster showing Paul and the flash of light and write under the picture: The Damascus Experience!

The **Damascus Experience** was a life-changing moment for Paul. He had a **conversion** to a different way of thinking and living, a way deeply rooted in Jesus Christ and the message of **Christianity**.

Paul spent fourteen years or more reflecting deeply on Jesus' life, death and Resurrection.

This prayer and reflection spurred him on to be a **missionary** – that means to travel to other lands to spread the message of Jesus to all peoples . . .

TO KNOW

Missionary = a person who goes on a religious journey to spread Jesus' message.

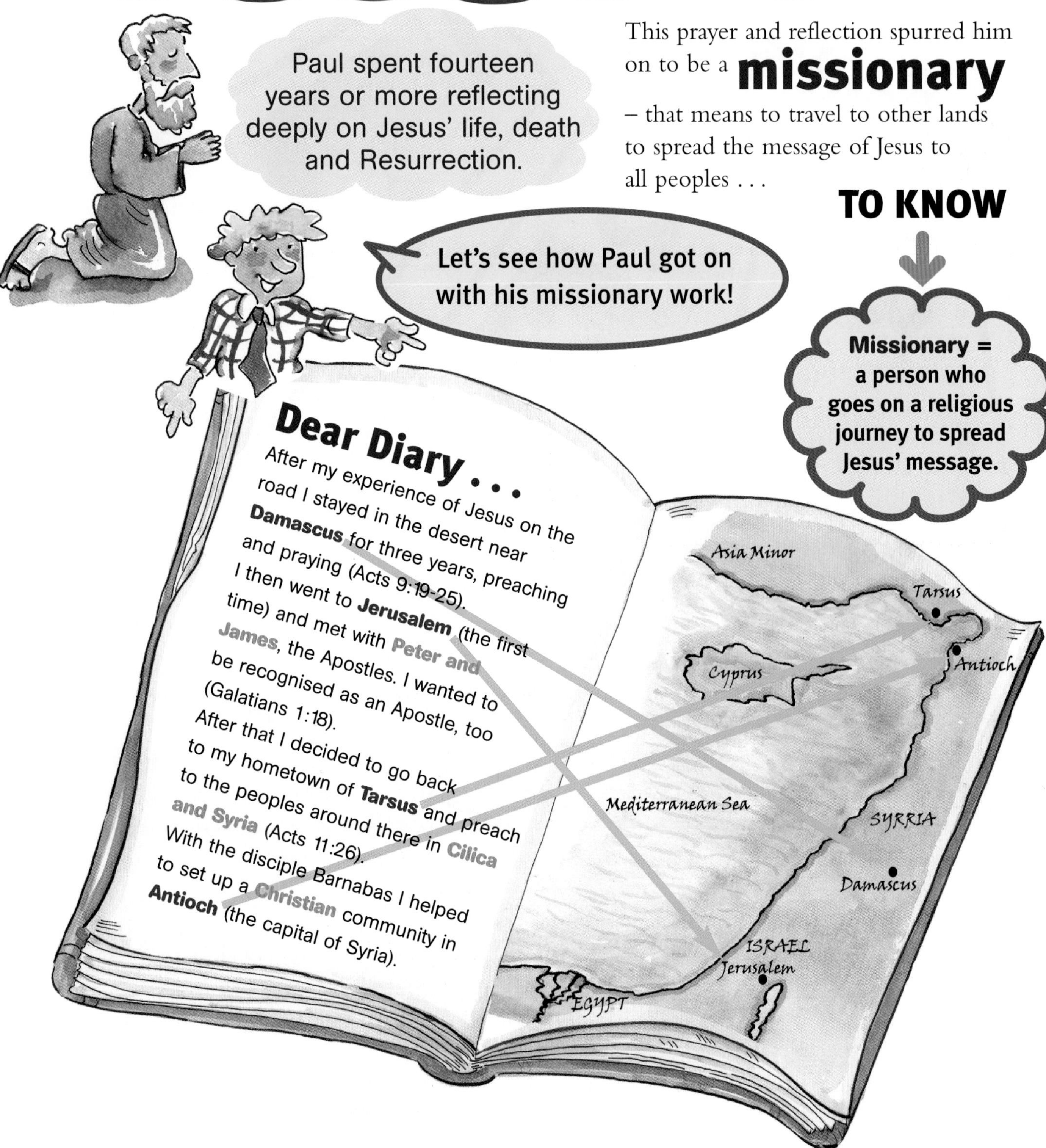

Let's see how Paul got on with his missionary work!
Dear Diary . . .
After my experience of Jesus on the road I stayed in the desert near Damascus for three years, preaching and praying (Acts 9:19-25).
I then went to Jerusalem (the first time) and met with Peter and James, the Apostles. I wanted to be recognised as an Apostle, too (Galatians 1:18).
After that I decided to go back to my hometown of Tarsus and preach to the peoples around there in Cilica and Syria (Acts 11:26).
With the disciple Barnabas I helped to set up a Christian community in Antioch (the capital of Syria).
Asia Minor
Tarsus
Antioch
Cyprus
Mediterranean Sea
SYRRIA
Damascus
ISRAEL
Jerusalem
EGYPT

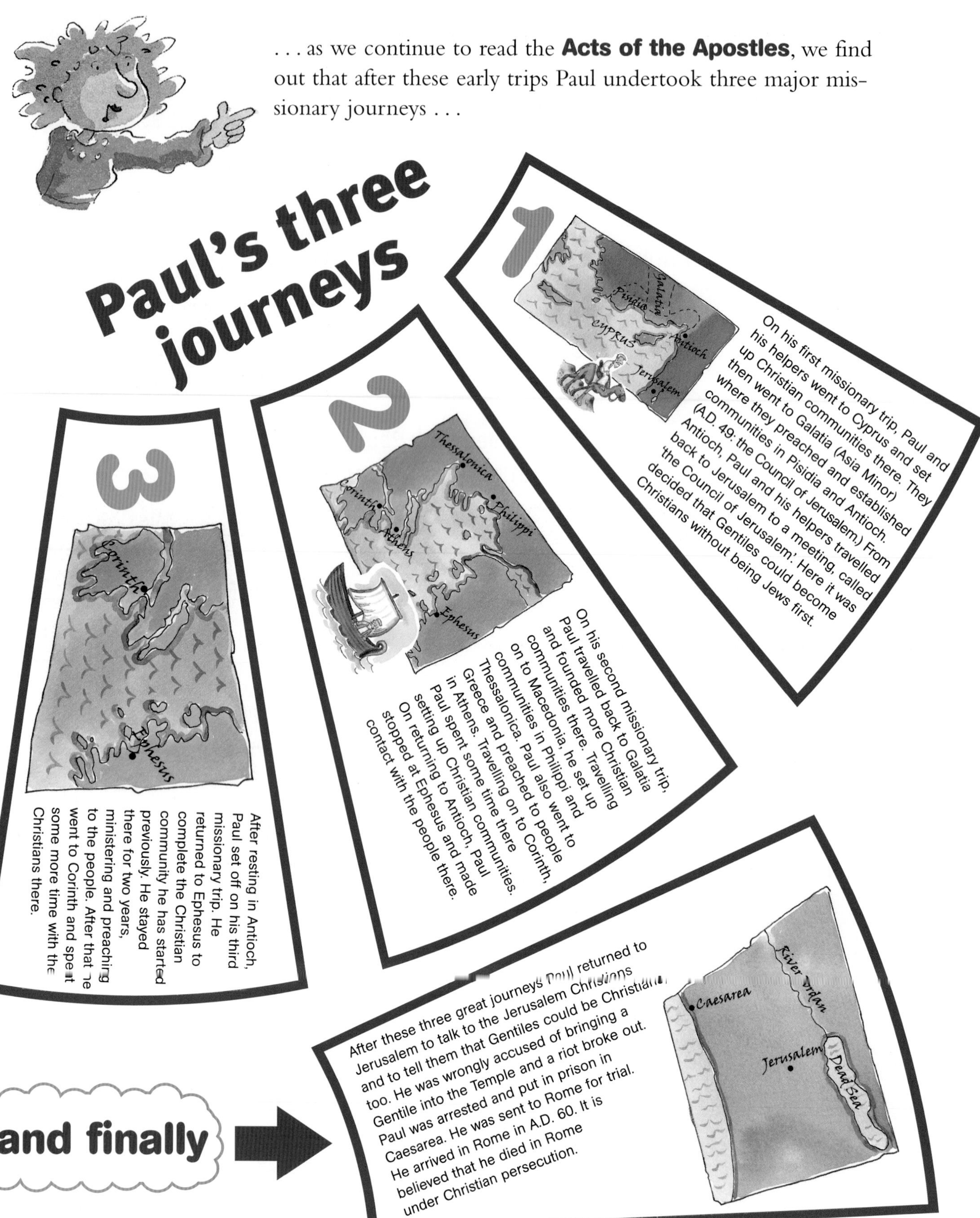
. . . as we continue to read the **Acts of the Apostles**, we find out that after these early trips Paul undertook three major missionary journeys . . .
Paul's three journeys
1
Galatia
Pisidia
CYPRUS
Antioch
Jerusalem
On his first missionary trip, Paul and his helpers went to Cyprus and set up Christian communities there. They then went to Galatia (Asia Minor) where they preached and established communities in Pisidia and Antioch. (A.D. 49: the Council of Jerusalem.) From Antioch, Paul and his helpers travelled back to Jerusalem to a meeting, called 'the Council of Jerusalem'. Here it was decided that Gentiles could become Christians without being Jews first.
2
Thessalonica
Corinth
Philippi
Athens
Ephesus
On his second missionary trip, Paul travelled back to Galatia and founded more Christian communities there. Travelling on to Macedonia, he set up communities in Philippi and Thessalonica. Paul also went to Greece and preached to people in Athens. Travelling on to Corinth, Paul spent some time there setting up Christian communities. On returning to Antioch, Paul stopped at Ephesus and made contact with the people there.
3
Corinth
Ephesus
After resting in Antioch, Paul set off on his third missionary trip. He returned to Ephesus to complete the Christian community he has started previously. He stayed there for two years, ministering and preaching to the people. After that he went to Corinth and spent some more time with the Christians there.
and finally
After these three great journeys Paul returned to Jerusalem to talk to the Jerusalem Christians and to tell them that Gentiles could be Christians too. He was wrongly accused of bringing a Gentile into the Temple and a riot broke out. Paul was arrested and put in prison in Caesarea. He was sent to Rome for trial. He arrived in Rome in A.D. 60. It is believed that he died in Rome under Christian persecution.
Caesarea
River Jordan
Jerusalem
Dead Sea

...some work to do...

Put these **Dear Diary** sentences in the right order!

- After that I decided to go back to my hometown of Tarsus . . .
- I helped set up a Christian community in Antioch.
- I then went to Jerusalem and met with the Apostles, Peter and James . . .
- . . . and preached to the peoples around there in Cilica and Syria.
- After my experience on the road I stayed in Damascus . . .
- . . . the Apostles. I wanted to be recognised as an Apostle, too.
- . . . and the desert for three years, preaching and praying!

Draw this map and indicate with labelled arrows all the sites mentioned by Paul.

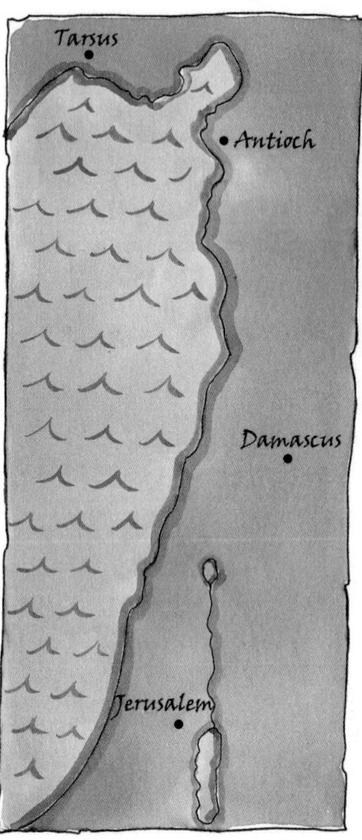

To Do

JOURNAL IDEA

Pretend you were one of Paul's companions on each of his three journeys. Write your own diary entries, detailing the journeys, Paul himself and how you felt being with him during this time!

Some art to do

Draw a big poster that shows all the places Paul visited on his three major missionary journeys. Make sure to name all the places!

Qqs

Q1. What did Paul spend fourteen years doing?
Q2. What does 'missionary' mean?
Q3. Why did Paul go to Jerusalem the first time?
Q4. Why did he go to Tarsus?
Q5. Where did Paul go on his first missionary trip?
Q6. When did the Council of Jerusalem take place? What was it about?
Q7. What did Paul do on his second trip?
Q8. Where did he stay for two years during his third trip?
Q9. What happened the last time he went to Jerusalem?

'Paul's Letters'

Just like Peter, Paul was filled with the 'Spirit of Jesus'. This gave him the strength, courage and conviction to bring Christ's message to the Gentiles of the surrounding areas and beyond!

TO KNOW

Epistle = an Apostolic letter.

As well as his very important missionary journeys, Paul also used letters to spread the message of Jesus Christ far and wide.

It was during his second trip that Paul began to write letters to the various Christian communities, explaining things and giving instructions and advice!

NB

These letters were addressed to people from different places and with different backgrounds, each having their own needs, wants and questions about Jesus.

Timothy and Titus were Paul's co-workers

NB

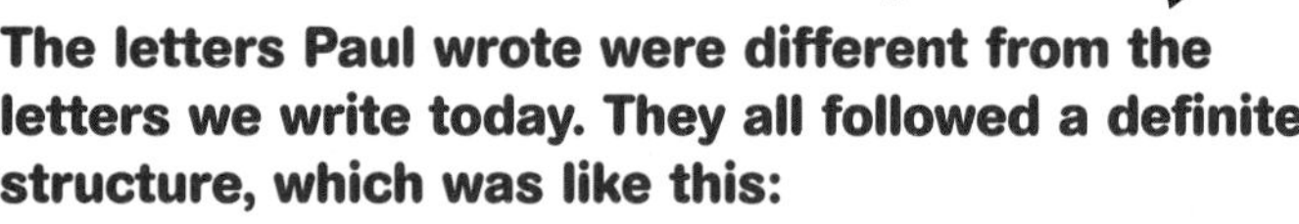

The letters Paul wrote were different from the letters we write today. They all followed a definite structure, which was like this:

A. Greeting from Paul to the people named and addressed.
B. Thanks for all the blessings received.
C. The main body of the letter – promoting an understanding of Jesus and the Good News.
D. Instructions for future events.
E. A goodbye and a prayer.

Main themes of the letters:

- Answers to questions about Jesus!
- Directions for how to live a good, moral and spiritual life!
- Proclamations about being saved by Jesus!
- Jesus is alive in the Christian community!
- Guidelines on worship and prayer!
- A personal encounter with God is possible!
- Sin and its consequences!
- The Church is the Body of Christ!

Paul Wordsearch

S	E	M	N	P	N	A	S	I	S	G	A
U	E	I	L	F	H	P	T	E	C	N	E
S	S	S	Y	S	I	I	L	H	T	T	S
E	I	S	H	R	U	I	L	I	E	R	S
H	R	I	T	T	T	C	O	L	E	N	N
P	A	O	E	N	N	C	S	T	I	L	S
E	H	N	E	J	H	I	T	A	L	P	D
O	P	G	E	C	E	E	R	G	M	G	I
A	P	O	S	T	L	E	S	O	L	A	L
M	E	L	A	S	U	R	E	J	C	B	D
X	A	I	T	A	L	A	G	D	E	K	P
H	T	A	R	S	U	S	P	A	U	L	I

ANTIOCH	LETTERS
CORINTH	PHARISEE
GALATIA	TRIPS
JERUSALEM	ATHENS
PAUL	EPHESUS
TARSUS	GREECE
APOSTLES	MISSION
DAMASCUS	PHILLIPI
GENTILES	

Qqs

Q1. What gave Paul the strength to do what he did?

Q2. What did Paul write?

Q3. When did he begin to write letters?

Q4. How were the letters constructed?

Q5. List four main themes of the letters.

Q6. Who were Timothy and Titus?

Pick one of the letters written by Paul. After reading it, complete this FACT FILE in your copy . . .

- Name of community.
- Country in which they live.
- Greeting.
- Problems mentioned.
- Advice about Jesus.
- Advice about living a good life.
- Advice about belief.
- Advice about worship.
- Advice about salvation.
- Advice about the Church.

Write a letter to one of the Christian communities mentioned. Pretend to be Paul, answering their questions and giving advice about a Christian life. Construct your letter according to the letter-writing format used by Paul!

Christianity

Grows and Splits

The Apostles Peter and Paul reached Rome – the centre of the Roman Empire – and brought Christianity with them!

. . . as well as Rome, small Christian communities began to spring up across the **Roman Empire** . . .

have a look at the missionary work of the disciples of Jesus!

Capital of the Empire

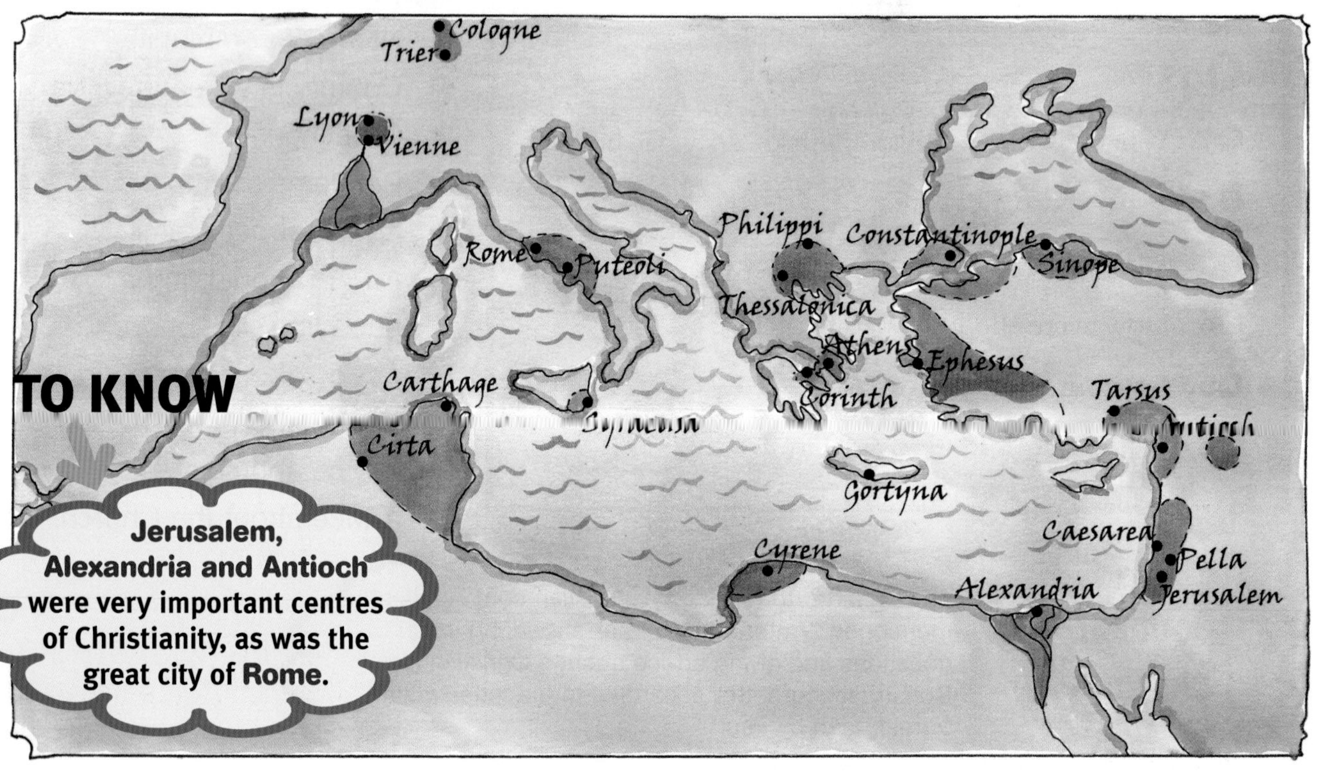

TO KNOW

Jerusalem, Alexandria and Antioch were very important centres of Christianity, as was the great city of Rome.

These **'early Christian communities'** had to meet in secret because the Roman Empire was suspicious of them.

As a group they . . .

- worshipped on Sundays, the day of **'Resurrection'**;
- met in each other's houses;
- listened to stories about the life, death and Resurrection of Jesus and sang from the **Book of Psalms** (Old Testament);
- remembered and celebrated what Jesus had asked them: to share in the breaking of bread and the drinking of wine;
- gave money to the poor and the sick.

It was also recognised that all members of the Christian communities had to use their **gifts and talents** for the good of the whole community! They received their gifts and talents from the Holy Spirit.

Over time, roles and responsibilities developed within the community . . . three important ones were:

Bishops:

Episcopos in Greek, meaning 'overseer', or 'guardian' because bishops oversaw an area called a **diocese**.

Deacons:

from the Greek meaning **'servant'** because they served presbyters and bishops in worship ceremonies.

Presbyters:

Greek word for **'Elder'**. The presbyters oversaw a group of believers.

TO KNOW

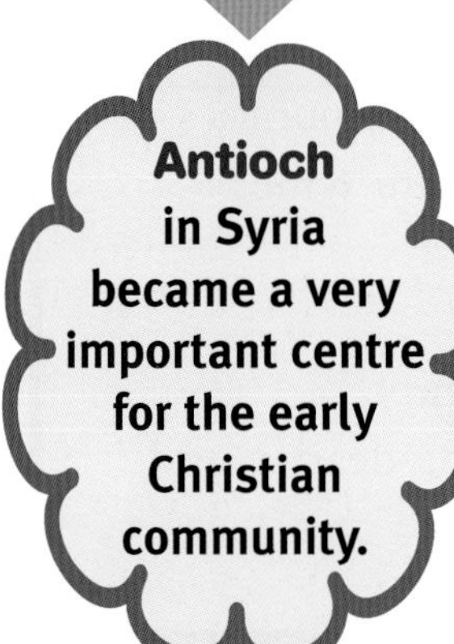

Antioch
in Syria
became a very
important centre
for the early
Christian
community.

These and all members of the Christian community worked together for God's Kingdom!

Q1. Who brought Christianity to Rome?
Q2. What was the capital of the Roman Empire?
Q3. Apart from Rome, name two other cities that were important centres of Christianity.
Q4. Judging from the map, how far did the Roman Empire spread?
Q5. Name some of the countries Rome conquered.
Q6. Name two things the early Christian communities did.

To Do

In your copy draw a picture to go with each of these things that the Christian communities did:

- listening to stories about the life of Jesus;
- breaking bread and sharing wine together;
- worshipping on Sundays in each other's houses;
- giving money to the poor.

Fill in the blanks:

Because of the _____, Peter and _____, Christianity reached the _____ Empire. The early _____ communities met together in their _____. They worshipped on _____, the day of _____. They _____ to stories about Jesus' _____, _____ and _____. They sang from the _____ of _____. They broke _____ and drank _____ because _____ asked them to do this in His name. They gave _____ to the _____.

Unmuddle each word and use it in a sentence

NRMAO PEMIER
ESLMJEARU
NTIANOCH
NEWI AND DRBEA
RSEPRBTEYS
NCEADO

More Qs . . .

A. Why, do you think, was it important for Christianity to reach Rome?
B. Name some things that the early Christian communities did.
C. Why was it important to break bread and share wine?
D. Why did they worship on a Sunday?
E. What did they do with their talents? Why?
F. Name another important centre of Christianity.
G. Name some differences between the role of a deacon and that of a bishop.

. . . for these early Christian communities it was very important that they looked after one another.

And one really important belief was that Jesus would eventually return to them!

. . . during this time life wasn't easy for the Christians living in the Roman Empire. The Christians wouldn't accept the Roman gods because they had only one God: the God of Jesus Christ. This belief got them into trouble with the Roman authorities.

. . . around A.D. 64 the Roman Emperor **Nero** was responsible for a huge fire in the capital. Rather than admit what he had done, he blamed the Christians who lived in Rome and ordered that they be persecuted!

Emperor Nero

During this time many Christians died for their beliefs.

TO KNOW

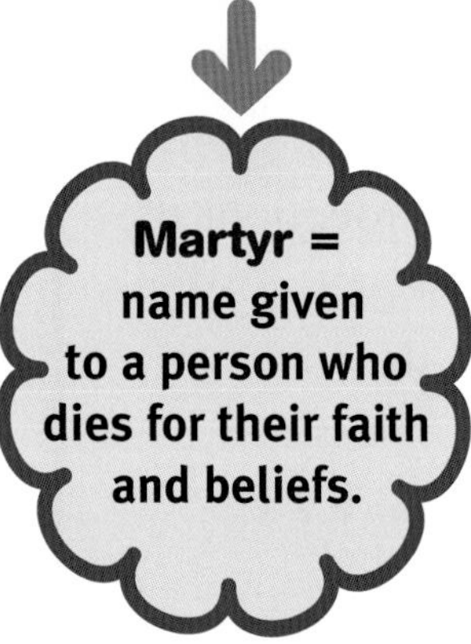

Martyr = name given to a person who dies for their faith and beliefs.

. . . the situation changed. Around A.D. 312 the Emperor **Constantine** was praying before a battle when he had a vision of a cross in the sky. Written on the cross was:

'In this sign, Conquer!'

The Emperor ordered that a cross be put on all the soldiers' shields. He won the battle and proclaimed that the Christian God was victorious!

...some work to do...

T	C	N	E	R	O	C	E	M	O	R	S
D	H	F	V	H	C	O	I	T	N	A	E
E	R	I	P	M	E	N	A	M	O	R	I
T	I	J	E	R	U	S	A	L	E	M	T
U	S	J	T	S	C	T	R	U	S	G	I
C	T	X	E	N	H	A	Y	A	P	G	N
E	I	P	R	O	A	N	T	P	L	D	U
S	A	A	L	C	R	T	R	N	I	I	M
R	N	C	I	A	I	I	A	Z	T	P	M
E	I	E	F	E	S	N	M	A	S	D	O
P	T	C	B	D	T	E	L	U	F	R	C
Y	Y	S	R	E	T	Y	B	S	E	R	P

Christianity Spreads Wordsearch

ANTIOCH	PAUL
CONSTANTINE	PRESBYTERS
ITALY	SPLITS
NERO	COMMUNITIES
PETER	EUCHARIST
ROME	MARTYR
CHRISTIANITY	PERSECUTED
DEACONS	ROMAN
JERUSALEM	EMPIRE

Qqs

Q1. What was a very important belief for the Christian communities?

Q2. Why was life hard for the Christian communities in Rome and in the Roman Empire?

Q3. Who was Emperor of Rome around A.D. 64?

Q4. What did he blame on the Christians?

Q5. What did he do to the Christians then?

Q6. What vision did Emperor Constantine have?

Q7. What decision did he make because of this vision?

Q8. Who did Constantine credit for his victories?

True / False ?

- The Christians didn't care about each other. **T / F**
- The return of Jesus was a very important belief for Gentiles. **T / F**
- The Christians accepted Roman gods. **T / F**
- They had one God, the God of Jesus. **T / F**
- The Romans loved the Christians. **T / F**
- Emperor Nero was responsible for a fire. **T / F**
- He took full responsibility for the fire. **T / F**
- Nero blamed the Christians. **T / F**
- The Christians were persecuted throughout the Empire. **T / F**
- A martyr is a person who wrote the Gospel. **T / F**
- Emperor Constantine had a vision. **T / F**

. . . because of this, **Christianity** was made the official religion of **the Roman Empire**!

TO KNOW

Church = the people of God, the followers of Jesus; also a building of Christian worship.

Also, the Bishop of Rome was seen as the direct successor of St Peter and became known as **'the Pope'** (Greek, '*Papa*' – father).

'The Split' begins

Around A.D. 330 Constantine decided to move the capital of the Roman Empire to **Constantinople** (now Istanbul, in Turkey). This left Rome without the imperial presence and therefore more vulnerable to attacks from barbarians.

With no emperor in Rome, the Pope became more powerful and became Head of Church and people.

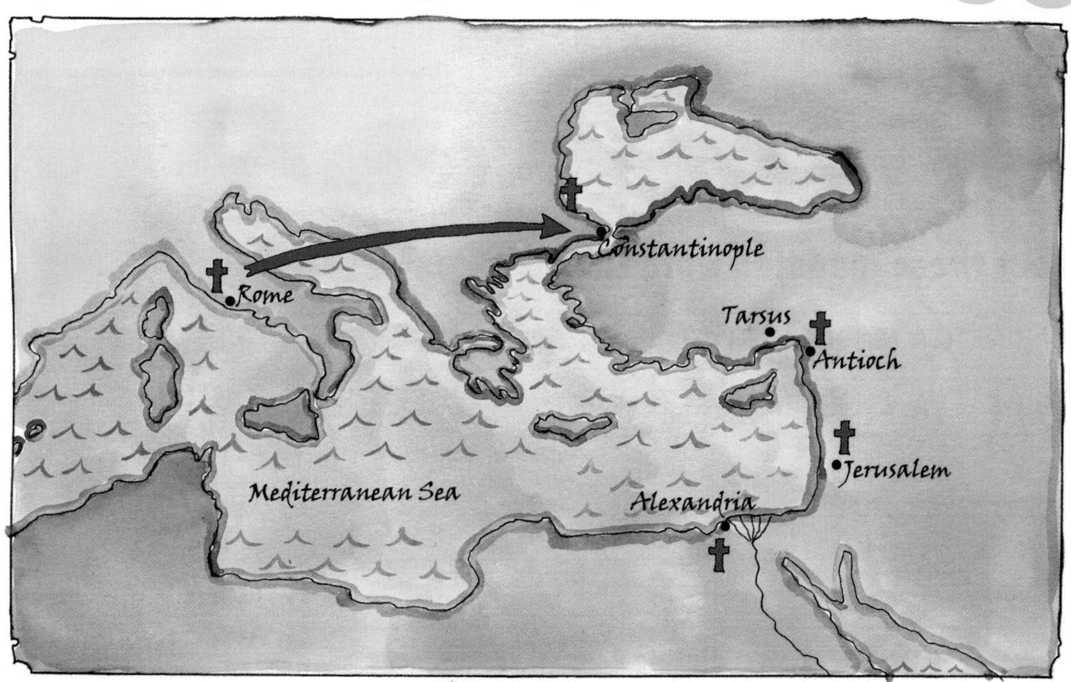

The move to Constantinople basically meant the beginning of two traditions in Christianity: one based around Rome and the Pope; the other based around Constantinople, in the east.

Those in Rome spoke Latin, while those in the east spoke Greek.

The eastern Christian communities of Antioch, Alexandria and Jerusalem were becoming concerned about the individual power of the Pope running the Church after the Emperor's move out of Rome. They believed that it should be the 'college' of Bishops that has governance and guidance over the church.

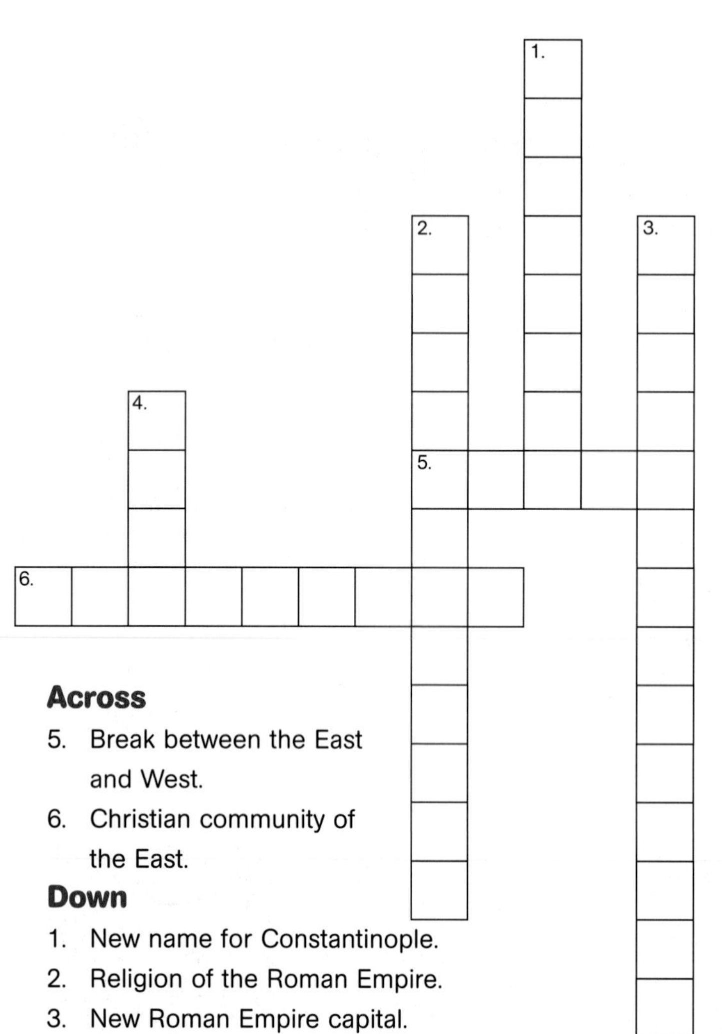

Across

5. Break between the East and West.
6. Christian community of the East.

Down

1. New name for Constantinople.
2. Religion of the Roman Empire.
3. New Roman Empire capital.
4. Name given to the Bishop of Rome.

Figure out these muddled word tiles

BE	PIR	CAM	HE	IGI	ICI	AL	ITY
OF	OFF	IAN	REL	THE	EM	E T	RO
CHR	E	IST	ON	MAN			

CON	ITA	E N	AME	L	BEC	STA	TH
NOP	NTI	LE	EW	CAP			

Fill in the blanks:

Because of Emperor ______'s vision and his victory in the ______, Christianity became the ______ religion of the Roman ______. The Bishop of ______ was seen as the direct ______ of St ______ and became known as the ______. Around ______ Emperor Constantine moved the ______ of the Empire to ______. Rome became open to ______ invasions. The Pope became more ______. The move to ______ meant the beginning of two ______ in Christianity: one based around ______; the other based around ______ in the ______. The Christians in the east became concerned about the ______ of the Pope.

A. Why was Christianity made the religion of the Roman Empire?

B. What does 'Pope' mean?

C. Who is seen as the successor of St Peter?

D. Give the two meanings for 'Church'.

E. What did the Emperor decide in A.D. 330?

F. What happened to Rome?

G. What two traditions began to develop?

H. What language did they speak in the east?

I. Name some eastern Christian communities.

J. What exactly does 'The Split' mean?

THE GREAT SCHISM

With continuing disagreement over who should be the leader of the Church and the development of the city of Constantinople, the East and West formally separated in A.D. 1054, a separation properly called **The Great Schism**.

NB

'... Christianity split into the Roman Catholic West and the Orthodox East.'

- The Eastern Orthodox Church was made up of the Christian communities of Constantinople, Alexandria, Antioch and Jerusalem.
- The leaders were, and still are, called Patriarchs.
- The Patriarchs of Constantinople, Alexandria, Antioch and Jerusalem are seen as important spiritual leaders and work with all the bishops in promoting religious laws and beliefs.

THE EASTERN ORTHODOX CHURCH

TO KNOW

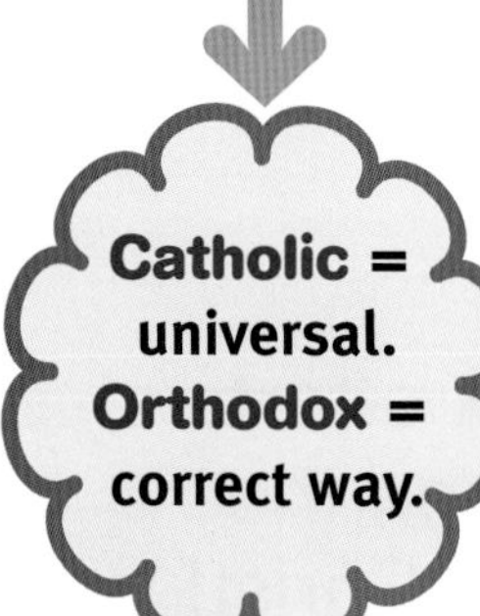

- In the Orthodox Church the Trinity of Father, Son and Holy Spirit is very important, as it is in Christianity overall.
- Its ritual for worship uses all the senses, with a lot of incense and candles, readings and chants, prayers and hymns. The floor of Orthodox churches is the world and the roof is Heaven. The followers use **'Icons'** to help them to pray to Jesus and the saints.

So the Eastern Orthodox Church grew and developed in countries such as ...
Russia • **Bulgaria** • **Greece** • **Romania** • **Georgia** • **Yugoslavia** • **Moldova** and others ...

TO KNOW

The Orthodox Church has around 175 million members.

And so the **Roman Catholic Church** grew and developed in most of the **European countries** and across to **the Americas and Australasia**!

NB Today, even though the Schism still exists, constant efforts are being made to focus on the similarities between the East and West and to grow together through Jesus Christ!

TRY THESE

Do this in your copy . . .

The Great Schism was...

finish this sentence and do the bubble writing!

Qqs

Q1. What does it mean to say, 'the East and the West'?

Q2. What did they separate?

Q3. What was this separation called?

Q4. What does the word 'Catholic' mean?

Q5. What does the word 'Orthodox' mean?

Q6. Name the Christian communities that were part of the Orthodox Church.

Q7. Give the title of the leaders in the Orthodox Church.

Q8. How does their worship use all the senses?

Q9. Name some countries where the Eastern Orthodox Church developed.

Q10. How many members are there in the Orthodox Church?

LFMNOPATRIARCHSWYABCONSTANTINOPLEFLTSCHISMSUCMORTORTHODOXBDWQRELEXANDRIAKSPLMTOCATHOLICZUVACDEASTERN

Find the words from this section in the word wheel and use each one in a sentence in your copy!

Fact File to Complete! (in your copies)

Religion: ____________________

Church name: ____________________

Year of Schism: ____________________

Reasons for Schism: ____________________

Leaders in the Church: ____________________

Countries where it is found: ____________________

Worship and ritual: ____________________

'Orthodox' means: ____________________

True / False?

- The Great Schism happened in A.D. 1200. **T / F**
- The Schism was between the Roman west and the Orthodox east. **T / F**
- Alexandria and Jerusalem were part of the Eastern Orthodox Church. **T / F**
- 'Catholic' means universal. **T / F**
- Leaders in the Orthodox Church are called cardinals. **T / F**
- Icons are used in Eastern Orthodox churches. **T / F**
- The Trinity is an important belief of the Orthodox Church. **T / F**

. . . this wasn't the end of splits and divisions within Christianity . . . have a  look!

Protestants

During the sixteenth century in Europe the Catholic Church had expanded and the Pope owned a lot of land and had power and money. Because of this, some people began to question this and say that the first **Christian communities** weren't like this. A German monk called **Martin Luther** raised questions about some Catholic Church practices. Other people agreed with him and began to protest against the Church. So began the **Protestant Reformation**. Luther and the Reformers rejected teaching around the Seven Sacraments, papal authority and the doctrine of indulgences (to a lesser degree). Luther and his followers also believed that people got to **Heaven** by belief (faith) alone and not by good works. Protestant beliefs began to spread across Europe and churches and communities for **Protestants** were set up; some became known as the **Lutheran Church**.

With this sixteenth-century Reformation well under way, the King of England, **Henry VIII**, began to get annoyed with the Pope as well. King Henry wanted to divorce his first wife, which, of course, the Church and the Pope wouldn't allow. As a result, Henry VIII rejected the rule of the Pope in England and set himself up as the Head of Christianity in England. Henry began what is now called the **Church of England** (in Ireland it is called the Church of Ireland), also known as the **Anglican Church**.

John Calvin

Another important person who helped the Protestant Church to grow was **John Calvin**. John Calvin was French and he developed many of the ideas of Martin Luther, especially in Switzerland. He believed that a person could only know God through the Bible and that there were only two sacraments: Baptism and Communion. He also believed that God already knew who would be saved! Calvin and his followers eventually became known as the **Presbyterian Church**.

NB: All these religions, or Churches, are officially called 'denominations of Christianity'.

Give these a go

Match the pairs into your copy

• Martin Luther	• Granting forgiveness
• Reformation	• Calvin accepted Baptism and Communion
• Papal Authority	• Follower of Luther from France
• Indulgence	• The Church of England
• John Calvin	• Began with Luther in the sixteenth century
• Two sacraments	• German monk
• King of England	• Rejected by Luther
• Anglican Church	• Henry VIII
• Wanted divorce	• Henry VIII

Qqs

Q1. What had happened to the Catholic Church during the sixteenth century?

Q2. Who was Martin Luther?

Q3. What questions did he raise?

Q4. What was the Protestant Reformation?

Q5. What did Protestants reject?

Q6. What did they believe?

Q7. Who was John Calvin?

Q8. Name three of his beliefs.

Q9. What was the name of the Church begun by Calvin?

Q10. What does 'Indulgence' mean?

Q11. How did the Church of England begin?

Unmuddle each word

and use in a sentence in your copy:

- TOSEPRTNATS
- MFAINORERT
- NAMTIR UHLERT
- NOJN LCAINV
- DEUGCSNLENE
- NFRAINCOMTIO
- OEPP
- GLCANIA HURCH
- RYENH VIII

Fill in the blanks:

During the _____ century the _____ Church had grown. The _____ had a lot of _____ and money. Some people raised _____ about this. A German _____ named _____ _____ questioned some Catholic _____. People began to _____ with him, so began the _____ Reformation. John _____ was another important part of the _____. He was _____ and spread Luther's ideas across _____. He believed you could only know _____ through the _____. In England, King Henry _____ broke from the _____ Church and started the _____ of _____.

The Anglican Church today

So, as we said, the **Anglican Church** really began with an English Reformation in the sixteenth century. This was based on the fact that King Henry VIII wanted a divorce, which caused him to split from the Roman Catholic Church **because it forbade divorce.**

NB: The Anglican Church has 80 million followers worldwide.
... and so the Anglican Church grew.

- The Anglican Church, or **'Anglican Communion'**, is the name given to Anglican Churches across the world.
- They all stem from the **Church of England**, but each has its own governing system, bishops and archbishops **(including the Church of Ireland)**.
- In some countries Anglican Churches ordain women as priests. This shows that the Anglican Churches don't always do the same as each other: there are some differences.
- The Anglican Communion always seeks unity of its Churches across the world.
- Although there is no specific leader (like the Pope), the Archbishop of Canterbury is seen as a spiritual leader with some influence on the Anglican Communion.
- The Anglican Church is the established Church in England and the Queen is its **'Supreme Governor'**.
- General Synod meets every year, made up of bishops and representatives.

Rowan Williams

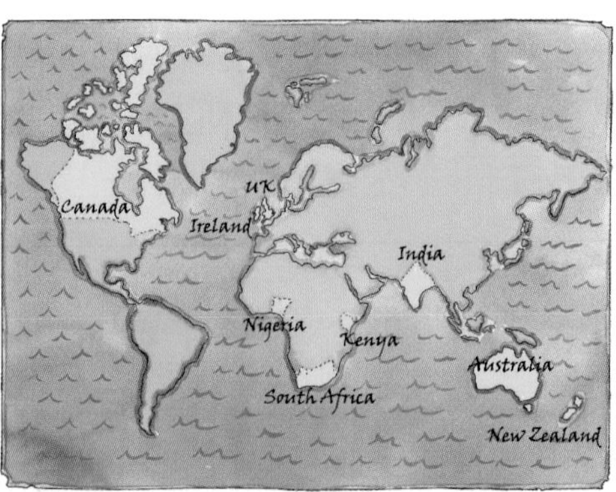

Anglican Communion

Some Anglican Churches focus intently on the Bible and Scripture. The Word of God is interpreted for the believers.

Other Anglican Churches may have a celebration more like the Catholic Mass, with bread and wine and incense, reading and singing.

In Ireland ...

NB:
Diocese = groups of parishes together overseen by a bishop for worship and administration.

- The Anglican Church of Ireland, more properly called **the Church of Ireland** (CoI), has been in existence since 1871.
- It has twelve dioceses throughout Northern Ireland and the Republic of Ireland.
- The Anglican Archbishop of Armagh is seen as the Church's leader.

Robin Eames

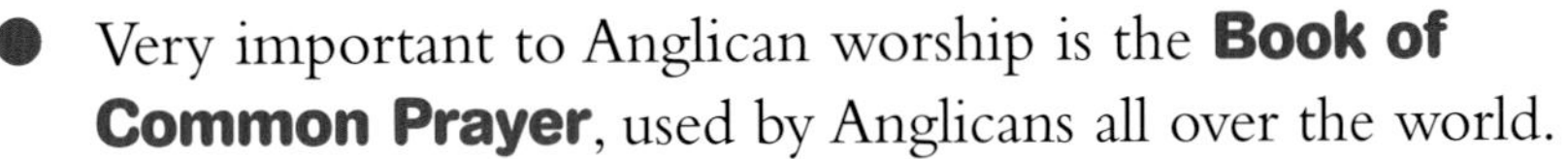

- Very important to Anglican worship is the **Book of Common Prayer**, used by Anglicans all over the world.

- Members of the Anglican Communion profess **the Nicene Creed and the Apostles' Creed** (as do Catholics).
- The Catholic and Anglican Churches work together closely to promote Christian values in Ireland.

NB: Ordained men and women are called 'vicars'.

Some Anglican churches can be plain on the inside, with just seats, a stand, an altar and cross. Others are more elaborate, with statues and gold, etc.

Over to you!

Complete this Anglican **Fact File** in your copy

- English King: ______________
- When it began: ______________
- Proper name: ______________
- All Churches stem from: ______
- Seen as Church Head: ______
- Supreme Governor: __________
- Meets every year: ___________
- Archbishop of Armagh: _______
- Dioceses in Ireland: _________
- Used in worship: ____________

Qqs

Q1. How did the Anglican Church begin?
Q2. What is the Church's proper name?
Q3. Where do the various Churches stem from?
Q4. How do you know that there are some differences within the Anglican Church?
Q5. Who is seen as its spiritual leader across the world?
Q6. Who is the Supreme Governor of the Church of England?
Q7. Where did the Church of Ireland begin?
Q8. Who is seen as its leader?
Q9. How many dioceses are there in Ireland?
Q10. What are Anglican priests called?

Figure out these muddled word tiles

FR	NGL	AND	ST	RCH	AN	EMS	CHU
URC	THE	ANG	CH	LIC	F E	H O	OM

THE	OF	IN	IS	E L	IRE	OP	ISH
AGH	EAD	ARM	CHB	D	LAN	TH	AR
ER							

True / False?

- Anglican Church began with Henry VIII. **T / F**
- He wanted a divorce. **T / F**
- He split from the Catholic Church. **T / F**
- All Churches stem from the Church of Ireland. **T / F**
- It is properly called the Anglican Society. **T / F**
- Archbishop of Dublin is its leader. **T / F**
- The Queen is the Supreme Governor. **T / F**
- There are eighteen dioceses in Ireland. **T / F**
- The Book of Common Hymns is used in worship. **T / F**
- Ordained men are called vicars. **T / F**

More Qs

A. What problem did Henry VIII have with the Catholic Church?
B. How do we know the Anglican Communion may differ on certain issues?
C. The Archbishop of Canterbury is not the same as the Pope: explain.
D. Why is it important that the Anglican Church expresses the Nicene Creed and the Apostles' Creed?
E. How do the interiors of its churches differ?

Quick word on the other

Protestant Churches

Society of Friends (Quakers)

- **Begun** in England in the seventeenth century by George Fox.
- He wasn't happy with Catholicism or Protestantism.
- Felt that the Churches focused on outward signs and displays rather than on inner goodness and spirituality.
- He and his friends and followers began the **Society of Friends**.
- The Church questioned Fox and his followers. To the judge Fox replied, 'Quake at the voice of the Lord'. Quakers stuck!
- Eventually settled in America.
- Believe there is no need for structures or rules. All people have Christ in them. No churches or ministers.
- Advocates of peaceful means in all things; non-violent.

GEORGE FOX.

Presbyterian Church

- **Begun** in the eighteenth century, in Geneva, by John Calvin. He was a Reformation follower of Martin Luther.
- Luther rejected the authority of the Pope and the idea of bishops.
- John Knox, an enthusiastic follower, brought these ideas to Scotland, where the Church became, and still is, very strong.
- Brought to Ireland in the seventeenth century; now a worldwide Church.
- Main idea is that all we need to know is to be found in the Bible.
- Church to be governed by **Presbyters** (elders).
- Plain churches – no statues or stained glass.
- Have a general assembly to make decisions.
- Predestination is one of its primary beliefs!

Christianity

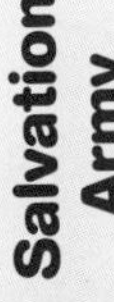

Salvation Army

- **Begun** in nineteenth century by William Booth, a Methodist minister in England.
- He saw that London's homeless and destitute needed help and so he set up the **Salvation Army**.
- Organised along military lines, but with Christian values.
- Spread across Europe.

Baptist Church

- **Begun** in Holland in the sixteenth century.
- Group of Christian people believed that baptising babies was wrong.
- They believed that only those who chose to follow Jesus should be baptised.
- They baptise adults by **immersion** (going totally under the water). This represents death of an old life, and the birth of a new life in God.
- Originally called **Anabaptists** (*ana* = again) because its followers were rebaptised as adults.
- Spread to England, America and Ireland.
- No priests or bishops; all members have a say in Church affairs and can express their opinions at regular meetings.

Methodist Church

- **Begun** in England in eighteenth century by John and Charles Wesley.
- They wanted to reform the Church of England (the Anglican Church).
- Following opposition from Church leaders, they split from the Church of England.
- They started the **Methodist Church, so-called** because they were very methodical (orderly) about Bible study and prayer.
- This attracted followers who were unhappy with the Church of England.
- They reject the authority of the Pope and do not have bishops.
- A Council of Church members meets and decides on important issues, with one person acting as chairperson.
- The Church teaches that all people are equal and can be called by God.
- Ministers lead the people in prayer, as equals.

TRY THESE

Pick three of the Protestant Churches and complete a FACT FILE for each one ...

Name: ____________
Begun: ________
By: ________
Rejected: ___
Beliefs: _______
Leader: _______
Countries: _______

×3

Bubble writing to do in your copy:

Protestant Churches

Methodist Church

Baptist Church

To Do

Design a poster, giving the name and details of one Protestant Church!

T C N E R O C E M O R S
T S I D O H T E M N Q N
G G A W E S L E Y A O E
C Y R N I O N L R I P T
B G N T A G J E T R L H
B I P A L I H A O E N E
I A S A M T M T N T A R
B A N H U R E W I Y C L
L D U L O S E P V B I A
E X O F T P O G L S L N
B U E A A P S I A E G D
Y R N C E L D K C R N S
G T Q U A K E R S P A Q

Protestant Churches Wordsearch

ANA	METHODIST
BIBLE	PRESBYTERIAN
ENGLAND	REFORMATION
LUTHER	BAPTIST
POPE	CALVIN
QUAKERS	GERMANY
ANGLICAN	NETHERLANDS
BISHOPS	PROTESTANT
FOX	WESLEY

. . . so as you can see, the religion of Christianity certainly took some twists and turns over the centuries, but always at the centre is Jesus Christ. Let's look at some of

The Titles of Jesus!

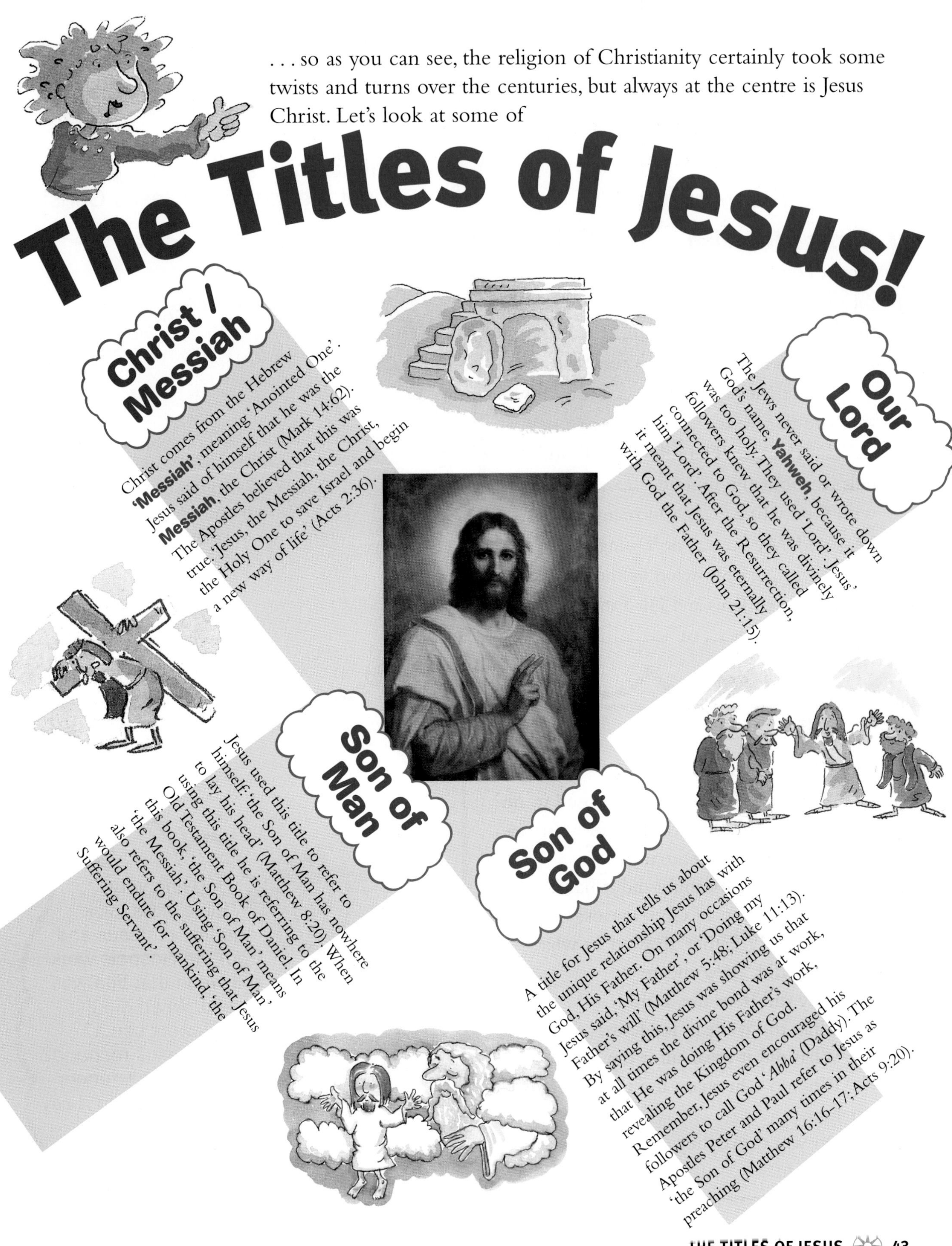

Christ / Messiah

Christ comes from the Hebrew **'Messiah'**, meaning 'Anointed One'. Jesus said of himself that he was the **Messiah**, the Christ (Mark 14:62). The Apostles believed that this was true. 'Jesus, the Messiah, the Christ, the Holy One to save Israel and begin a new way of life' (Acts 2:36).

Our Lord

The Jews never said or wrote down God's name, **Yahweh**, because it was too holy. They used 'Lord'. Jesus' followers knew that he was divinely connected to God, so they called him 'Lord'. After the Resurrection, it meant that Jesus was eternally with God the Father (John 21:15).

Son of Man

Jesus used this title to refer to himself: 'the Son of Man has nowhere to lay his head' (Matthew 8:20). When using this title he is referring to the Old Testament Book of Daniel. In this book, 'the Son of Man' means 'the Messiah'. Using 'Son of Man' also refers to the suffering that Jesus would endure for mankind, 'the Suffering Servant'.

Son of God

A title for Jesus that tells us about the unique relationship Jesus has with God, His Father. On many occasions Jesus said, 'My Father', or 'Doing my Father's will' (Matthew 5:48; Luke 11:13). By saying this, Jesus was showing us that at all times the divine bond was at work, that He was doing His Father's work, revealing the Kingdom of God. Remember, Jesus even encouraged his followers to call God '*Abba*' (Daddy). The Apostles Peter and Paul refer to Jesus as 'the Son of God' many times in their preaching (Matthew 16:16–17; Acts 9:20).

Over to you!

Fill in the blanks:

Christ / Messiah

Christ comes from the ______ for ______, meaning ______ One. Jesus said of himself that he was the ______, the ______. The Apostles were sure that this was true. ______, the Messiah, the ______, the Holy One are to save ______ and begin a new ______ of ______. The title Son of God tells us about the unique ______ Jesus had with God, His ______. On many ______ Jesus said 'My ______' or 'Doing my ______'s ______'. Showing us the ______ bond between Jesus and His Father, revealing the ______ of ______.

To Do

Using the titles and the information given above, write a one-page essay about the identity of Jesus Christ.

VWANOINTEDLMNYAHWEHPQSTDANIELBLDECHRISTFGUTITLESQBLMESSIAHCXTUVLORDCFGHIJSONKSRQPOGODTMOSMANEROTSERVANTUX

Find the words in the Word Wheel and use in a sentence in your copy.

Q.

A. What does 'Christ' mean?
B. What was the Messiah supposed to do?
C. When using the title 'Son of Man', to what was Jesus referring?
D. What other meaning did it have?
E. The title 'Son of God' means?
F. Using 'My Father' showed us what?
G. What did '*Abba*' mean?
H. Why did Jesus use 'Lord'?
I. What did it mean for Jesus?
J. What did it mean after the Resurrection?
K. Why do Christians use these titles for Jesus?
L. Do you think they are important? Explain.

RESEARCH
JOURNAL IDEA

Using your Bible skills, pick one title of Jesus and from the Gospels work out when that title was used. When did the followers use it? How did Jesus respond? How did the listeners respond? What did it say about Jesus?

The Christian Community You Are In!

. . . finally, it is important to look at a Christian community at work on our own doorstep . . .

By this I mean the **Parish.**

The parish is the local Christian area to which you belong.

TO KNOW

Faithful = those in the community who are part of the religion.
Lay = people who are not ordained to priesthood.
Liturgies = the worship and prayer celebrations in the church.

Every parish has a priest, or priests, to help lead the Christian people in their worship and their lives.

Some parishes have a parish sister to assist within the parish.

Some parishes have a Parish Council to help with the organisation and decision-making of the parish. Laymen and laywomen serve on the Council as is obligatory.

Laypeople assist with the Mass and other liturgies in the parish church, for example, reader/eucharistic minister/deacon/acolyte/server. They also collaborate and participate in spreading God's word.

Parishes usually have groups of singers and musicians who use their talents to help celebrate the Mass and the Sacraments in the church.

Parish church: the place where all worshippers go to pray and celebrate the Sacraments in the home of Jesus Christ (Sundays and weekdays), for example, Eucharist, funerals, marriages, baptisms, Communion, Confirmation, etc.

In parishes laymen and laywomen help out with other jobs in the church as well, for example, cleaners, sacristan, flower-arrangers, etc.

Parishes are very lively places, with lots of people doing lots of things. These people love what they do because they do it for their faith, for other people and for the love of God.

Time To Think and Pray

We offer these prayers to God . . .

For us –
that we will each try to respect and live our faith.

For all Christians –
that they will constantly be an example of Jesus' unending love to those around them.

For Christian Churches –
that they will continue to strive for unity and work on those things that bring them closer together.

For Church leaders –
that they will constantly be open to the voice of the Spirit in the communities they serve.

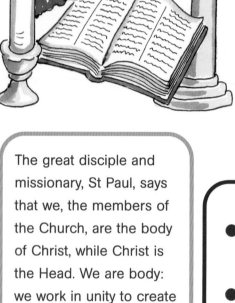

Read from Scripture:

1 Cor. 12:4-11

1 Cor. 12:14-27

The great disciple and missionary, St Paul, says that we, the members of the Church, are the body of Christ, while Christ is the Head. We are body: we work in unity to create God's Kingdom in this world, to create a place of peace, love and joy, where we can exist in the presence of God forever. The Holy Spirit is given to us to help us to be the body of Christ and to show God's love to the world. **AMEN**

Let us Pray

- that we will play our part in being Christ's body;
- that we will listen to the Spirit of Christ, the Head;
- that we will reveal Christ's love to the person beside us;
- that we will see those in need and reach out to them always.

AMEN

Section 2

Looking up a Bible Reference

The Religion of Israel – Judaism

- How did it all begin?
- Abraham's Journey from Ur to Hebron (in Canaan)
- The Covenant
- The Israelites in Egypt
- Moses
- The Passover
- The Exodus
- The Ten Commandments
- Living in the Promised Land
- King David
- Joshua
- King Solomon
- Exile and Return
- History of Israel Timeline

The Beliefs, Worship and Traditions of Judaism

- The Torah
- Judaism and Food
- The Jewish Sabbath

- The Synagogue
- Synagogue Worship
- The Messiah
- Jewish Rites of Passage
- Special Clothes of the Jewish Faith
- Festivals of Judaism
- Judaism and the World
- Judaism in Ireland
- Varieties of Judaism
- Judaism and Christianity
- Jewish Holy Places
- Time to Think and Pray

Looking up a Bible Reference

Before we delve into the history and development of the religion of Israel, it's important that we know **how to look up stories** in the Old Testament.

To Do

Here is a typical Bible reference:

Genesis 12:1

It tells you:

The name of the Book to look up;

the chapter number (it's the big number, in this case: 12);

the number of the line/sentence (it's the smaller number, in this case: 1).

So, keep in mind that you are looking for **the name of the Book**, for example, Genesis, Exodus, Deuteronomy and so on. You are looking for the **chapter number** – the big number on the page – and you are looking for the **sentence number** – the smaller number beside the lines.

Sometimes the Book name will be shortened. For example, Exodus may be shortened to EX, Genesis shortened to GEN, and so on.

Try looking up these:

Genesis 12:1;

Genesis 15:4;

Exodus 2:1;

Exodus 3:1-15.

The Religion of Israel

Words to remember:
Polytheism
Greek Civilisation
Monotheism
Covenant
Passover
Decalogue

For thousands of years human beings have believed there is something greater than them, something that exists beyond their sphere of experience. This being, or beings, they called 'god', or 'gods'.

The Greeks believed in many different gods, each with responsibility for a specific area. For example, Zeus was the overseer of all the gods, Athena was the goddess of war and Poseidon was the god of the sea.

The Romans also believed in many different gods, to whom they prayed and made sacrifices.

Belief in many gods is called

POLYTHEISM

Civilisations like these believed that the gods had control over the world and needed to be pleased, or else they would become angry and punish the people with famine, or war, or death.

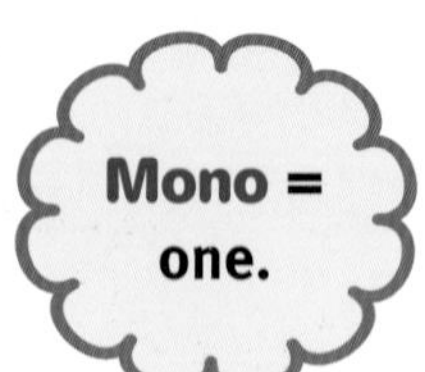

However, the developing religion of Israel was very different. It was a religion that held the belief that there was only **one God**. This God would show His people how to live good lives. Belief in one God is called

Monotheism

How did it all begin?

Well, it all began with a man called **Abraham** (or Abram, as he was called originally). If you want to learn more about Abraham, read Genesis 12:1 and a few of the chapters that follow it.

Almost **4,000 years ago** Abraham had a unique experience – he heard God speaking to him.

Abraham and his wife, Sara (later Sarah), lived in **Ur**, a city in **Mesopotamia** (part of what is now Iraq). On the map shown you will see that Ur is near the mouth of the **River Euphrates**, at the top of the **Persian Gulf**. From Ur, Abraham and his family (his father was called Terah) moved to **Haran**, travelling along the Euphrates. From there they went to **Hebron** in **Canaan** (the ancient name for Israel). There Abraham spent most of his life.

TO KNOW →

Canaan is the name of the grandson of Noah, and the name given to the land in which he settled.

Abraham's journey from Ur to Hebron (in Canaan)

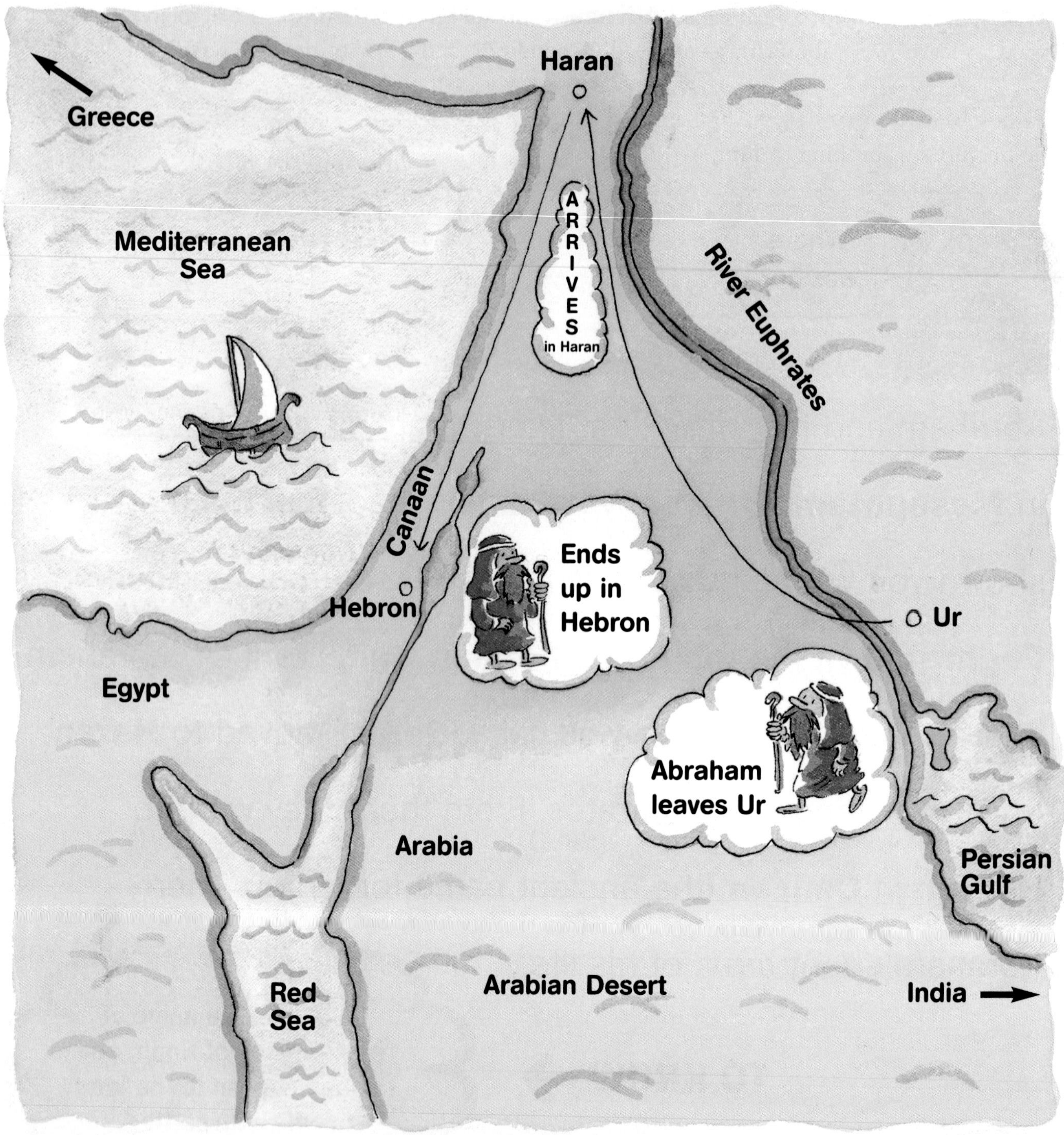

So, Abraham lived in the city of Ur. It was an ancient city where tribes called **CHALDEANS** lived. It was famous for its **ziggurat**, made by the Chaldeans.

People in Ur had good jobs and nice houses ...

...they also had trading links with their neighbours and good markets ...

Come on, Sarah. God will show us the way.
CANAN
Few miles

God chose Abraham because he was a good, holy and devout man. He chose him to go on this journey to the Promised Land.

...from UR, ABRAHAM AND SARAH moved to HARAN. It was here that God spoke to Abraham:

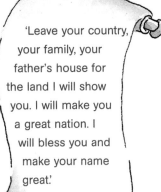

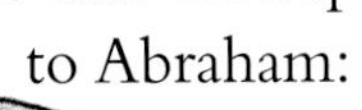

'Leave your country, your family, your father's house for the land I will show you. I will make you a great nation. I will bless you and make your name great.'
(Gen. 12:1)

TO KNOW

The word 'HEBREW' comes from the name given to people who lived across the River Euphrates. The Israelites were known as Hebrews.

Abraham's Journey Wordsearch

```
S K B H O N G H V C K D L F S I M N P L H B K J C
I E B C K M U I X L V W L P A G R E E M E N T T O
N C T U H Y O N J Z G U H E I J L O L Q B G U I V
Q A O A I A P T P U G E A J X X E Z J Q R T C L E
T G N C R N L E C N E I R E P X E S I S E N E G N
N K P N O H G D A A O A A C Z A N N S G W H J U A
E F R R A A P I E K I Z S I I J P U U J V U V M N
A P B N E R S U O A H B G V R N J L V G Z S W X T
D E H K Y R J U E L N G A C A A P E W J A Q T G A
H X I P E E L C J R U S R R O A V Y X L A J V Y Q
G E F P G O I B D R E V V W A N N Z S B R M S Z M
K X M W Z L O S A D U V E M I A Q A L W F T C G O
T N B D H H Z T Z F I N I Q M C R Y R C W E Y N L
J G N D N J R F T O R W F R A Y L E Q A W B A B W
N P W I W U A W N E Q R E B T T K J E W H V D B L
M A H A R B A U O D A K Q Y O O T V Y B A A S A O
K Q B A L M W Z T B O D X B P N V L W A T T Y W G
J E J H W W V R R M X M Q D O P M L L N G Q O P E
B J M D N W G A Z P C J N O S V R H O Z U I K Y Y
G A H O O R M U T F F P J Q E N Q X K F J F B X U
T G F O X W J J S X B W Q A M I M U W Y O J C S Y
C J P P K Q J R I W C N Z S R E D S E A P H E R D
P L K Q N A G R Q F G S F S F Z F V Y Z J T I U I
U O C Q R Q U X W H O V R O Z G R S Z V L J U O E
P U T G S W J D B X H M A N E Q J F J B W J V P E
```

ABRAHAM
ABRAM
AGREEMENT
ARABIA
CANAAN
CHALDEANS

COVENANT
EGYPT
HARAN
HEBREW
HEBRON
GENESIS EXPERIENCE

MESOPOTAMIA
PERSIAN GULF
RED SEA
RIVER EUPHRATES
SARAH
ZIGGURAT

TO KNOW

What happened next is called the

'Covenant'

COPY AND COLOUR

NB a **Covenant** is an agreement between two people – a bond, or a link.

This was the beginning of the religion of Israel. Abraham trusted God and did as God asked of him. This 'One God' was very important to Abraham and he worshipped him.

While Abraham was in Hebron, in Canaan, God promised him that he would have a son.
'Then the word of **Yahweh** (God) was spoken to him again:
"A child will be born of you, your own flesh and blood."' (Gen. 15:4)
This was God's **Covenant** with Abraham, and Abraham was very happy.

Q1. Who was Abraham's wife?

Q2. Where did they live originally?

Q3. Where did they travel to first?

Q4. Where did Abraham and Sarah end up?

Q5. What did God want Abraham to do?

Q6. What Covenant did God make with Abraham?

Q7. Why did Abraham worship and trust God?

- God's Covenant came true and Sarah had a son, whom they named Isaac. Sarah and Abraham continued to trust and worship God and thus began the relationship between **God** and the **Israelites**.

- The descendants of Abraham, namely Joseph, his brothers and his father, Jacob, eventually settled in Egypt. They moved there because of famine in Israel (Gen. 25, and following chapters).

TO KNOW

Israelites didn't like to use the name of God because it was so sacred. What they called God was a word based on 'YHWH' (with vowels: Yahweh). Also they preferred to use the word Adonai, meaning Lord.

'The Israelites in Egypt'!

COPY AND COLOUR

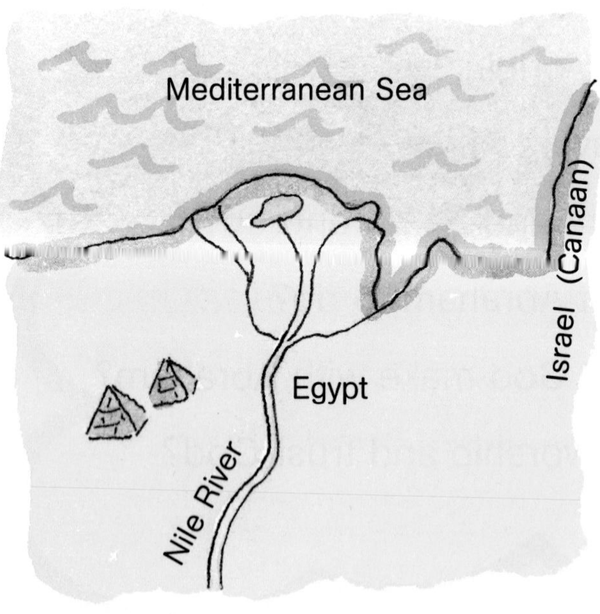

What Happened Next?
Exodus
Genesis
The next part of the relationship between God and the Israelites focuses on Moses.

Words to remember
Pharaoh • Exodus • Goshen
Canaan • Passover
Genesis • Exodus

MOSES

- In the Book of Exodus, in the Old Testament, we can read that a new king (or pharaoh) took over Egypt. This king was a very selfish man who forced the Israelites into slavery, making buildings and temples for him. At this time most of the Israelites lived in a place called **Goshen**.

- Many writers and historians say that this period of rule began around 1300–1250 B.C.

- After a time the pharaoh became concerned that there were too many Israelites. He felt they would rise up against him and refuse to obey him anymore.

- He ordered all first-born Israelite boys to be killed. One person escaped this terrible fate. His name was **Moses**. Moses' mother hid her baby son and put him in a basket, which she put in the River Nile. The basket floated to safety, with Moses in it (Exodus 2).

Q1. In which Old Testament book can we read about Moses?

Q2. What is the proper name for the king of Egypt?

Q3. Where in Egypt did most of the Israelites live?

Q4. As far as historians know in what period did all this all happen?

'God made sure Moses Survived'!

COPY AND COLOUR

Unmuddlo these words and use them in a sentence in your copy.

- EOSMS
- HAROAPH
- HSEGON
- DSOXEU
- STROHINAS
- RLITEASIE
- DLO
- ETMSANTE

Moses' basket floated into the Pharaoh's palace. The Pharaoh's daughter found him and took him home. She looked after the baby and he became part of the Pharaoh's family.

This is how Moses grew up as an Egyptian prince, educated by the best teachers and enjoying all the luxuries of the palace.

His name meant:
MOSHE (Hebrew) = is born from the water,
and **MOSE** (Egyptian).

Eventually Moses realised he was not an Egyptian but an **ISRAELITE** (a Hebrew).

Moses opened his eyes and began to really look at how the Israelites were being treated. They were slaves, whipped and starved and treated badly. Moses felt very sorry for his people. One day he witnessed a soldier whipping an Israelite unmercilessly and Moses lost his temper. He hit and killed the soldier in his efforts to protect the slave.

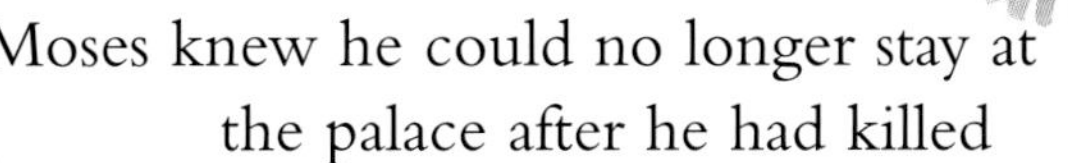

Moses knew he could no longer stay at the palace after he had killed one of the Pharaoh's soldiers. He left and travelled to Midian. There he met a man called JETHRO and his daughters. He stayed with them, helping to work the land and tend the sheep.

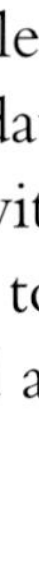

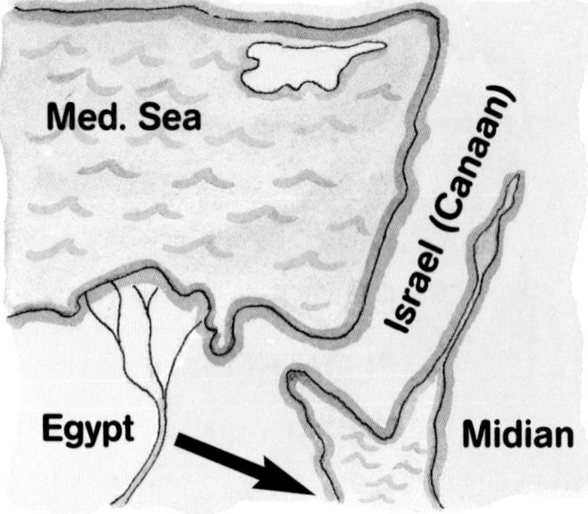

Moses Wordsearch

Z	H	P	L	F	D	S	H	X	C	Y	W	J	P	E
T	S	O	E	B	X	E	E	E	S	G	E	R	H	A
C	Q	H	H	Z	W	R	T	R	B	T	E	A	Q	N
E	D	V	S	T	T	V	C	A	H	R	R	V	F	S
M	T	Q	O	N	A	A	Q	R	E	O	E	L	V	T
I	W	I	M	A	V	N	O	Z	P	R	O	W	E	N
D	T	H	L	N	P	T	I	P	S	A	T	K	J	E
I	X	C	F	E	D	H	I	D	T	E	S	M	T	H
A	H	M	I	V	A	Z	A	E	C	A	S	P	U	S
N	B	R	G	O	G	R	D	R	B	G	Y	O	P	O
X	Y	G	Q	C	H	Q	S	V	A	G	X	M	M	G
M	O	D	E	E	R	F	J	I	E	O	B	H	K	P
O	Q	P	A	L	A	C	E	D	P	N	H	H	C	E
A	E	S	D	E	R	P	B	L	M	G	X	B	I	W
I	D	E	N	T	I	T	Y	X	P	N	H	C	C	X

COVENANT
EGYPT
FLOATED
FREEDOM
GOSHEN
HEBREW

IDENTITY
ISRAELITE
JETHRO
MIDIAN
MOSES
MOSHE

PALACE
PHARAOH
RED SEA
SERVANT
TREATED
ZIPPORAH

Over to you!

Q1. Where did Moses' basket float into?

Q2. Who found the basket?

Q3. What did the Pharaoh's daughter do with Moses?

Q4. What did Moses grow up as?

Q5. Where does the name Moses come from?

True / False ?

- Baby Moses was put in a pram. **T / F**
- The Pharaoh's mother found Moses. **T / F**
- Moses grew up as a prince of Egypt. **T / F**
- Moses means 'from the palace'. **T / F**
- Moses realised that he was an American. **T / F**
- He became angry. **T / F**
- He murdered an Egyptian. **T / F**
- Moses ran away to Turkey. **T / F**

Complete this cloze test:

Moses' basket f_______ into the Pharaoh's p_______. The Pharaoh's d_______ found baby M_______. She a_______ him. Moses grew up in the Pharaoh's p_______. He was a p_______ of E_______. Later he realised that he was in fact an I_______. He m_______ an Egyptian soldier and then r_______ away. He ended up in M_______.

Just as with **ABRAHAM** before him, God had a special mission for Moses.

One day Moses was tending the sheep and he led them to fresh grass. Suddenly a bush was consumed by flames – with no explanation. Before Moses could figure out what had happened, he heard a voice. It was God speaking to him.

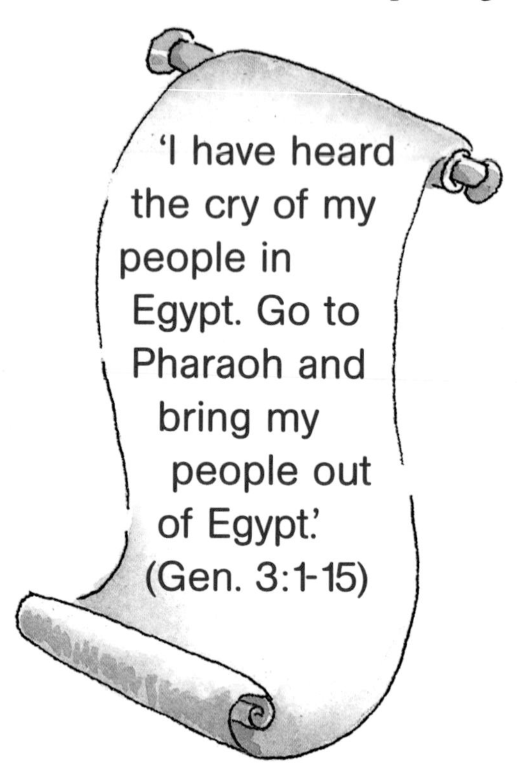

'I have heard the cry of my people in Egypt. Go to Pharaoh and bring my people out of Egypt.'
(Gen. 3:1-15)

Moses was afraid and puzzled. He asked who was speaking to him. God replied,

Moses then knew that this was the One God of Israel who had made a Covenant with Abraham. The One God who was unchangeable, reliable, present and active. Moses agreed to save his and God's people from Egypt.

- Moses immediately did as God had asked him and went to the Pharaoh to demand that the Israelites be set free. The Pharaoh refused. God sent down **plagues** on the Egyptians and their land.

- The tenth and last plague was too much for the Pharaoh and forced him to change his mind and set the Israelites free. God finally chose that all **first-born Egyptian children** were to be killed, including the son of the Pharaoh.

The ten plagues on Egypt:
EX 7:14-29;
EX 8:1-28;
EX 9:1-35;
EX 10:1-29;
EX 11:1-10.

COPY AND COLOUR

What happened next is called ...

'The Passover'!

God instructed Moses to tell all the Israelites that on the fourteenth day of the month they were to to sacrifice a lamb that was a year old (or less) and smear its blood over their doors. Then, they were to roast the lamb whole and eat it with unleavened bread, herbs and spices.

Moses also told the Israelites how to eat their sacrificial lamb: with a belt around the waist, sandals on the feet and a staff in the hand. On that night, the night of the fourteenth day, all first-born Egyptian males would be struck down by God and killed. Houses with blood smeared on their doors would be spared and God would spare and care for the Israelites. (Exodus 12:1-14).

TO KNOW

'Unleavened bread' = bread that doesn't rise when it is baked because it has no yeast. It's much quicker to bake than dough, which rises!

For you to do

Make a list of the ten plagues (look them up first) and then draw a picture for each one.

1. __________
2. __________
3. __________
4. __________
5. __________
6. __________
7. __________
8. __________
9. __________
10. __________

1.	2.
3.	4.
5.	6.
7.	8
9.	10.

Some Qs:

Q1. Why did the Pharaoh refuse to free the Israelites?

Q2. How did the plagues affect the people of Egypt?

Q3. What finally made the Pharaoh free the Israelites?

Q4. Explain the Passover.

Q5. What is left out of unleavened bread?

Q6. How were the Israelites to eat the Passover meal?

The Passover Meal

(on the night to freedom)

Label each item.

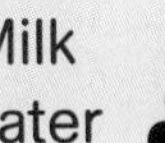

They drank one of the following:

Wine

Milk

Water

So, the Pharaoh let the Israelites go, and the next important moment is ...

THE EXODUS

COPY AND COLOUR

Moses led his people as they set out for a place called **Succoth**. When they got to the **Red Sea**, they realised the Pharaoh and his army were coming after them. Then God performed a miracle at the Red Sea – the waters dried up and the Israelites crossed the seabed and walked to freedom. When the Egyptians attempted to follow them across, the water just as suddenly returned and drowned them.

TO KNOW

EXODUS = leaving a place in great numbers.
RED SEA = properly called the Sea of Reds.

So, the Israelites travelled to the Promised Land: **Canaan**!

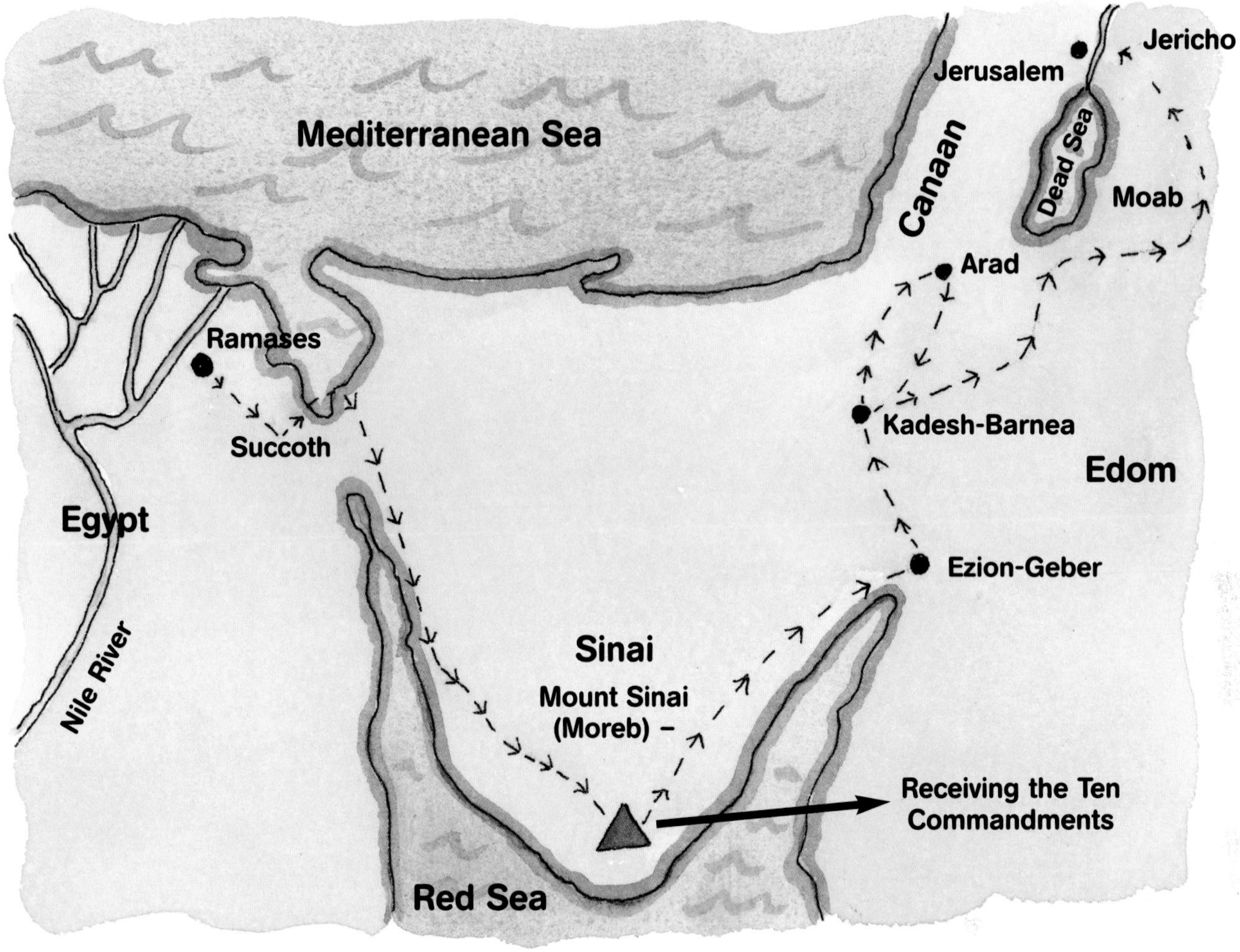

The Journey of the Exodus to Canaan.

When Moses and the Israelites reached Mount **Sinai**, a new **Covenant** was made between God and his people. This took the form of the …

Ten Commandments

(in Greek, the Commandments are called the Decalogue).

COPY AND COLOUR

God called Moses onto **Mount Sinai** and told him he must always look after his people. He then gave to Moses the **Ten Commandments** as a new Covenant **(Agreement)**. In doing this, God was revealing his will to his people.

TO KNOW

The stone tablets on which were written the Ten Commandments were placed inside the Ark of the Covenant, which was sealed shut (EX 25:10).

God's Commandments to His people were (EX 20:1-21):

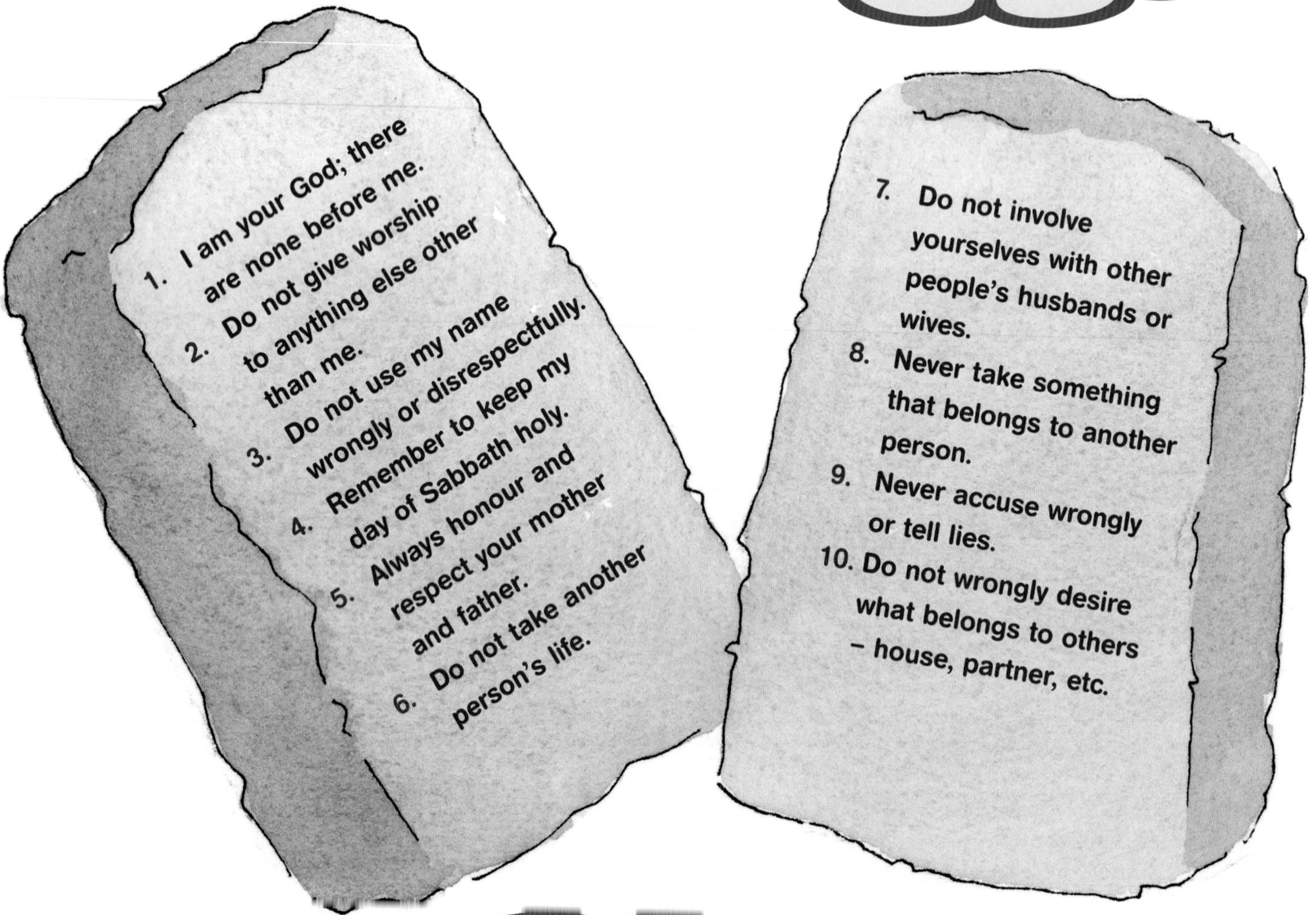

1. I am your God; there are none before me.
2. Do not give worship to anything else other than me.
3. Do not use my name wrongly or disrespectfully.
4. Remember to keep my day of Sabbath holy.
5. Always honour and respect your mother and father.
6. Do not take another person's life.
7. Do not involve yourselves with other people's husbands or wives.
8. Never take something that belongs to another person.
9. Never accuse wrongly or tell lies.
10. Do not wrongly desire what belongs to others – house, partner, etc.

TO KNOW

In the Book of Exodus, it says that Moses wrote down the laws and that later the Commandments were written on slabs, or stone tablets. Above is a traditional presentation of the Decalogue on stone tablets.

NB

The Ten Commandments comprised the continuation and renewal of the **Covenant** between God and His people.

Over to you for some work

Draw a cartoon strip in your copy, based on the following series of events:

1. Moses put in basket	2. Floats into palace	3. Grows up a prince	4. Runs away from Egypt
5. Shepherds sheep	6. Returns – asks to free people	7. Leads people to freedom	8. Gets Ten Commandments

Q1. Why was he called 'Moses'?

Q2. Why did he have to run away from the palace?

Q3. Where did he run away to? Where is it?

Q4. In the story of the burning bush, what did God say to Moses?

Q5. How did Moses feel in his heart?

Put yourself in the shoes (or sandals!) of

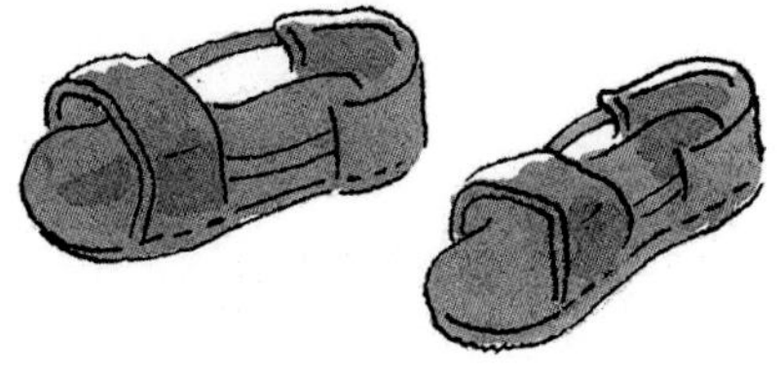

Tell his story from the time he was placed in the basket by his mother to the moment when he received the Ten Commandments from God.

There are some very important points we need to remember about God's relationship with the Israelites and the beginnings of the religion of Israel.

These are:

Isaac

Ten Commandments

1. God called ordinary people to give a message and mission to them.
2. God made an agreement **(Covenant)** with them.
3. The Israelites saw themselves as the **'Chosen People'**, as God's people.
4. God gave them a place to stay, a country of their own.
5. He looked over them and guided them and made wonders happen that seemed to be unnatural.
6. He gave strength to their leaders.
7. God gave them rules to live by and asked them to live good lives.
8. Through these works God slowly revealed himself to the Israelites.

You are my people

Go to Canaan

Do not be afraid. I am with you

Never lie ...
Never disrespect ...
My name is holy ...

Exodus Wordsearch

T	L	V	R	R	X	V	I	S	V	A	F	Z	F	D
P	J	I	Y	P	G	E	Z	A	G	D	Z	G	M	E
S	U	O	I	R	O	L	G	R	N	S	W	O	Y	C
S	I	A	C	A	Z	A	E	Y	E	I	D	B	E	A
T	C	R	M	I	X	E	V	T	P	E	S	L	G	L
N	G	K	B	S	M	W	I	I	E	T	I	J	G	O
E	N	W	X	E	E	L	G	R	P	N	I	W	C	G
M	O	G	N	I	E	A	F	N	Z	Y	N	A	W	U
D	S	T	K	A	D	I	S	C	I	P	L	I	N	E
N	Y	E	R	E	U	R	T	O	D	V	R	T	P	S
A	F	S	C	O	D	E	E	V	B	G	A	E	E	W
M	I	J	C	N	T	F	L	D	O	E	O	E	J	J
M	E	X	O	D	U	S	B	D	S	P	Y	G	L	P
O	H	E	W	H	A	Y	A	M	L	E	L	C	F	Q
C	E	U	W	V	K	L	T	E	S	R	A	S	M	I

AGREEMENT
ARK
CODE
COMMANDMENTS
DISCIPLINE
DECALOGUE
EGYPTIANS
EXODUS

FREEDOM
GLORIOUS
GOD
ISRAELITES
LEAVING
NILE
OBEY
PEOPLE

PRAISE
RED SEA
SONG
TABLETS
YAHWEH

A. According to the Exodus story, how did God help the Israelites to escape from the Egyptians?

B. Why was Moses such an important person?

C. Where were the Israelites travelling to?

D. What was so important about the Ten Commandments?

E. What sort of a code are the Ten Commandments?

F. What is another name for the Ten Commandments?

G. What does the word 'Exodus' mean?

H. Create your own Ten Commandments to live by.

I. Name another religion that follows the Ten Commandments.

Fix the following sentences (rewrite them in your copy):

- God called ordinary / special people to give a message to them.
- The Israelites saw themselves as being the ignored / chosen people.
- God weakened / gave strength to their leaders
- God hid away / revealed himself to the Israelites.
- God avoided / looked after them on their journey to the Promised Land.
- God made deals / Covenants with the Israelites.

LIVING IN THE PROMISED LAND

In order to find out how the Israelites fared in the Promised Land of **Canaan**, we read the Old Testament, especially the Book of **JOSHUA** and the Book of **JUDGES**.

JOSHUA

After Moses' death, Joshua was chosen to be the Israelites' leader in the Promised Land. Once he and the Israelites arrived in Canaan, he divided the land into twelve separate areas, each one for a tribe of Israel.

The Book of Joshua tells us that the Israelites took over the city of **JERICHO** and the towns of **SHECHEM**, **GIBEON**, **MAKKEDAH** and **HAZOR**. They claimed this land for God because God had given it to them.

When Joshua was dying, he demanded that the Israelites always love and obey God, as Moses had told them to do.

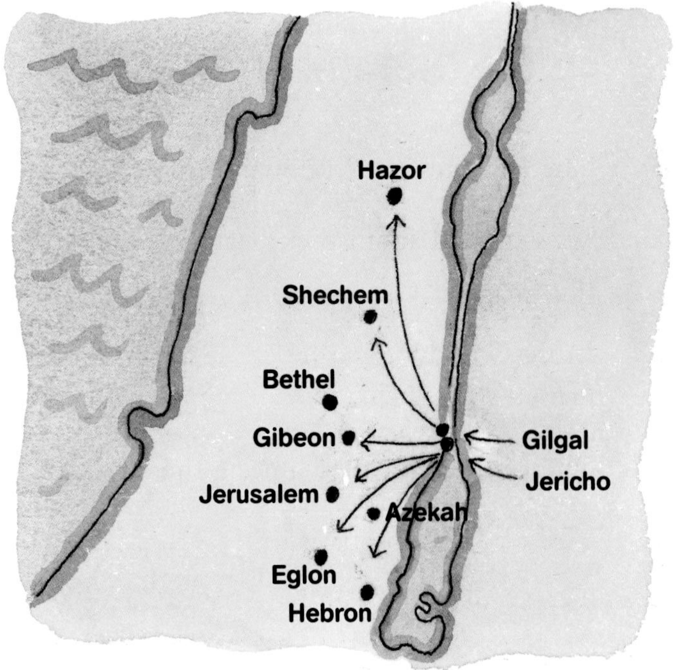

Over to you

Q1. If you were a historian, which books would you read to find out about the Israelites settling down in the Promised Land?

Q2. When did Joshua become leader of the Israelites?

Q3. Where did he lead the people?

Q4. What happened when the Israelite people claimed the land?

Q5. What was Joshua's last request to his people?

Q6. Which Book tells us about Joshua and claiming the land?

Q7. Name some of the cities and towns taken by the Israelites.

Q8. What did they believe about the land they took?

Complete these sentences:

A. The Israelites settled down in the ______.

B. We can read about them claiming the land in ______.

C. Moses was dying, so he chose a new leader, named ______.

D. The land was divided among the ______.

E. The Book of Joshua is in the ______.

Unmuddle these:

- AHJSUO
- SELIRAISTE
- ΠEBITS
- OHEJRCI
- NCAANA
- HESCHME
- HWEYAH
- SEMSO

As well as the Book of Joshua, the Book of Judges tells us about the Israelites in their new land.

The Book of Judges covers the period 1250–1050 B.C.

The Book of Judges gives us a lot of information about about the twelve tribes settling in the Promised Land.

TWELVE TRIBES OF ISRAEL

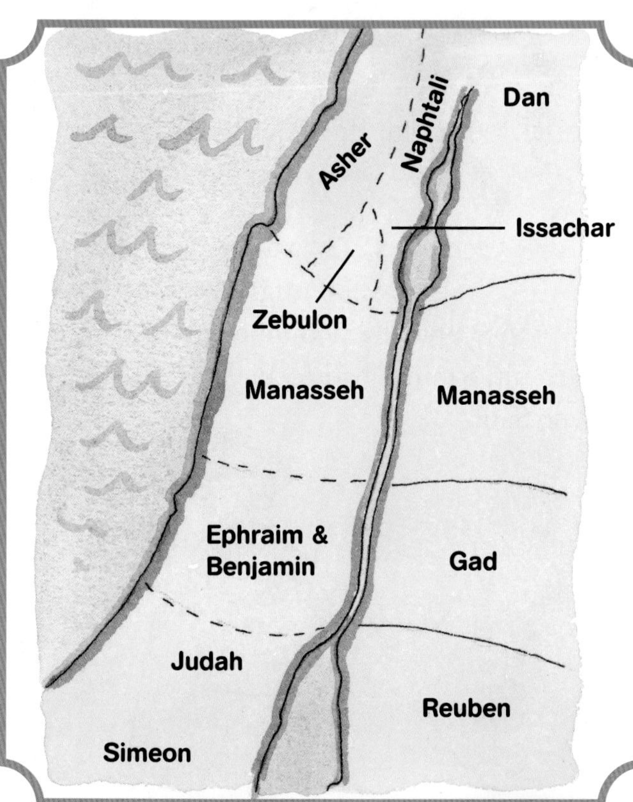

According to the history relayed in the **Book of Judges**, the Tribes picked twelve Judges. These twelve men were more than legal judges, they were leaders of their tribes, people of honour and courage who helped their tribes during battles and hardship. Moses himself would have been considered a Judge.

The **Book of Judges** further records that there were six minor Judges and six major Judges.

NB:
Throughout all this time the Israelites continued to believe that they were God's people and they obeyed the Ten Commandments.

To Do

Q1. What land did the Israelites settle in?
Q2. Who was their leader?
Q3. Name the Twelve Tribes of Israel.
Q4. What was a Judge?
Q5. Read Deut. 16:18-20 and 17:2-3.
What instructions did Moses give to the people?

Of course, time moved on and the people of Israel began to want to organise things a little differently.

They still believed God had given them the land!

And they still followed the Ten Commandments and had a strong belief in their Covenant with God.

... but they looked to the countries near them that had KINGS and they wanted their own king ...

...one of the last Judges, **SAMUEL**, was sent to find a man suitable to be a King of Israel.

God sent Samuel to a man called **SAUL**. He was to be the **first King of Israel**. Saul was in his mid-thirties, handsome, tall and seemed to possess the qualities of a good leader. He agreed to go to Canaan and be the King of the Israelites.

Saul defended the land against many invasions, but he became power-hungry, ignored Samuel's good advice and the people came to hate him. As a result, Samuel had to pick a new king to replace Saul.

In *c.*1000–961 B.C. Samuel anointed **DAVID** as the new King of Israel in Bethlehem.

Complete this Cloze test:

Throughout all this, the I______ believed that G______ was with them, especially through the T____ C______. God had given this L______ to them and allowed them to c______ it. The tribes p______ and continued to w______ God and give t______. The next important stage in their development was the T______ of the K______.

BIBLE MOMENT

Read Samuel I:16 in the Old Testament. Say how David was made King.

Qqs

Q1. What did the Israelites believe about the land?

Q2. What was the next stage in Israelite history?

Q3. Who was the last Judge?

Q4. What did he do?

Q5. Why did the Israelites want a king?

Q6. Who was Saul?

Q7. What did he do?

Q8. What happened to Saul?

Q9. How were kings anointed?

In this box, draw a picture of how King Saul might have looked.

So, the next King of Israel was ...

COPY AND COLOUR

King David!

David the Shepherd

David was the youngest of eight sons. His father was called **Jesse**. The family lived near Bethlehem. David was a shepherd and worked in the fields with the sheep, looking after them and keeping them safe. David had two great skills: using a sling-shot and playing the harp. Tradition also says that David wrote the psalms contained in the **Book of Psalms**, though some disagree.

David was crowned **King of Israel** in the southern region called Judah (Israel was north), and thus became King of the entire region. He made Jerusalem his capital and planned to build a great temple there to honour God.

David the King

TO KNOW

Bethlehem is sometimes called 'The City of David'.

David never got to build his temple, however. He had a number of sons – Absalom, Adonijah and Solomon were three of them. Solomon was his immediate heir.

David was looked upon as:

- a great king;
- a great soldier;
- a king who brought God to Jerusalem in the Ark of the Covenant;
- a king and a man who remained faithful to God and to the Covenant with God.

TO KNOW

The Ark of the Covenant was the specially designed container for the Ten Commandments.

TO KNOW

God made a promise that David's kingdom would last forever and his kingship would never end. The people always tried to remain faithful to this.

The next important king was ...

King Solomon!

(*c.*1000 B.C.)

King Solomon is probably the most famous of all the Kings of Israel. You can read about him in the Old Testament, Book 1, Kings 2:12 and in the chapters that follow.

KING SOLOMON

- When Solomon became King, there was peace in the land of Israel. Solomon wanted to keep this peace, so he made the army bigger and built stronger fortresses.

- As King, he made Israel a rich country. He traded with neighbouring countries, exchanging horses and copper for jewels and gold. Solomon ensured he maintained good relations with the neighbouring countries, and even married the daughter of the Pharaoh of Egypt.

- Solomon was famous for his **'God-given wisdom'**. His great wisdom was known and respected far and wide, from Egypt to Turkey. During Solomon's reign, the great and first temple dedicated to God at Jerusalem was built. This was a sign of how much Solomon worshipped and loved the God of Israel. For 400 years this temple stood as a symbol of the Israelites' loyalty and obedience to God.

COPY AND COLOUR

The Temple of Solomon

TO KNOW

This temple was central to the religious beliefs of Israel.

Front of Solomon's Temple in Jerusalem (950 B.C.).

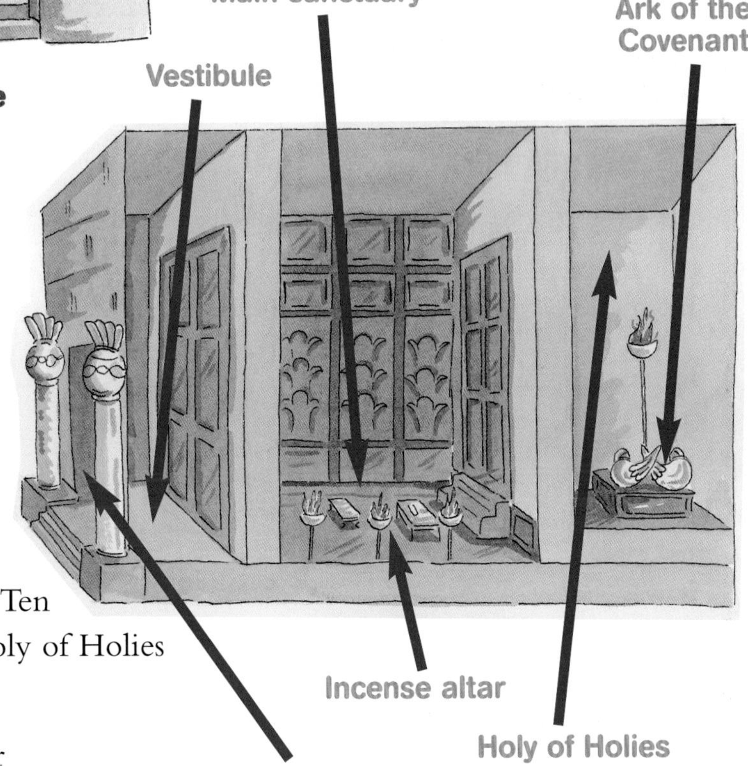

- Made from limestone.
- 55m (180ft) long, 27.5m (90ft) wide, 15m (50ft) high.
- Lit by small windows.
- Floor made of Cypress wood.
- Inside were incense, altars and steps and pillars, gold and silver.
- Ark of the Covenant, containing the Ten Commandments, was kept in the 'Holy of Holies (at the back).
- **'Holy of Holies'** entered once a year by Temple priest.

Some work to do

Q1. Who was David's father?

Q2. What did David do as a boy?

Q3. What were his two great skills?

Q4. What did he write?

Q5. What is Bethlehem sometimes called?

Q6. What city did David make the capital city?

Q7. What did he plan for the capital city?

Q8. David was seen as what?

Q9. Who was David's heir?

Q10. What was God's promise to David?

Complete these sentences:

You can read about Solomon in ________.

When Solomon became King there was ________.

He made bigger and stronger ________.

He traded ________ for ________.

He was famous for his ________.

He built the ________.

It was a sign of ________.

And a symbol of ________.

He married ________.

Put the tiles together to make a sentence

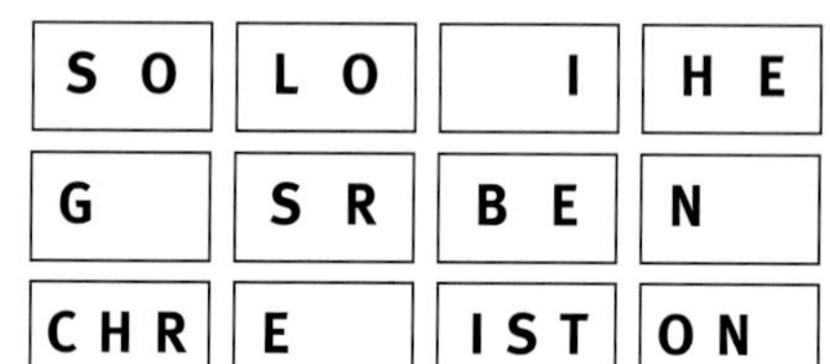

K	T	I N	A E	M O	L
C A	M E	O F			

____

____

____

Solomon died and following his death there began religious and political unrest in the land over territory and power and the peace was threatened. The country was divided between the north and the south.

COPY AND COLOUR

The northern area was **Israel!**

The southern area was **Judah!**

The Split of Israel and Judah

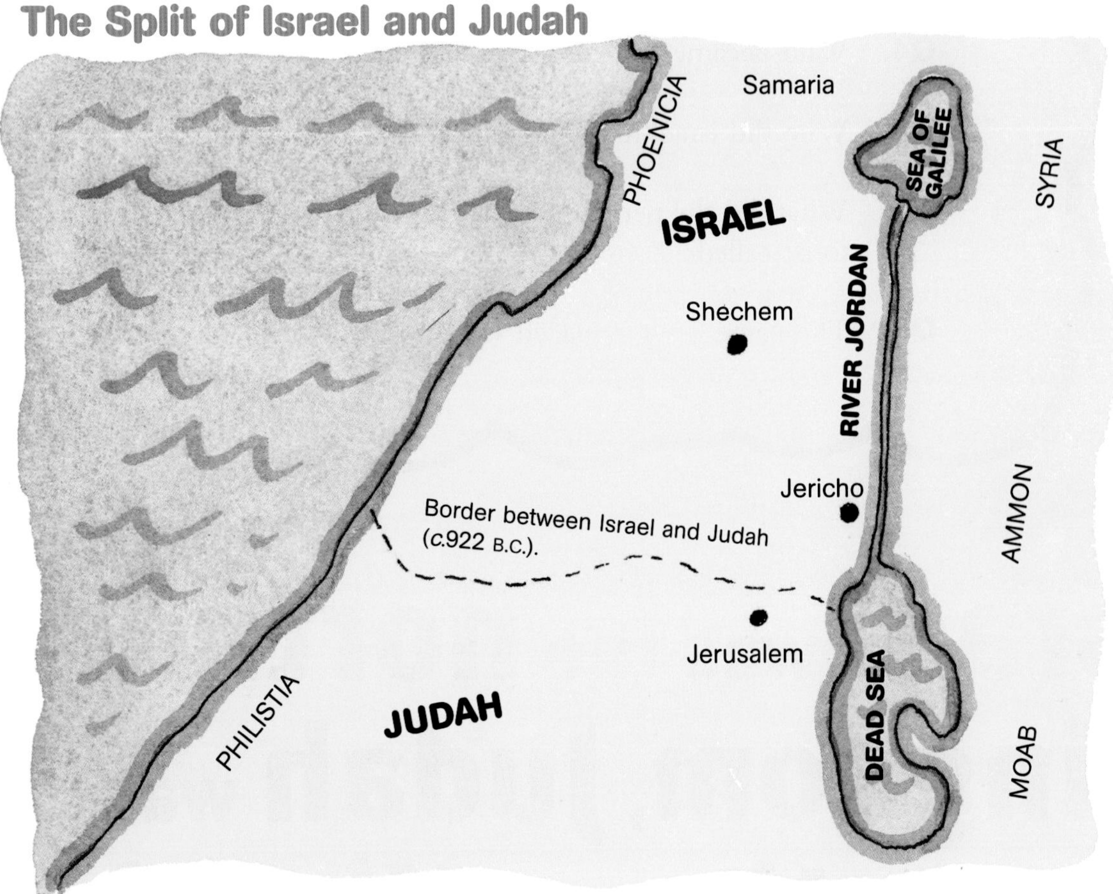

The people of Judah were called **'Jews'**. They were seen as the protectors of the ancient beliefs and traditions. These beliefs and traditions became known as **Judaism**, the religion of the Jewish people.

The people of Judah, in the south, continued the family line of David for their king. Accordingly, they chose Solomon's son, **Rehoboam**, as king. Israel in the north, on the other hand, took on a new king, King Jeroboam. The people never forgot that God had promised David that his family would rule forever **(2 Samuel 7:16)**.

Qqs

Q1. What happened when Solomon died?

Q2. What was the name of the northern area of the country?

Q3. What was the name of the southern area of the country?

Q4. Who became the king of Judah?

Q5. Who did Israel have as its king?

Q6. What did the people in Judah eventually come to be called?

Q7. The name 'Jews' replaced what other name?

'Israel was the northern Kingdom, Judah was the southern Kingdom'

COPY AND COLOUR

EXILE and RETURN

Words to remember
Exile • Samaria • Assyrians • Prophet

TO KNOW

EXILE = **removal or banishment from your country.**

Moses had said that if the people forgot God, **they would lose their land** … and so it happened!

This is the next important event in the history of Israel.

ISRAEL WAS EXILED!

PROPHETS EMERGE

During the time when Samuel was a Judge, a group of the people had urged the Israelites never to forget God. These people were the **PROPHETS**.

AMOS and **HOSEA** preached in Israel around the eighth century B.C. and **JEREMIAH**, among others, preached in Judah around the seventh century B.C.

Prophets appeared when the people began to forget about their duties to God, and also during times of crisis and trouble.

All the Prophets called on the people to turn back to God and to remember God's love and promises. They criticised:

- sins of the people and their leaders;
- unfaithfulness to God;
- greed and corruption;
- wrongdoing against good people;
- social inequality.

The prophets **Amos** and **Hosea** warned the northern kingdom of Israel that disaster would strike if the people did not mend their ways. But the people ignored the warning. In 721 B.C. the neighbouring kingdom of **Assyria** (west of the River Tigris) invaded Israel.

Assyrian attacks on Israel

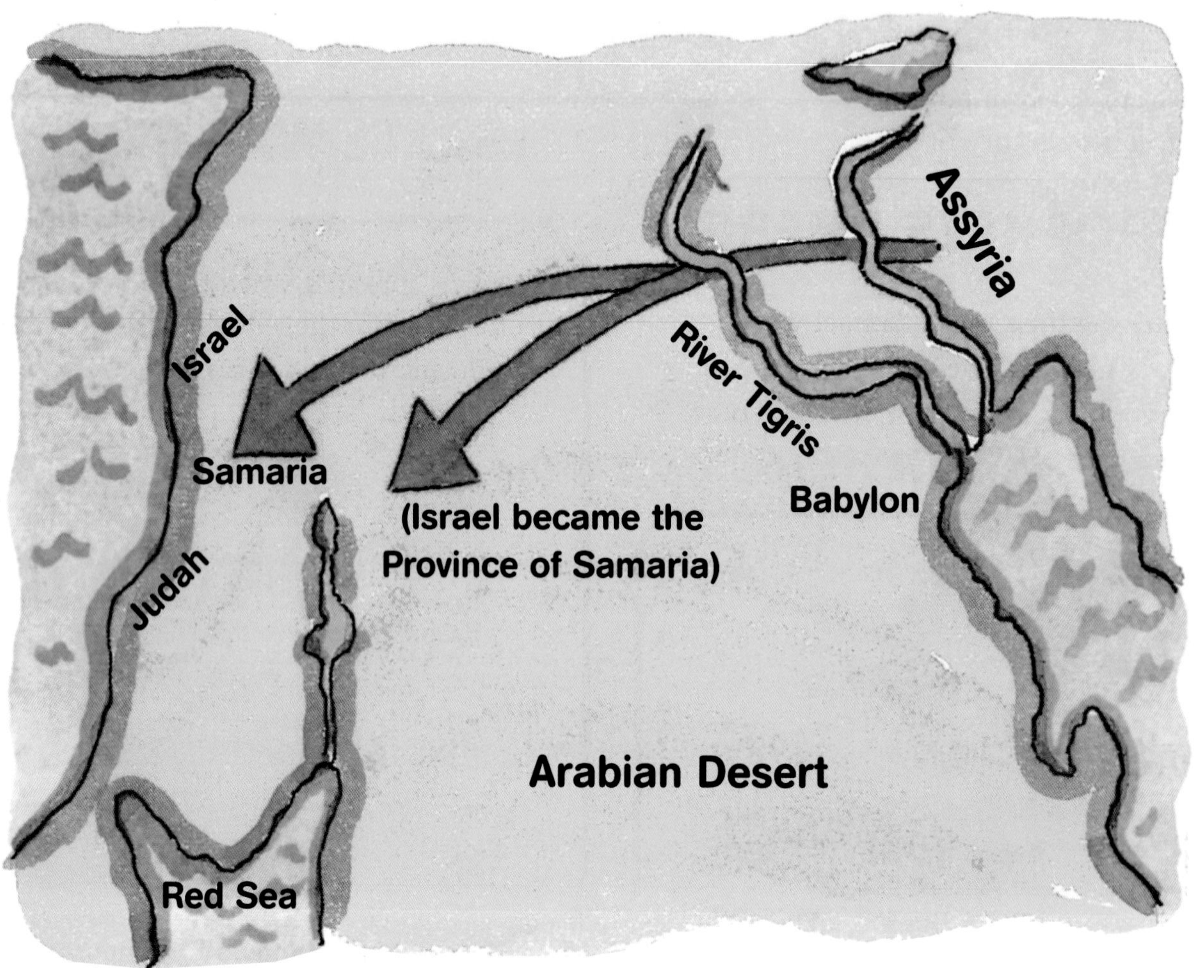

The Assyrians captured Samaria, the capital of Israel. The people of Israel were deported (exiled) and scattered throughout the Assyrian Empire. Foreigners then settled in the land of Israel, and it became the Province of **Samaria**. The Twelve Tribes of Israel were never heard of again (Deut. 8:19-20; 2 Kings 17; Amos 2-9; Hosea 9).

Exile Crossword

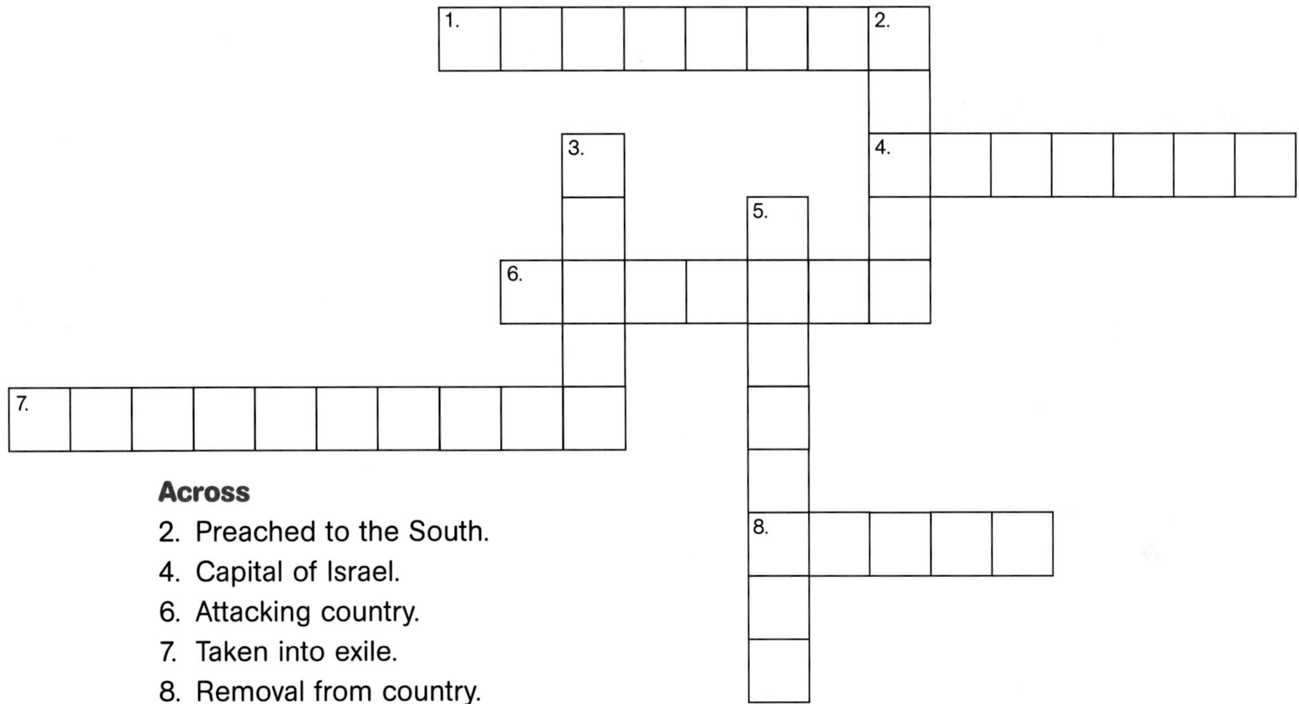

Across

2. Preached to the South.
4. Capital of Israel.
6. Attacking country.
7. Taken into exile.
8. Removal from country.

Down

2. Preached to the North.
3. Told them not to forget God.
5. Warned of exiles.

Over to you!

Q1. What does 'exile' mean?

Q2. What would happen if the Israelites forgot God?

Q3. Who continually warned them about the dangers of forgetting God?

Q4. Who were the Prophets?

Q5. What did they do?

Q6. Which Prophets preached in the north?

Q7. What did they criticise?

RESEARCH
JOURNAL IDEA

Find out about some other prophets from the Old Testament.
Who where they?
When did they preach?
What did they do?
Who are present-day prophets?
Find out about them.

Get more information about Amos, Hosea and Jeremiah (look them up in the Old Testament). Put the information you find in your copy.

The Exile of Judah!

(597 B.C.)

The southern Kingdom of Judah was also threatened by neighbouring armies. But the King, **KING HEZEKIAH**, trusted God and also listened to the **PROPHET JEREMIAH** and therefore they were saved from invasion at that time.

But a new enemy loomed on the horizon: the **BABYLONIANS**. These were the people from **BABYLON**, a city on the River Euphrates. Their king, **KING NEBUCHADNEZZAR**, was a great leader and had successfully invaded and captured many cities.

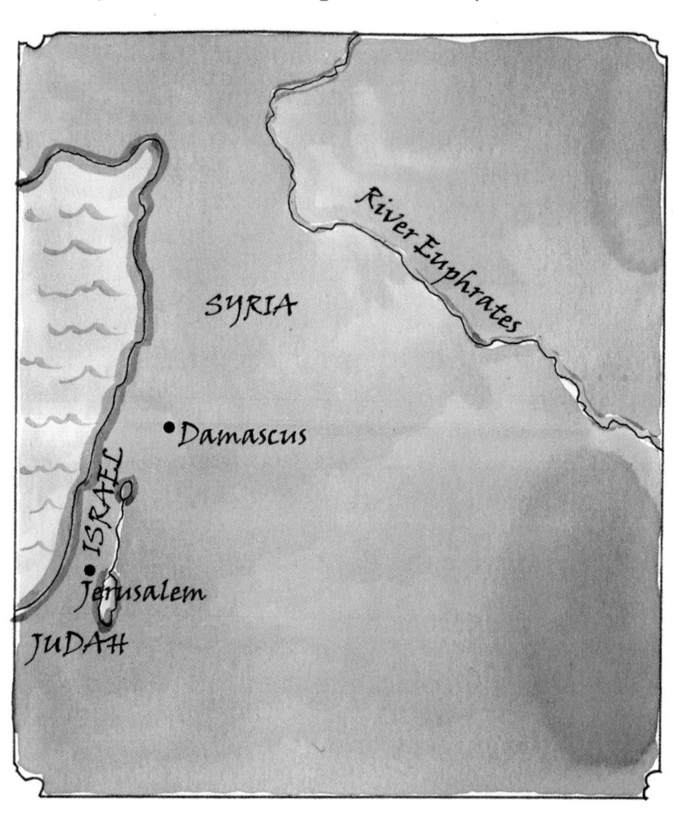

The Babylonian army first took Syria, in the north, then moved south and captured Judah.

Then, in the summer of 587 B.C., the capital of Judah – **Jerusalem** – was taken over. The Temple was looted and burned and the Jews were transported into exile in Babylon!

In Babylon the Jews were allowed to live in their own settlements. They were also allowed to earn money and keep their own religious customs and beliefs.

However, many of them longed to return to the land that God had given them and to rebuild his holy temple. For them, the temple had been the centre of their religion.

So, they began to put extra importance on the following:

- A special day of rest dedicated to God, called the Sabbath.
- Circumcision – the physical sign of God's Covenant with them.
- The laws concerning what was clean and what was unclean.
- Places of prayer and worship: synagogues developed.

They also began to write down God's message to them and to study the laws; many of the Books of the Old Testament were written down at this time.

TO KNOW

It was now even more important for theJews to keep their religion alive: with no temple, they had to look at their faith differently.

Let's do some work!

Complete this cloze test:

The southern K________ of J________ was under threat from the N________ armies. The people and King H________ trusted G________. They had listened to the w________ of the Prophet J________. They were saved from i________. Another enemy loomed close – the B________. Babylon was a city on the R________ E________. The people of Judah were taken into E________.

Q1. Whose warnings did the people of Judah listen to?

Q2. What was Judah under threat from?

Q3. Which army overthrew Judah?

Q4. Where is Babylon?

Q5. When did Jerusalem fall to the Babylonians?

Q6. Where were the Jews taken into exile?

Q7. Explain how the Jews kept their religion alive while in exile in Babylon?

Q8. Why was the temple in Jerusalem so important to them?

What happens next is called …

'The Return'

How did it happen?

RETURN TO JUDAH

In the year 539 B.C., almost fifty years after **King Nebuchadnezzar** had captured Jerusalem, the Babylonian Empire was taken over by the Persian Empire (which lay south-west of the rivers **Euphrates** and **Tigris**).

In 538 B.C., Cyrus, the King of Persia, declared that the Jews could leave Babylon and return home. He gave them money and supplies – everything they needed to return to the land of Judah. One of the first things the Jews did on their return was to rebuild the temple. The descendant of the last King of Judah, **Zerubabel**, and the priest **Joshua** took charge and the work of rebuilding the temple and the Kingdom of Judah began.

TO KNOW

The prophets saw the Exile as God's punishment because the people had disregarded the laws. After tnever to let this happen again. People called scribes (recorders of law and history) made a careful study of the law and drew up strict rules for the people.

TO KNOW

Synagogues (places of worship) began to spring up across the land.

History of Israel Timeline

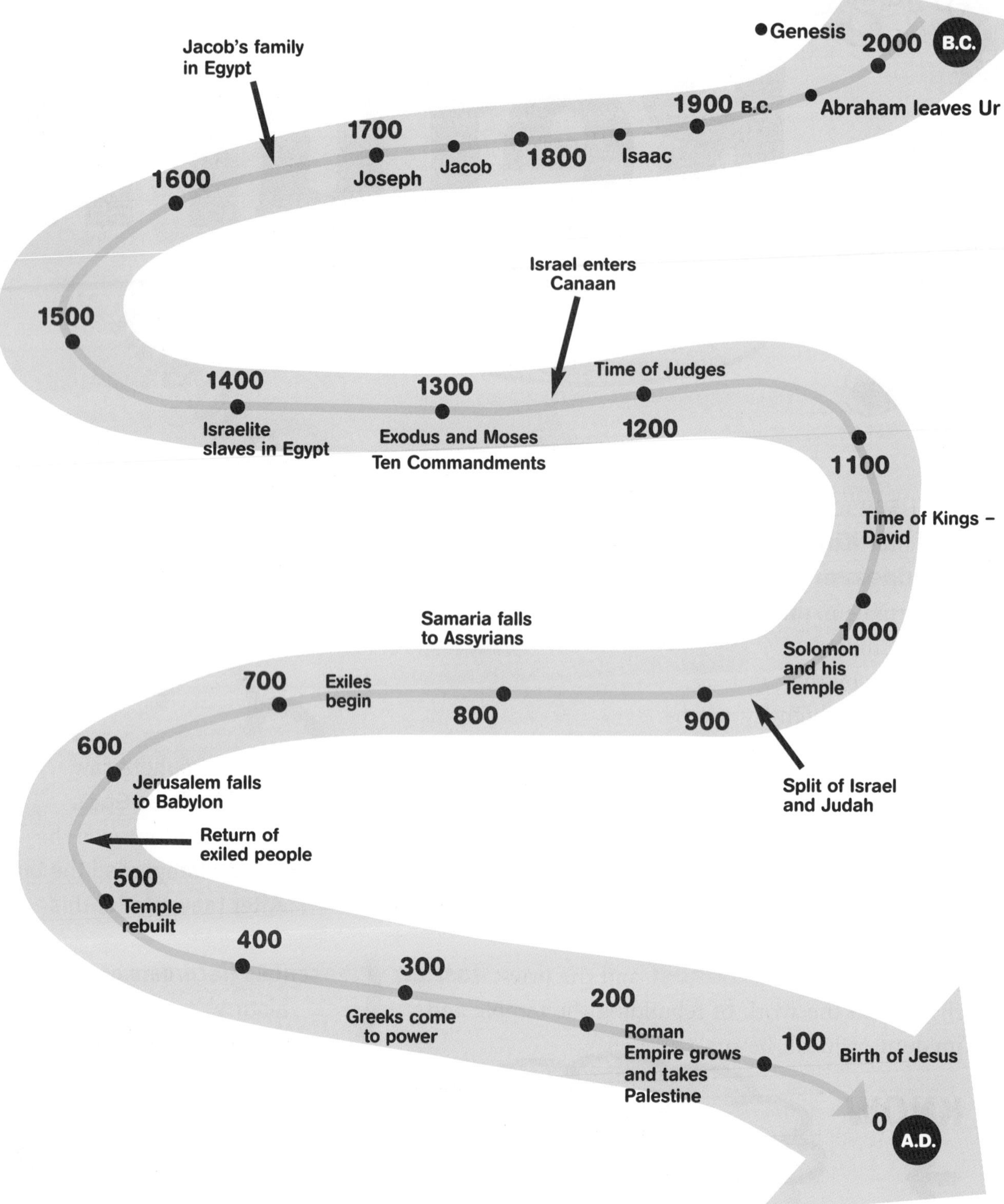

Genesis
2000 B.C.
Abraham leaves Ur
1900 B.C.
Isaac
1800
Jacob
1700
Joseph
Jacob's family in Egypt
1600
1500
1400
Israelite slaves in Egypt
1300
Exodus and Moses
Ten Commandments
Israel enters Canaan
Time of Judges
1200
1100
Time of Kings – David
1000
Solomon and his Temple
Split of Israel and Judah
900
800
Samaria falls to Assyrians
Exiles begin
700
600
Jerusalem falls to Babylon
Return of exiled people
500
Temple rebuilt
400
300
Greeks come to power
200
Roman Empire grows and takes Palestine
100
Birth of Jesus
0
A.D.

History Wordsearch

A	A	I	R	A	M	A	S	G	H	R	Q	R	K	J
N	S	V	V	K	P	G	Y	E	I	I	S	O	U	N
M	O	S	S	Y	N	H	Z	N	U	Y	A	D	Y	T
T	O	L	Y	N	S	K	E	E	R	G	A	R	E	C
B	G	S	Y	R	A	Q	U	S	C	H	N	M	S	A
H	J	A	E	B	I	M	I	I	P	A	P	E	W	A
P	W	U	P	S	A	A	O	S	B	L	V	R	P	S
E	X	O	D	U	S	B	N	R	E	A	Q	E	H	I
S	H	U	M	G	O	S	A	S	L	E	Q	T	M	I
O	Y	B	O	C	E	H	O	S	D	Z	G	U	D	R
J	R	P	A	F	A	S	I	Q	L	P	L	R	K	K
U	R	J	H	M	G	O	Y	C	B	M	L	N	I	X
T	J	C	E	G	Y	P	T	E	L	I	X	E	N	D
C	O	M	M	A	N	D	M	E	N	T	S	S	G	P
F	W	R	Q	M	A	P	F	D	A	X	L	H	S	Q

ABRAHAM
ASSYRIANS
BABYLON
COMMANDMENTS
EGYPT
EXILE
EXODUS
GENESIS
GREEKS
ISAAC
JACOB
JOSEPH
JUDAH
JUDGES
KINGS
MOSES
RETURN
ROMANS
SAMARIA
SLAVES
TEMPLE

Q1. Who took over the Babylonian Empire?

Q2. Who was the King of Persia?

Q3. What did he declare?

Q4. What was one of the first things the Jews did on return to Judah?

Q5. Who was the new King of Judah?

Q6. How did the prophets view the Exile?

Q7. What did scribes do?

The Beliefs, Worship and Traditions of Judaism

Words to remember:
Judaism • Monotheistic
Torah • Mishnah
Talmud • Gemara

Judaism took centuries to develop fully. Its practices and traditions were added to over the years. At the centre of this development was the belief in God and the relationship the Jewish people had with God.

Let's look at  their beliefs, worship and traditions!

One very important thing to remember is that Judaism was the first religion that was **MONOTHEISTIC** (belief in one God). This God was the Creator of the Universe ...

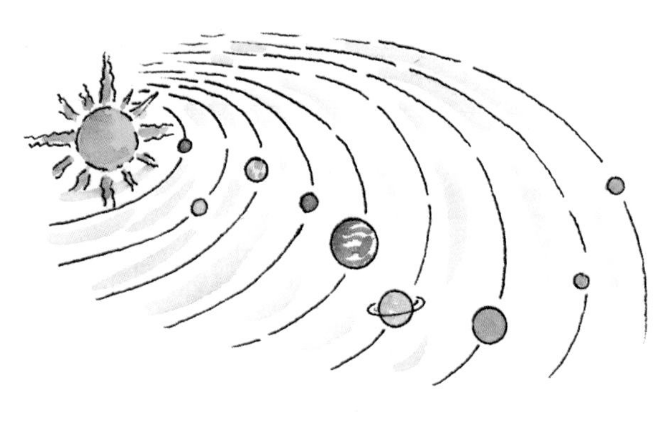

The **COVENANTS** between God and the forefathers of Israel (**ABRAHAM** and **MOSES**) and the **TEN COMMANDMENTS** sealed the relationship between God and His Chosen People.

These **COVENANTS** created a strong bond between God and His people. Because of this the beliefs, worship and traditions of Judaism became an essential part of the lives of all believers.

All this history and the relationship between the Jews and God is called the **Torah**.

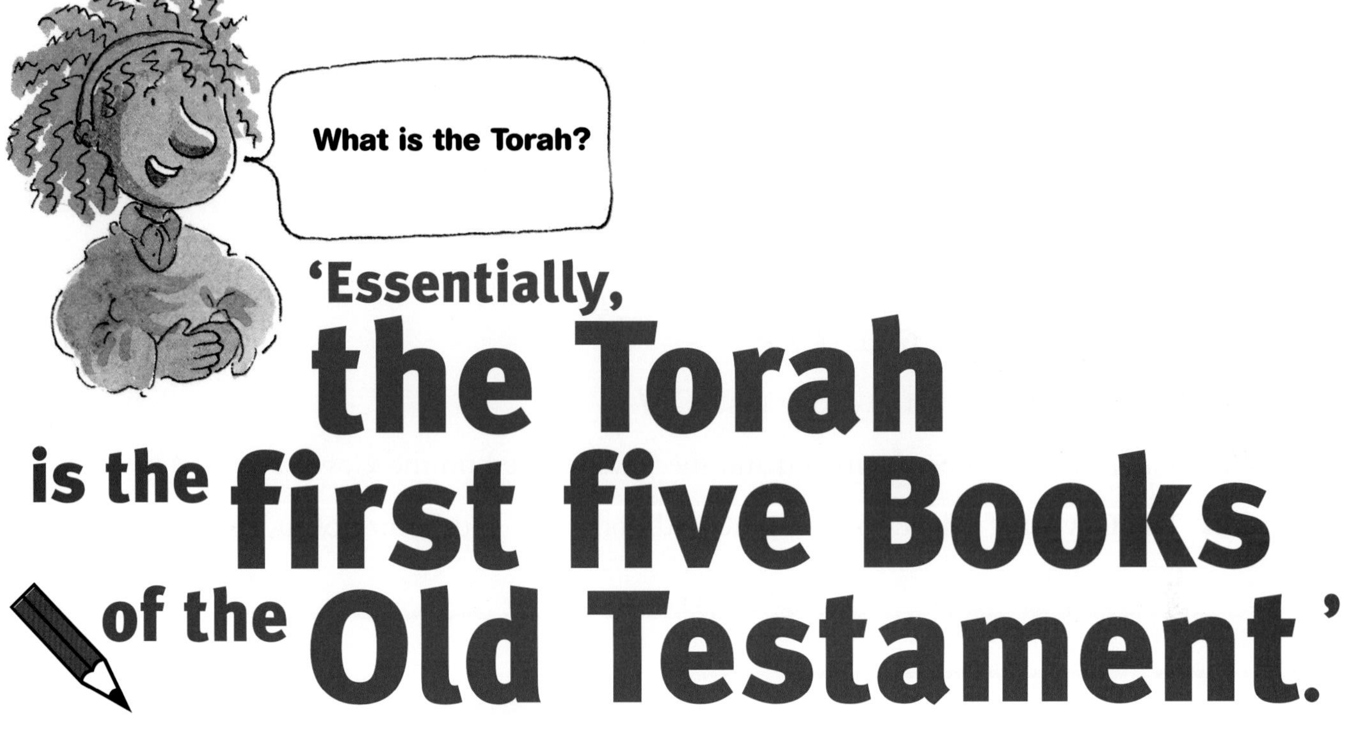

'Essentially, the Torah is the first five Books of the Old Testament.'

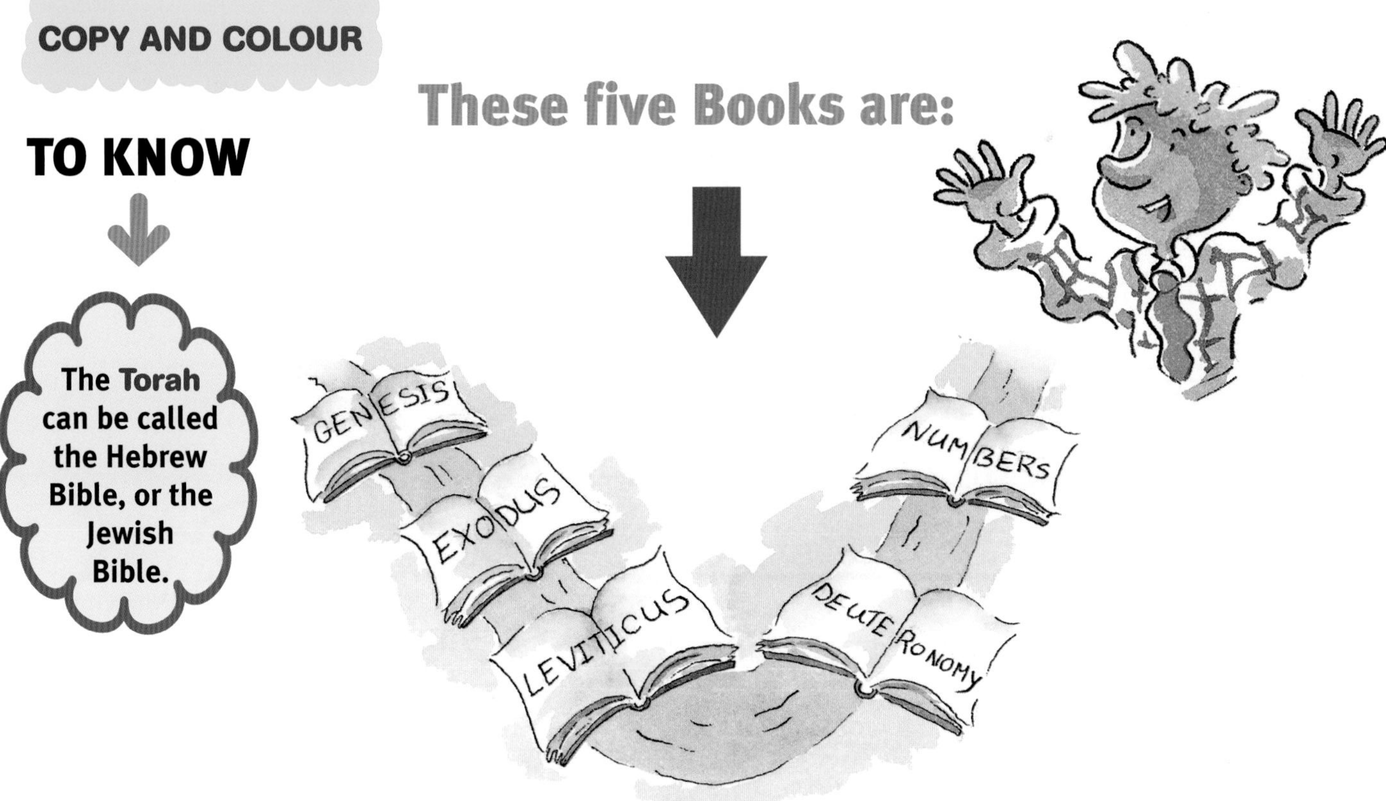

COPY AND COLOUR

These five Books are:

TO KNOW

The Torah can be called the Hebrew Bible, or the Jewish Bible.

Your Turn!

True / False?

(Write the answers in your copy.)

Q1. Judaism took about ten years to develop. **T / F**

Q2. The Jewish religion is polytheistic. **T / F**

Q3. Jews believe in one God. **T / F**

Q4. Polytheism is a belief in strong glue. **T / F**

Q5. The relationship between God and the Jews is based on the Covenant. **T / F**

Q6. The Covenant helped to create the traditions, laws and history of Judaism. **T / F**

Unmuddle these

OSXDUE

ITEVLCSUI

RNSEMBU

GESNSI

TDRONYMEUE

Q1. What is the Torah? Name the Books it comprises.

Q2. What else can the Torah be called?

RESEARCH
JOURNAL IDEA

Describe what each of these Books contains (just the important points).

Torah means 'instruction' (or law) and while relating particularly to the first five Books of the Old Testament, the word 'Torah' also includes the **Books of the Prophets** and the **Wisdom Writings** in the Old Testament.

TO KNOW

The first five Books can also be called 'The Pentateuch' – *Penta* is Latin for 'five' (e.g. a pentagon has five sides).

Jewish tradition also calls these five books
The Books of Moses!

As well as the history of Israel and Judaism, the Torah also sets out **613 commandments**.

These rules concern social and daily life and religious practices.

Around A.D. 200 a Jewish man called **Rabbi Judan** wrote Mishnah.

This book was an addition to the laws contained in the five Books of the Old Testament.

Other writers studied the **Mishnah**, and from that study they wrote the **Gemara** (a critical study of the Mishnah). Later, the Mishnah and the Gemara were put together to form the **Talmud** (A.D. 500), a book of the law for Jews to study.

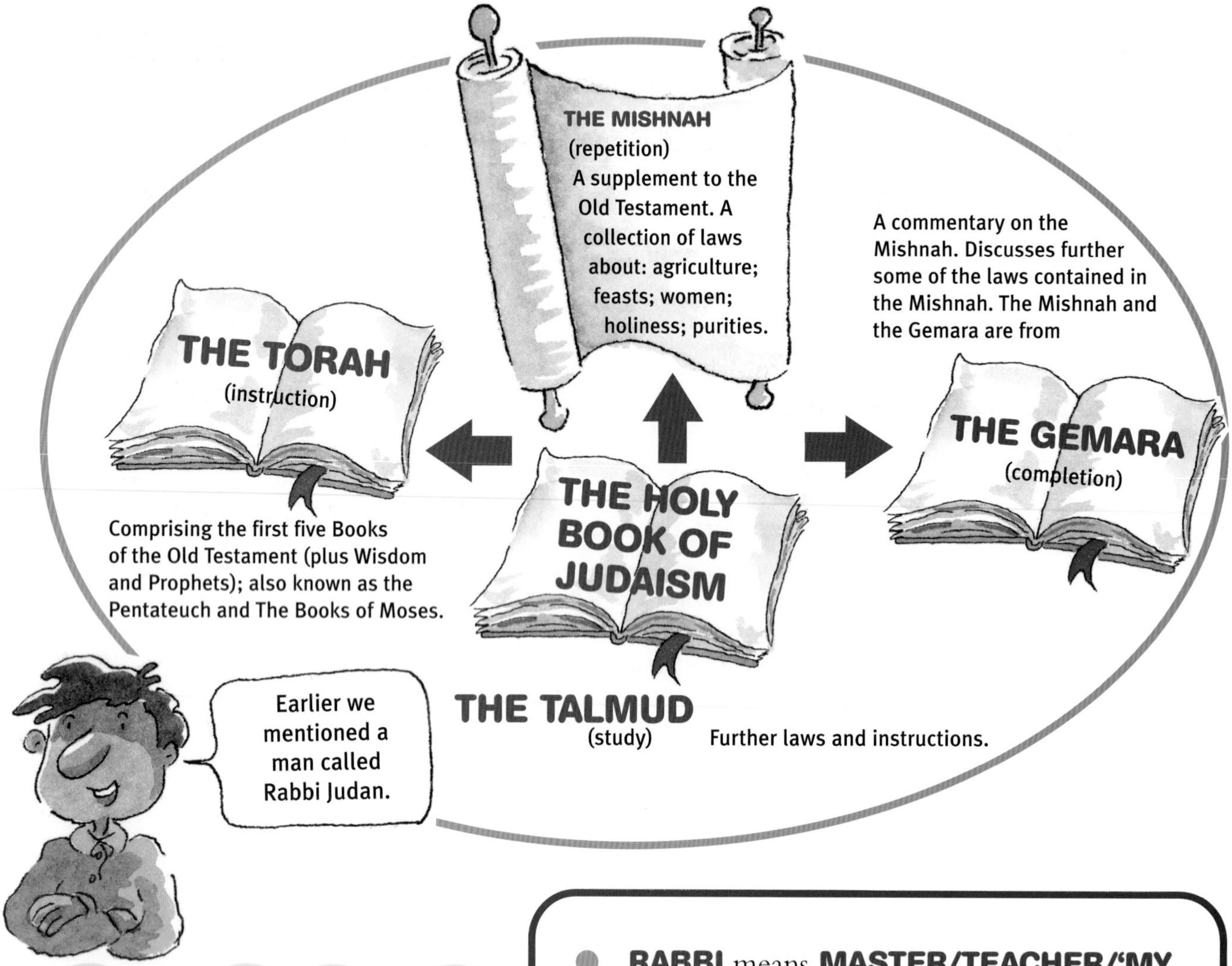

THE MISHNAH
(repetition)
A supplement to the Old Testament. A collection of laws about: agriculture; feasts; women; holiness; purities.

THE TORAH
(instruction)

Comprising the first five Books of the Old Testament (plus Wisdom and Prophets); also known as the Pentateuch and The Books of Moses.

THE HOLY BOOK OF JUDAISM

THE GEMARA
(completion)

A commentary on the Mishnah. Discusses further some of the laws contained in the Mishnah. The Mishnah and the Gemara are from

THE TALMUD
(study) Further laws and instructions.

Earlier we mentioned a man called Rabbi Judan.

Let's have a look at a **RABBI**.

- **RABBI** means **MASTER/TEACHER/'MY LORD'** in **HEBREW**.
- He is a teacher of the Jewish faith.
- After *c*. A.D. 70 it also meant a man who was a **JUDGE**.
- In the **NEW TESTAMENT** Jesus was called **RABBI (MASTER)**.
- The Books listed above would all have been written by **RABBIS**.
- Today, **RABBIS** continue their teaching role as well as working in the community with Jewish believers and writing books about Judaism and its beliefs.
- Every synagogue has a **RABBI**.

Qqs

Q1. What does the word 'Torah' mean?

Q2. What other books and writings can the Torah include?

Q3. What does the Greek word '*Penta*' mean?

Q4. How many commandments does the Torah set out?

Q5. What do its commandments concern?

Complete this cloze test:

Around A.D. 200 Rabbi _________ wrote the _____________. This book was an _________ to the laws in the Torah. Other writers studied the _________ and from that study wrote the ____________. These were then put together to form the _________________, a book of the ____________ to be studied.

MOSESUXTORAHOMEUROPEELAWSTUSTBOOKSLUSKETVFIVECEFPENTATEUCHOPMISHNAHCOSTGEMARATKABTALMUDUUOPENTALPT

Find the words hidden in the word wheel

When you find the words, write sentences in your copy using each one.

More Qs

A. What is the Mishnah?

B. What makes up the Talmud?

C. Who sets out religious teachings?

D. Who wrote the books?

E. What does 'Rabbi' mean?

F. What does a Rabbi do today?

Judaism and Food!

The Jewish religion has important laws concerning food. Collectively, these laws are called

Words to remember:
Kashrut • Kosher
Shochet • Treifa

'The Kashrut'

The laws of the Kashrut set out which food is

COPY AND COLOUR

Kosher food that Jews are free to eat and which food is

Treifa food that Jews are forbidden to eat.

COPY AND COLOUR

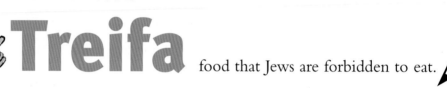

Here are some examples of Kashrut Kosher law:

A. Only animals that chew the cud and have cloven hoofs (e.g. cows and sheep) may be eaten.

B. They must be killed by a skilled **Shochet** (a person educated in Jewish food law) and the killing must be in a manner that causes the least amount of pain.

C. Most of the blood has to be drained from the animal.

D. The only fish that may be eaten are fish with fins and scales (no eels and no shellfish). Birds of prey are **Treifa** (not allowed).

E. Milk and meat (and foods made using them) are not to be prepared together, and are not to be eaten at the same meal.

Kosher Wordsearch

X	S	H	E	L	L	F	I	S	H
A	H	J	K	S	C	D	I	S	O
E	T	E	W	I	E	N	I	H	K
A	R	O	L	L	L	W	Q	E	A
F	C	E	L	L	E	L	B	E	S
I	S	E	H	J	F	I	E	P	H
E	D	W	A	S	R	I	K	D	R
R	F	K	A	D	O	L	S	N	U
T	E	N	S	L	I	K	K	H	T
S	L	A	M	M	A	M	E	A	L
M	E	X	T	E	H	C	O	H	S

BIRDS
COWS
FISH
JEWISH
KASHRUT
KILLED
KOSHER
LAWS
MAMMALS
MEAL
MILK
SHEEP
SHELLFISH
SHOCHET
TREIFA

Q1. What are the laws about food called?
Q2. What does it say in the **Kashrut**?
Q3. What does **'Kosher'** mean?
Q4. What does **'Treifa'** mean?
Q5. Give two examples of **Kosher** law.
Q6. Name two **Treifa** foods.

Design a poster, with words and pictures, describing and showing **Kosher** foods and **Treifa** foods.

The Jewish SABBATH

TO KNOW

Sabbath, or Shabbat = rest or cessation in Hebrew.

The commandment to keep the Sabbath is set down in Exodus 20.8 and in Deuteronomy 5.12. All instruct that **THE SABBATH** must be celebrated and observed!

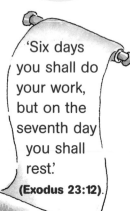

'Six days you shall do your work, but on the seventh day you shall rest.' **(Exodus 23:12).**

For Jews, the Sabbath day starts at sunset on Friday. The Jewish week begins on Sunday, which means the Sabbath day is **SATURDAY**, so therefore it begins on Friday evening and ends at sunset on Saturday night! The **SABBATH** is a reminder that God rested on the seventh day after he had created the world (Genesis).

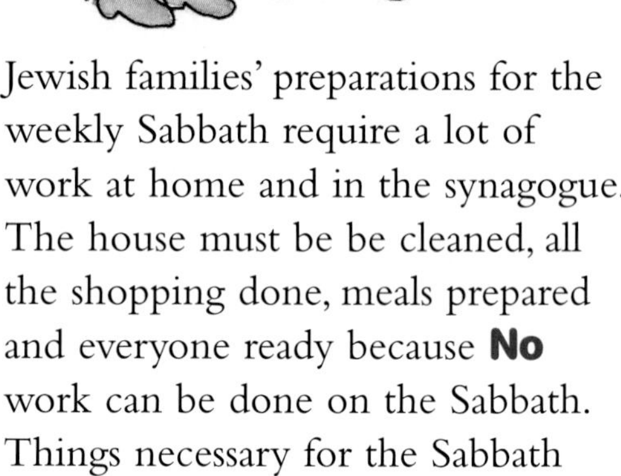

Jewish families' preparations for the weekly Sabbath require a lot of work at home and in the synagogue. The house must be be cleaned, all the shopping done, meals prepared and everyone ready because **No** work can be done on the Sabbath. Things necessary for the Sabbath and the meal are:

- A white tablecloth.
- Two candles and candlesticks.
- Two loaves of bread (*challot* – covered).
- Salt.
- Wine.
- Fresh flowers.

If celebrating the Sabbath at home, the family members will also bathe or shower and put on clean clothes before it begins.

The Sabbath is welcomed on Friday evening by:

A The woman of the house lighting the candles.

B She then covers her eyes and says this blessing: 'Blessed are you, O Lord our God, King of the Universe, who have hallowed us by your commandments and commanded us to kindle Sabbath lights.'

C The father then blesses his children and reads a passage praising the woman of the house (the passage is from Proverbs 31:10-31).

D Just before the meal is eaten, a blessing is said, called the **'Kiddush'**. This is said over the bread and wine.

E Everyone then greets one another with the words **'Shabbat Shalom'** (which means, 'Have a peaceful Sabbath').

F The meal is eaten and then songs are sung, stories are told and the Torah is read aloud.

For you to do

Q1. What does Exodus 23:12 say about the seventh day?

Q2. What other Book speaks of the Sabbath?

Q3. At what time of the day does the Sabbath start?

Q4. In the Book of Genesis, what did God do on the seventh day:

a) go shopping;
b) work;
c) rest?

Q5. If you were shopping in preparation for the Sabbath, which of the following items would be on your list?

PICNICKUBASKETFUSALTXYPEPPERUVWINETYORANGEPOJUICEJHBREADEDOOLOAVESUZWAFFLESFFCANDLESTICKSSIWHITEYTABLECLOTH

HATSICANDLESGUPICNICNJFRESHPFLOWERSUUPLASTICIQFLOWERSBNPASTAPQPARTYJJ

SHOPPING LIST

A. ______________________

B. ______________________

C. ______________________

D. ______________________

E. ______________________

F. ______________________

Q

In your own words, describe how the Sabbath is welcomed on Friday evening.

The MORNING of the SABBATH!

TO KNOW

Synagogue = meeting place.

This is usually spent in the **SYNAGOGUE**. The synagogue is where Jewish people pray, worship and study the Torah.

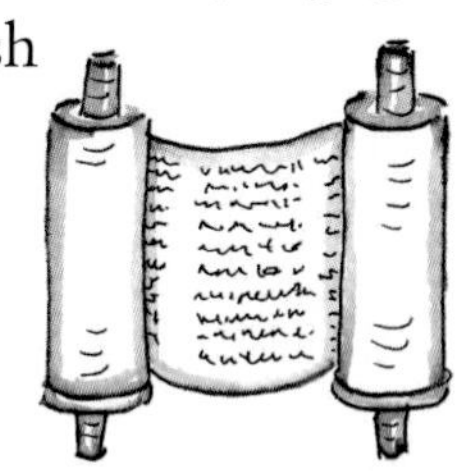

Later on the Sabbath they go home and share a meal together as a family.

The rest of the evening is spent studying the **Torah**.

When the sun is setting it is time to say goodbye to the Sabbath in word and song, prayers and blessings, by burning oil and lighting a candle so that the Sabbath can light the week ahead.

The Torah instructs Jewish people what not to do on the Sabbath, so that all people will be free from work:

- not to light a fire;
- not to do productive work;
- not to carry things;
- no writing;
- no cooking;
- no travelling.

NB:
Today some of these rules have been relaxed and families make decisions for themselves.

FOR JEWISH PEOPLE OF FAITH THE SABBATH IS IMPORTANT BECAUSE:

IT IS PART OF THEIR IDENTITY

→ wherever they are, they celebrate their relationship with God on the Sabbath.

IT STRENGTHENS FAMILY TIES

→ families come together to eat and pray and worship God.

IT IS TIME TO STUDY THE SCRIPTURES

→ reflection on the Torah and contemplation of God's relationship with them.

IT LENDS DIGNITY

→ life is not all about work, but also about personal development and prayer.

Let's do some work!

Q1. Where do Jews spend the Sabbath morning?

Q2. Where do Jews go after they leave the synagogue?

Q3. What do Jewish families do when they get home?

Q4. What happens when evening comes?

Q5. How do they say goodbye to the Sabbath?

Q6. According to the Talmud and the Torah, what are you not allowed to do on the Sabbath?

Q7. What were the reasons for the laws forbidding work on the Sabbath?

Keeping the Sabbath as a day of rest and as a holy day is important because ... (give four reasons!)

1. ______________________________

2. ______________________________

3. ______________________________

4. ______________________________

Q Do all Jewish families celebrate the Sabbath in this way? Explain your answer.

For you to do!

Draw a picture of a Jewish family at dusk, saying goodbye to the Sabbath.

The synagogue is 'none other than the House of God' **(Genesis 28.17)**.

The Synagogue

NB: The synagogue is also a place for study and teaching.

From Jewish history we read about the **TEMPLE OF SOLOMON**. This was the centre of religious worship for the Jews ... but when the Exile occurred and the Temple was destroyed, they had nowhere to worship God. It was at this time that **SYNAGOGUES** appeared. They were like miniature, portable temples and they allowed the Jews to keep their worship practices and therefore their religious identity. When the Jews returned to their own land, synagogues were built across the land of Israel.

To Know!

- A synagogue always faces towards **JERUSALEM**.
- So does the **ARK** (which holds the Torah).
- The curtains in front of the Ark are called **PAROCHET**.

- A light burns (*ner tamid*) to remind people of God's presence (His eternal light).
- The **TORAH** is read from the **BIMA**.
- People stand for the Torah Procession and sit for the readings.
- Pictures are not allowed on the walls of the Synagogue.
- Women sit upstairs, men sit downstairs (in Orthodox synagogues).

Some work for you to do

What is the function of each of the following (explain each one):

1. The Ark: ______________________
2. *Parochet*: ______________________
3. Eternal Light: ______________________
4. The *Bima*: ______________________
5. Seats upstairs: ______________________

Q Explain, in your own words, how synagogues came about.

Q1. What does Genesis 28:17 say about the synagogue?

Q2. In which direction does a synagogue face?

Q3. What is inside the Ark?

Q4. What does the Eternal Light serve to remind people of?

Q5. Where do women sit in Orthodox synagogues?

Q6. What are strictly law-abiding Jews called?

Find out about your local synagogue – the one nearest to your area. Where is it? How old is it? What happens there?

Synagogue Worship

TO KNOW

Shema = Hebrew for 'hear'

Synagogue gatherings and prayer services are held in the **morning**, **afternoon** and **evening**.

The SHEMA

is a very important part of all Jewish prayer, it says:

'HEAR O ISRAEL: THE LORD OUR GOD; THE LORD IS ONE.' (First line of Shema)
(Deuteronomy 5)

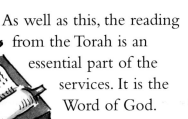

As well as this, the reading from the Torah is an essential part of the services. It is the Word of God.

NB: All Jewish men, women and children are encouraged to join together in daily prayer.

Let's have a look at morning prayer ...

Morning Prayer

in the synagogue

Men usually wear:

- **kippah**
- **tallit**
- **tefillin**

The service includes the following:

- The **SHEMA** is recited, followed by a morning blessing called '**BIRKOT HA-SHAHAR**'.
- Passages are read from the Torah and the Talmud.
- Psalms are sung and prayers are said, requesting help with different needs.
- Final Torah readings: this ends morning prayer and worship in the synagogue.

Over to you!

Q1. At what time of day are the synagogue services held?

Q2. The Shema is a special saying at which of these times: morning, afternoon, or evening?
The Shema is the main belief of the Jewish faith: write it out.

Q3. True or False:

a) People gather outside the synagogue to worship. **T / F**

b) There are three services a day. **T / F**

c) During the services, the Torah is read. **T / F**

d) Psalms are sung. **T / F**

Q. In your own words, describe Morning Prayer in the synagogue.

The Passover Festival

(Feast of Unleavened Bread)

TO KNOW

or **pesach**, is especially important to Jewish people. It celebrates their freedom from slavery in Egypt and their exodus to the Promised Land (with Moses). It is celebrated from 15 to 22 Nisan (spring) and lasts for eight days. The family celebrates at home with the **Seder** meal at which they usually eat unleavened bread (matzah), roast lamb, bitter herbs, eggs and spices. They also drink wine. During the **Seder meal** blessings and dialogue take place between the guests and the **Haggadah** is read (the story of the Exodus). It is also customary to leave a seat vacant for the **Prophet Elijah**, who will return to the Jews before the Messiah arrives.

Unleavened = no yeast, does not rise.
Seder = order.

The Messiah

COPY AND COLOUR

In Hebrew, the word is **Masiach!**

In Greek, it is **Christos!** Overall, the meaning is '**Anointed One**'!

In biblical times this term was used for ...

 Kings  Priests  Prophets

In Jewish thinking the **Messiah** is not a divine creature/person, nor the object of religious worship.

Despite all the differences, the basic belief focuses on the arrival of God's Kingdom on Earth through the Messiah. Then, God's rule will be active in human life. Jewish believers are called to be prepared at all times for the coming of the Messiah.

Expectations of what the Messiah will do differ among believers.

The Messiah could be ...

1. A historical figure who brings a new age of peace and justice.
2. A bringer of a new age for all believers.
3. A person who creates a new biblical age.
4. A person who gives Israel prominence over other countries.

Figure out these muddled sentences

THE	MES	FO	WAI	WS	JE	SIA	R T
HE	H	TED					

M	RING	THE	IAH	GOD	TO B
WAS	MESS	NGDO	S KI		

Q1. What is 'Anointed One' in Greek and Hebrew?

Q2. The name **Messiah** was used for which persons in biblical times?

Q3. In Jewish thinking, what is the **Messiah**?

Q4. The general belief in the **Messiah** focuses on what?

Q5. What do people expect of the **Messiah**?

Q6. Why would a believer want the **Messiah** to arrive on Earth?

Q7. What issues/problems do you think the **Messiah** would face in today's world?

Jewish RITES of PASSAGE

TO KNOW

Rite = a religious ceremony.

A rite of passage refers to those special moments in life when big changes happen. Religions celebrate those moments by performing special ceremonies, called 'rites'. Religious rites celebrate the life-changing moments of: **BIRTH, GROWING UP, MARRIAGE, DEATH,** etc.

A **MOHEL** performs circumcisions.

One Jewish rite of passage celebrates BIRTH! Eight days after the birth of a boy, the baby is **CIRCUMCISED** – '**BRIT MILLAU**' in Hebrew.

1. CIRCUMCISION

Circumcision is the removal of the foreskin from the penis. This is a sign – in the flesh – of the relationship between the child and God, that he is one of God's chosen people. The circumcision can take place in the **HOSPITAL**, at **HOME**, or in the **SYNAGOGUE**. After the circumcision the child is blessed and named.

Girls celebrate their Bar Mitzvah at twelve years of age, but usually don't read from the **TORAH** and have a low-key party.

2. BAR MITZVAH

Another rite of passage is '**BAR MITZVAH**' ('son of the law' in Hebrew). At thirteen years of age a boy celebrates his **BAR MITZVAH**. He is seen as an adult Jew who is now responsible for his own faith and who has an understanding of the law and his religion. An important moment is when the boy is permitted to read from the Torah in the synagogue! The **BAR MITZVAH** boy is surrounded by family and friends and has a big party to celebrate his passing into adulthood.

Rites of Passage Wordsearch

S	M	A	R	R	I	A	G	E	H
L	Y	R	I	T	E	S	D	A	C
I	D	N	O	W	E	J	V	S	E
Y	E	R	A	L	H	Z	L	P	R
A	A	B	A	G	T	L	A	Q	E
H	T	F	I	I	O	S	I	W	M
C	H	G	M	R	S	G	B	W	O
T	I	R	C	A	T	E	U	T	N
A	A	S	G	P	W	J	K	E	Y
B	R	E	L	I	G	I	O	U	S

BAR MITZVAH
BATCHAYIL
BIRTH
CEREMONY
DEATH
JEW
MARRIAGE
PASSAGE
RELIGIOUS
RITES
SCROLLS
SYNAGOGUE
TORAH

Q1. Name some important moments in life that you have experienced.
Q2. Name some other Rites of Passage that you know about.
Q3. What is a rite?
Q4. What is circumcision?
Q5. What does 'circumcision' mean?
Q6. Where does circumcision take place?

More Qs

A. What does 'Bar Mitzvah' mean?
B. How old is a Jewish boy when he celebrates his Bar Mitzvah?
C. What is one of the most important parts of the ceremony?
D. Name a girl's coming-of-age ceremony.

3. MARRIAGE

Marriage is another important ceremony that Jewish people observe.

● On their wedding day, the couple fast: they don't eat anything until after the ceremony.

● The wedding ceremony takes place under a **Chuppah** (a canopy) held up on four poles decorated with flowers.

What happens?

Well, there are a few things that have to be done.

A. A cup of wine is blessed by the Rabbi and the couple drink it. Thus, they are blessed.

B. The bride then enters the Chuppah and joins the groom and the Rabbi.

C. The groom places a ring on the bride's right-hand ring finger.

D. Then the bridegroom says:

'Behold, you are consecrated to me by this ring according to the Law of Moses and Israel.'

E. The marriage agreement (contract), the **Ketubah**, is read and signed by the couple.

F. The ceremony ends with the couple drinking from another cup of wine and listening to the final **'Seven Blessings'**. These blessings make a link for the couple to the story of creation, the history of Israel and hopes for the future.

G. The Rabbi says a few words, there is singing, and then the groom steps on a glass and smashes it!

This breaking of the glass reminds all the people of the destruction of the Temple in Jerusalem ... and so the ceremony ends.

4. DEATH and BURIAL

Q. Check again how Jesus Christ was buried.

- When a person is dying, his or her family and friends gather round. A Rabbi is present, too.
- If possible, a person's last moments are spent saying the Shema and making a final confession.
- When the person has died, the eyes and lips are closed. It is usual for the body to be tied up, arms and legs straightened, and (if death has occurred in hospital) tubes removed.
- The body is wrapped in a plain white sheet and placed in a mortuary.
- Later, the body is prepared for burial by being washed and wrapped in a new plain shroud. (A man wears the Tallith as his death shroud.)
- The body is then placed in a simple, plain, wooden box. The funeral usually takes place twenty-four hours after death, with psalms and prayers for resurrection.

OVER TO YOU

Complete this cloze test:

On their wedding day, the couple f__________ until after the c________. The ceremony takes place under a C__________ held on four p________________, decorated with f__________. A few things have to be done. A cup of w______ is b_________ by the R_______ and drunk by the couple. The bride enters the C____________ and joins the g_________ and the Rabbi. The groom places a ring on the b_________ finger (r______ h_____). The bridegroom says, 'Behold you are c_________ to me by this r_______ according to the L______ of M______ and I__________.'

Q Describe, in your own words, what happens at a Jewish wedding ceremony.

Q1. What do the Seven Blessings represent?

Q2. What does breaking the glass represent?

Q3. What is the canopy called under which the ceremony takes place?

Q4. On which finger is the ring placed?

Q5. What does the bridegroom say to the bride?

Q. Explain what happens when a Jewish person dies. (Check the Gospels to compare with the way in which Jesus was buried.)

Special Clothes of the Jewish Faith

For members of the Jewish faith, special ceremonial clothes are an important part of the rituals. These ceremonial clothes remind people of their beliefs, their religious faith and their closeness to God.

During prayertime Jewish men wear a '**TALLIT**' (prayer robe). This is square and made from wool or silk. The fringes remind people of God's law.

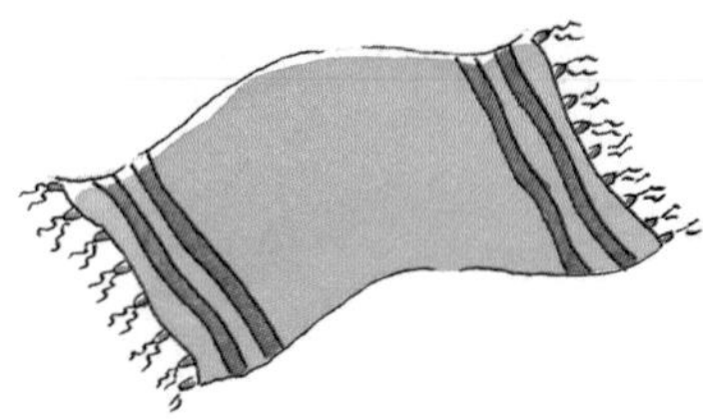

At all times (although for some, just during prayers) Jewish men wear a '**KIPPAH**' (prayer cap). It is *always* worn in the synagogue and for praying. It is a sign of respect for God and his Covenant to have one's head covered.

Another special item is the '**TEFILLIN**'.
This is two leather boxes holding parchment containing extracts from Deuteronomy 6:4-9 and 11:13-21; Exodus 13:1-10 and 11-16.
One box is tied to the forehead; the other is tied to the left arm.
Orthodox Jews wear these boxes during prayer times every day (although usually excluding the Sabbath and festivals).
The writings on the parchment in the **TEFILLIN** constantly remind believers of God's law.

Let's do some work!

In this box, draw a Jewish man wearing a **Tallit** / **a Kippah** / **a Tefillin**.

Find the words hidden in the word wheel:

APRSSHAWLDOTEFILLINCDESHEMAFITISABBATHABSPECIALVOTXECLOTHESUSETAUITLMOKIPPAHCTWOC

Q1. What is a Tallit?

Q2. What is a Kippah?

Q3. What's inside the Tefillin?

Q4. What does the writing in the Tefillin remind people of?

Q5. Where do Jewish men wear the Tefillin?

More Qs

A. What's the reason for wearing the **Tallit**?

B. Read Deuteronomy 6:4-9; Exodus 13:1-10; Deuteronomy 11:13-21. What do these passages mean to the believing Jew?

C. Why do Jewish men wear the **Tefillin**?

Festivals of Judaism

PESACH
15–22 Nisan
Passover: the meal to commemorate the Exodus.

The Passover meal and remembering freedom from Egyptian slavery.

YOM HASOAH
27 Nisan
Memorial for the Jews killed in the Nazi Holocaust.

YOM HA'ATZMA'UT
5 Lyyar
The creation of the Jewish State.

New Additions to the calendar

SHAVUOT
6–7 Sivan
Pentecost: remembers the receiving of the Torah.

FAST OF AV
9 Av
Fast: remembering the destruction of the Temple.

ROSH HASHANA
1–2 Tishri
New Year: birthday of the world. Ram's horn is blown to remember Abraham's Covenant with God.

YOM KIPPUR
10 Tishri
Praying for forgiveness of sins.

SUKKOT
15–22 Tishri
Tabernacles: remembers the forty years of wandering to find Canaan.

SIMCHAT TORAH
22–23 Tishri
End of the cycle and progression of readings from the Torah.

HANUKKAH
25 Kislev–3 Tevet
Festival of lights: remembers the reconstruction of the Temple (Menorah) used.

TU B'SHEVAT
15 Shevat
Trees are planted.

PURIM
14 Adar
Giving of gifts: remembers God saving the Jews from destruction.

The Jewish months are ...

Nisan (March–April)
Lyyar (April–May)
Sivan (May–June)
Tammuz (June–July)
Av (July–August)
Ellul (August–September)
Tishri (September–October)
Cheshvan (October–November)
Kislev (November–December)
Tevet (December–January)
Shevat (January–February)
Adar (February–March)

TO KNOW

The normal Jewish year has twelve lunar months of twenty-nine or thirty days each.

Let's Work!

True / False?

- Trees are planted during Shevat. **T / F**
- Kislev takes place around November/December. **T / F**
- 15–22 Tishri is the Feast of Pentecost. **T / F**
- 27 Nisan is the memorial for Jews killed in the Holocaust. **T / F**
- Yom Kippur celebrates praying for forgiveness. **T / F**
- Rosh Hashana is the New Year. **T / F**
- The creation of the Jewish State is celebrated on 14 Adar. **T / F**

Unmuddle these words and briefly explain the celebration

ANISN ____________________

NVAIS ____________________

VA ____________________

HTSRII ____________________

SLKVIE ____________________

RDAA ____________________

RLAYY ____________________

Give the date

New Year ____________________

Tabernacles ____________________

Festival of Lights ____________________

Planting trees ____________________

Creation of Jewish State ____________________

Passover ____________________

Pentecost ____________________

JUDAISM and the WORLD

TO KNOW

Ghetto = originally an area inhabited by Jewish people, a separated area.
Anti-Semitism = anti-Jewish feeling around the nineteenth century.

The spread of the Jewish religion and its people across the world is a very detailed and complex part of human history. Here we'll have a brief look at what happened. The spread is called '**DIASPORA**'.

- From the second century onwards the religion of Judaism spread to Europe.
- Jewish communities sprang up across Europe, in places like Rome and Cologne, and further afield, in Poland and the Baltics.

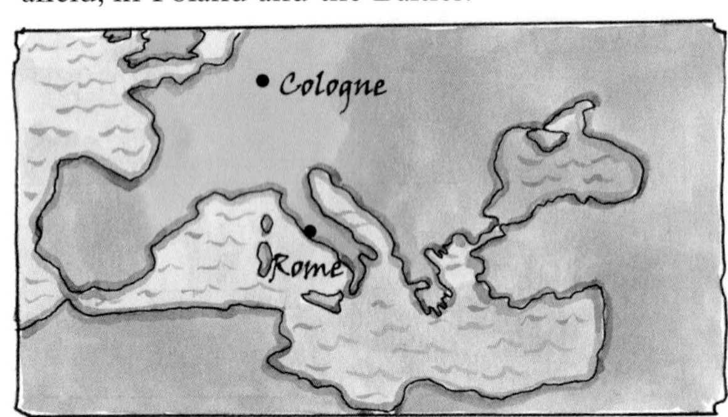

- Jewish people were regarded as being good economists, so they were able to get good jobs across Europe and move around with ease.
- In the eleventh century things changed for Jewish people. Their economic skills were no longer in demand and the Catholic Pope ordered that no other religion be allowed in Europe apart from Catholicism. This narrow-minded view also resulted in the Crusades.

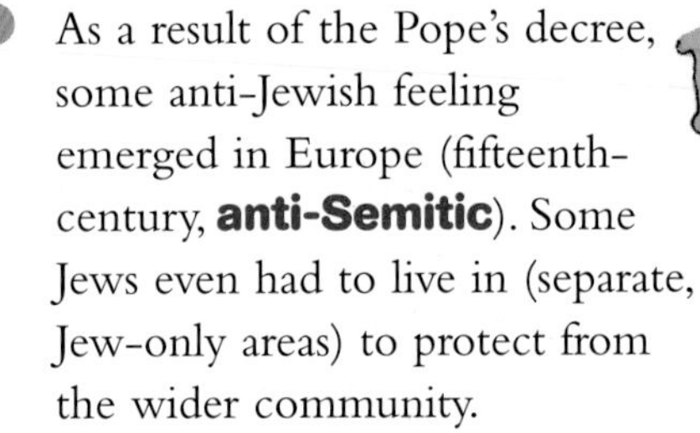

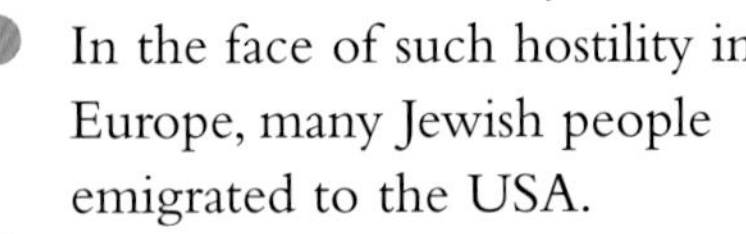

- As a result of the Pope's decree, some anti-Jewish feeling emerged in Europe (fifteenth-century, **anti-Semitic**). Some Jews even had to live in (separate, Jew-only areas) to protect from the wider community.
- In the face of such hostility in Europe, many Jewish people emigrated to the USA.
- Anti-Semitism spiralled in Europe and culminated in the devastating **Holocaust** of the Second World War – when Nazi Germany attempted to kill all Jewish people. (By 1945, six million Jews were dead as a result of the Nazis' 'Final Solution'.) Because of all this, Jewish people called for a return to their homeland in order to create a Jewish State. This was called '**ZIONISM**'.
- In 1948 the UN supported the establishment of the Jewish State, now known as '**ISRAEL**'.

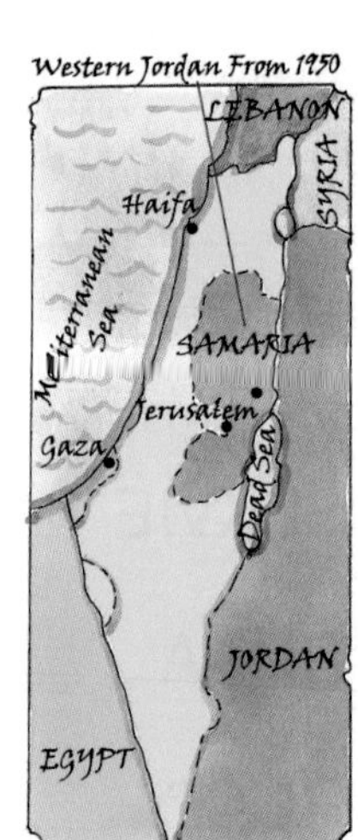

Over to you!

Q1. Where were the earliest Jewish communities in Europe?

Q2. To which countries did Jewish people emigrate?

Q3. What happened in the eleventh century that was bad for Jewish people?

Q4. Around Europe, where were Jews confined?

Q5. What is a ghetto?

More to Do!

A. Explain anti-Semitism.

B. What is it based on?

C. What was the Holocaust?

D. Why did it happen?

E. Explain Zionism.

Q. Does anti-Semitism still exist in Europe today? Explain.

Q. Why is anti-Semitism wrong? Explain.

Judaism in Ireland

Let's see how Judaism got on in Ireland ...

The earliest reference to Jews living in Ireland is in the **Annals of Inisfallen**,

in the year **1079**! (They may have arrived from France as merchants.)

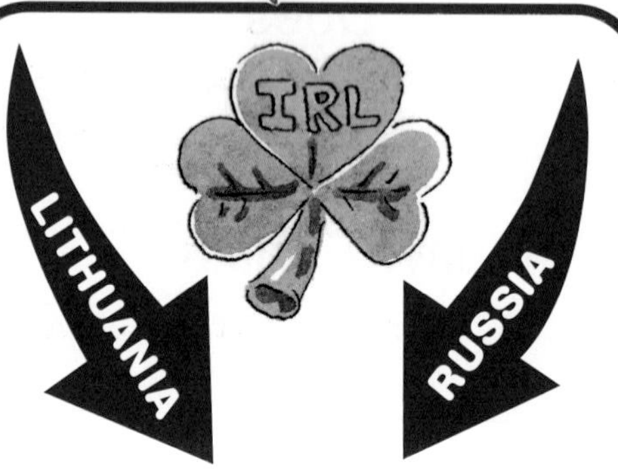

During the late 1800s Jewish people escaping from oppression in Russia, Lithuania and Latvia arrived in Ireland, landing in Cork and Dublin, and formed the basis of the Jewish communities that survive today.

- According to historical records, there have been small Jewish communities coming and going since the mid-seventeeth century.
- More Jewish people probably arrived in Ireland after they had been forced out of European countries around the late 1400s.
- Historical records indicate that the earliest synagogue was set up around 1660 in Crane Lane, opposite Dublin Castle.
- The oldest Jewish cemetery dates from the early 1700s. It is located near Ballybough Bridge in Clontarf, Dublin.

The years between 1880 and 1910 saw the greatest number of Jews arriving in Ireland. Approximately 2,000 Jewish people arrived from **Eastern Europe** and settled in Belfast, Dublin, Cork, Limerick, Waterford, Derry and Drogheda. At present, there are about 2,000 Jews in total in the Republic and Northern Ireland. The numbers of Jewish people in Ireland have declined since the mid-1940s.

This is because:

1. Young Jews who wished to marry Irish Catholics were forced to convert to Catholicism.

2. In 1948 the State of Israel was founded and many Jews returned 'home'.

DESTINATION: ISRAEL

3. From the 1960s onwards, Jews moved for economic reasons – and there were more jobs in other countries.

Cork has a synagogue, too. The Jewish population in Cork is estimated at fifty people.

- At present, there is one Kosher butcher shop in Dublin. It is on Lower Clanbrassil Street and is called B. Ehrlich's. It was opened in 1926.

- Despite its small number, the Jewish community has had representatives in Irish politics, including Mervyn Taylor and Ben Briscoe, who both served as TDs (Teachtaí Dála) in Dáil Éireann.

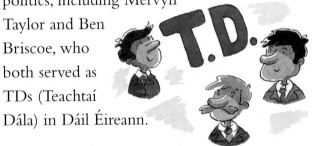

- Chaim Herzog, a former president of Israel, grew up in Dublin, where there is a monument in memory of him.
- Judaism in Dublin is mostly Orthodox, but is still more liberal than in other countries, such as the United States. The Jewish community in Dublin have their own synagogue and a progressive temple.

The Chief Rabbi in Ireland is Yaakov Pearlman.

Let's Work

Complete this Cloze test:

The earliest reference to Jews living in Ireland is in the A ________ of I________ in 10__. According to the history, Jewish people have been coming and g________ to and from I________ since the s____________ c____________. More Jews came, leaving L____________, L____________ and R________, and settled. These formed the basis of the current J____ C______. The earliest s________ was set up in 16________ in C______ L______, opposite D________ C__________.

Complete these sentences:

Reference to Jews living in Ireland can be found in ________.

More Jewish people came after running away from ________.

These Jews formed the ________________.

The earliest synagogue was located on __________.

Oldest cemetery dates back to __________.

Between 1880 and 1910 ________________.

There are 2,000 Jews ______________.

Numbers have fallen because __________.

In Dublin, there is one ____________.

Judaism in Dublin is mostly ____________.

Q. Explain in your own words why the Jewish population in Ireland has declined.

RESEARCH
JOURNAL IDEA

- Find out about the influence of Jewish people on Dublin City.
- Do you know anyone who is Jewish? If so, interview them about their lifestyle and beliefs.

Varieties of Judaism

COPY AND COLOUR

It's fair to say that until the nineteenth century, Judaism was united. All its followers accepted the Torah and Scriptural Law as authority, albeit with possible differences over interpretation. But things have changed, especially regarding the question of authority (leadership), and from that have stemmed differences in faith and practice.

Reform Judaism

- Began in Western Europe, particularly in Germany.
- It focuses on confession and atonement.
- Prayer services are short and more artistic, using people's native language and not always Hebrew.
- Rejected many old laws and customs.
- Spread to France, Denmark and Britain.
- Liberal and non-authoritarian.
- Has the Bar Mitzvah.
- First female Rabbi in 1972.

Atonement means 'being sorry for sins'.

Orthodoxy

- Originated with Samson R. Hirsch. It opposes Reform Judaism.
- Comprises a blend of traditional Judaism and modern thinking and learning.
- Contains a range of groups within it, from modern Orthodox to Hasidic Sect (who shut out the modern world).
- In Israel, Orthodoxy is the only recognised Judaism.
- Women are supposed to work only within the home and must occupy separate seating areas in the synagogue.

Conservative Judaism

- Founded by Solomon Schechter.
- Respects traditional Jewish law and practice.
- Recognises modern literary criticism of the Bible and sacred writings.
- Voted in women **Rabbis** in 1983.
- Largest Jewish group in the United States.

Reconstructionist Judaism

- Based around thinking of Mordecai Kaplan.
- Focus on reconsideration of Jewish core beliefs – God, Israel, Torah, synagogue – incorporating modern philosophy, theology and social theories.
- Emphasis on Jewish identity and culture.
- Female members are treated as equals.

Varieties Crossword

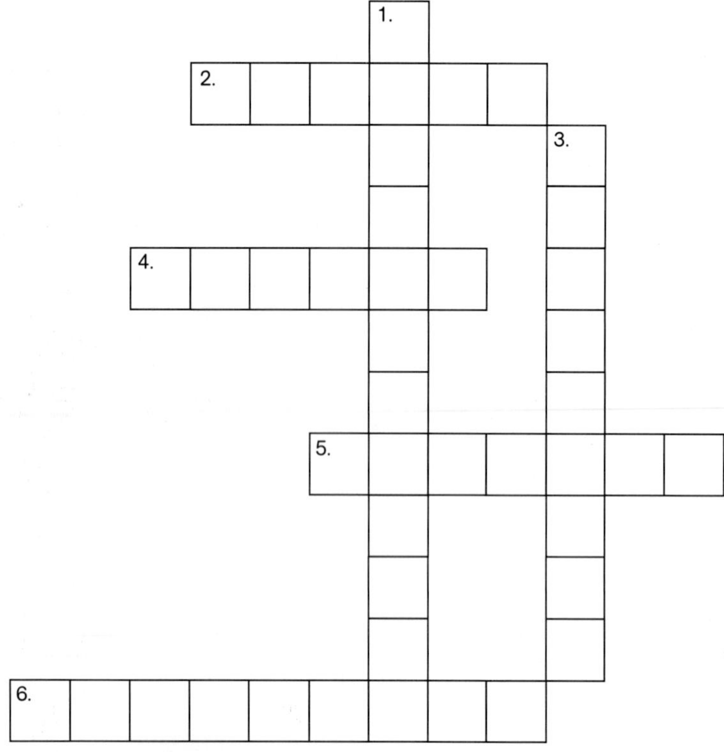

Across

2. Began in West Europe.
4. Official in this country.
5. Within orthodoxy.
6. Sorry for sins.

Down

1. Founded by S. Schechter.
3. Began with Samson Hirsch.

Q1. When did splits in Judaism begin?
Q2. Where did Reform Judaism begin?
Q3. What does it focus on?
Q4. Do they always use Hebrew?
Q5. When did they first have a female Rabbi?
Q6. What is Orthodoxy a blend of?
Q7. Name two groups within Orthodoxy.
Q8. How does it view women?
Q9. Who founded Conservative Judaism?
Q10. How is it different from the other traditions?
Q11. What is the focus of Reconstructionist Judaism?

More Qs

A. Why did the splits occur, do you think?
B. Why did the followers make changes to Judaism?
C. Are there differences in relation to women's roles? Explain.

COPY AND COLOUR

JUDAISM and CHRISTIANITY

It's clear from history that Christianity has not always been good to Judaism. Indeed, there have been instances of anti-Jewish sentiment down through the ages. However, since the Second World War and the Holocaust, Jews and Christians have been trying to rectify decades of misunderstanding.

TO KNOW

Liturgy = celebration of worship by believers.

The relationship between Judaism and Christianity has been expressed in changes in worship and liturgy (Good Friday intercession prayers, for example) and in official statements made by Christian Churches.

Second Vatican Council Statement about non-Christian religions

'The Jews still remain most dear to God because of their Fathers, for he does not repent of the gifts He makes nor of the calls He issues. In company with Prophets and the Apostle Paul, the Church awaits that day, known to God alone, on which all peoples will address the Lord in a single voice and 'serve him' with one accord. Since the spiritual patrimony common to Christians and Jews is so great, this Synod wishes to foster and recommend that mutual understanding and respect which is the fruit above all of biblical and theological studies, and of brotherly dialogue.' (Nostra Aetate 4, 1965)

Nostra Aetate = Declaration of the relationship of the Church to non-Christian religions.

TO KNOW

Patrimony = inherited from father (ancestors).

In 1965, at the **Second Vatican Council** (meeting of Catholic bishops, cardinals, theologians and laypeople), the members issued this document, the **Nostra Aetate**, which promoted respect, understanding and cooperation between Christians and Jews. The other Christian Churches have also promoted better relations with the Jewish people.

Today, the Catholic Church believes that:

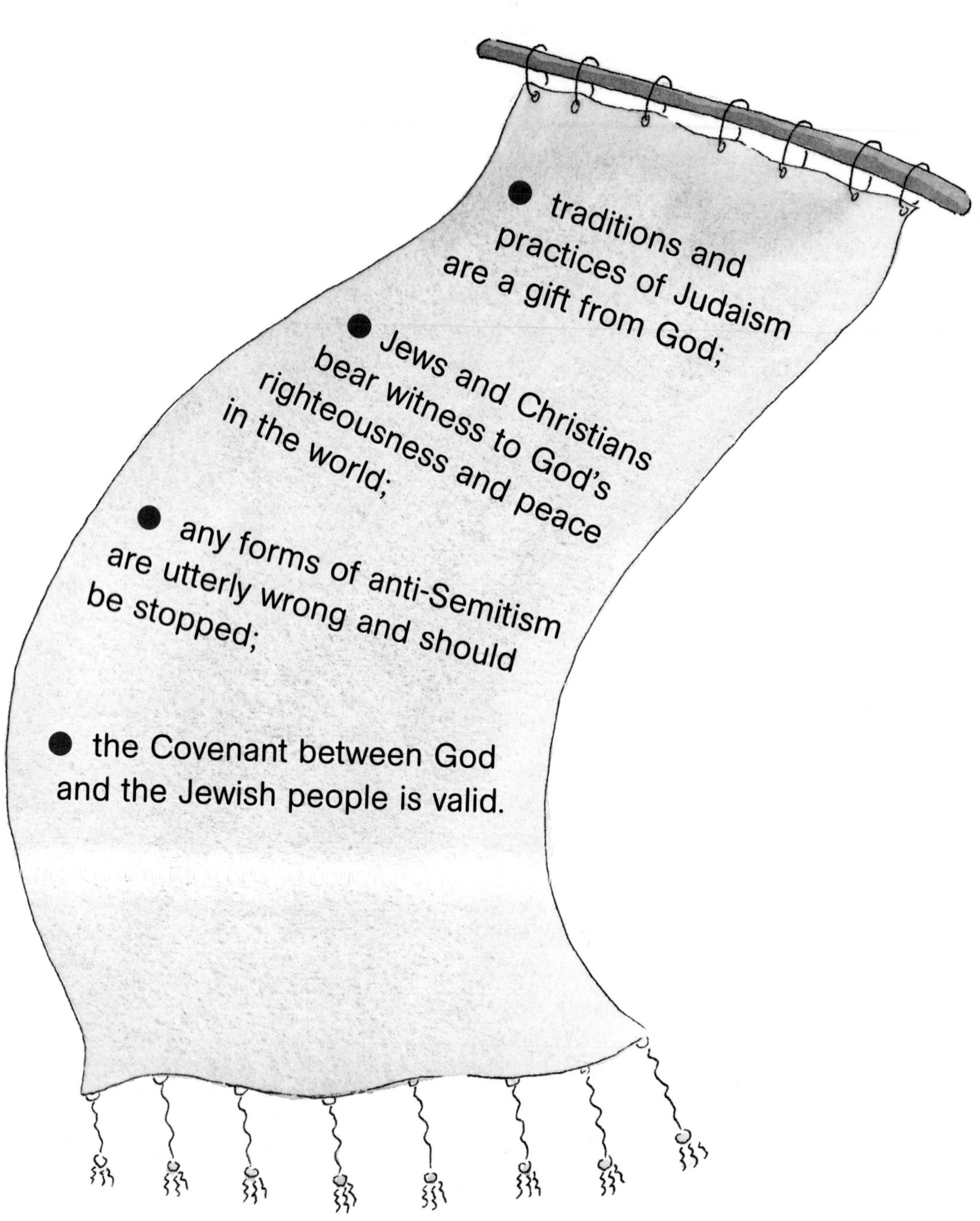

● traditions and practices of Judaism are a gift from God;
● Jews and Christians bear witness to God's righteousness and peace in the world;
● any forms of anti-Semitism are utterly wrong and should be stopped;
● the Covenant between God and the Jewish people is valid.

Work for you to do!

Q1. What does 'liturgy' mean?

Q2. What has happened since the Second World War?

Q3. How have changes occurred?

Q4. What document was issued by Catholics to promote better relations with non-Christians? In what year was it issued?

Q5. What did this document say?

Q6. What can we say about Judaism today?

More Qs

A. Why is it important to remember that Jesus was a Jew? Explain.

B. What was so important about Nostra Aetate?

C. Why, do you think, might Christians have been involved in anti-Jewish sentiment?

D. What is the situation today between Christians and Jews?

How does the Jewish community get on with other religions in your local area or region?

Complete this **Nostra Aetate** cloze test:

The ______ still remain most ______ to God because of their ______ for He does not ______ of the gifts He makes nor of the ______ He issues. In company with the ______ and the ______ ______, the Church awaits that day, known to God ______, on which all ______ will address the ______ in a single ______ and serve Him with one ______. Since the spiritual ______ common to ______ and ______ is so great, this Synod wishes to ______ and recommend that mutual ______ and ______ which is the fruit above all of ______ and theological studies and of ______ dialogue.

Jewish Holy Places

Many religions have towns and places that are considered holy. They are usually connected to the founding of the religion and the worship of God. Here are some of the Jewish holy places:

Mediterranean Sea

ISRAEL

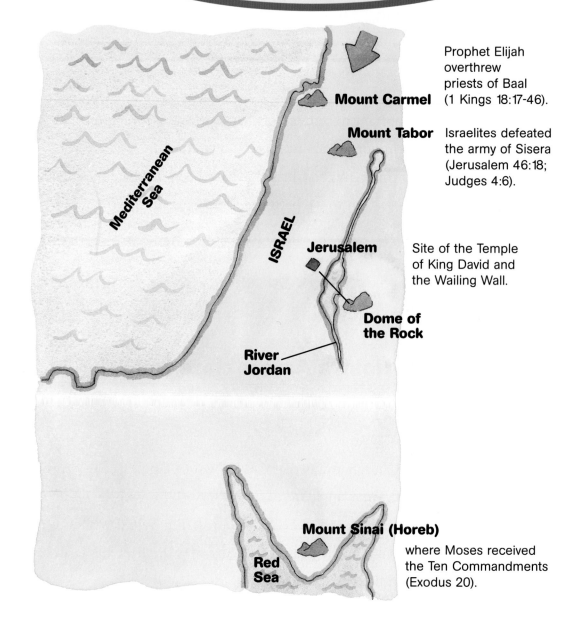

Mount Carmel Prophet Elijah overthrew priests of Baal (1 Kings 18:17-46).

Mount Tabor Israelites defeated the army of Sisera (Jerusalem 46:18; Judges 4:6).

Jerusalem Site of the Temple of King David and the Wailing Wall.

Dome of the Rock

River Jordan

Mount Sinai (Horeb) where Moses received the Ten Commandments (Exodus 20).

Red Sea

Time to Think and Pray

'I lift my eyes Heavenward.'

What does respect mean?

Well, it means accepting someone for who they are! Looking at a person with human dignity! Seeing a person in the image of God! Standing beside them! Shaking their hand! Seeing differences in them as a good and interesting thing! Loving them!

Let us pray ...

- That we will always treat other people with respect – Amen.
- That we will see people as being the same as us – Amen.
- That differences among people are cherished – Amen.
- That love makes us human – Amen.
- That love is a gift from God – Amen.

Read and reflect on the New Testament Gospel of Matthew 25:35-45.

Section 3

The World Religion of Islam

- Looking deeper… at a Community of Faith
- Muhammad
- Revelation to Muhammad
- The Koran
- Muhammad in Mecca
- Hijra
- The Five Pillars
- The Hajj
- Islamic Religious Leaders
- The Sunni and the Shiite
- The Mosque
- Festivals of Islam
- Food, Drink and Dress
- Islam in Ireland
- Time to Think and Pray

The World Religion of Islam

Looking Deeper . . . at a Community of Faith

The religion of Islam began with a man called **Muhammad** in the year A.D. 622. Let's see how it happened!

TO KNOW

ISLAM = submission (to Allah). **ALLAH =** name of God.

ISLAM

Muhammad's early life!

According to family accounts, Muhammad was born on Friday, 17 Rabi'ul Awwal in A.D. 570. After his birth he was named **Muhammad**, meaning 'praiseworthy'.

Muhammad's father died young, at twenty-four, when Muhammad was still an infant. His mother, Aminah, died when he was six. His grandfather, Abd al-Muttalib, became his foster-father and his only family.

As a young boy growing up he helped his uncle, Abu Talib, tend his sheep and travelled with him on trading journeys. For many years he lived and worked in Mecca **(Makkah)**.

At the age of twenty-five Muhammad married Khadija. He had worked for her on a trade journey and she was impressed by his truthfulness, honesty and trustworthiness. She was forty at that time when she married the young Muhammad.

Saudi Arabia

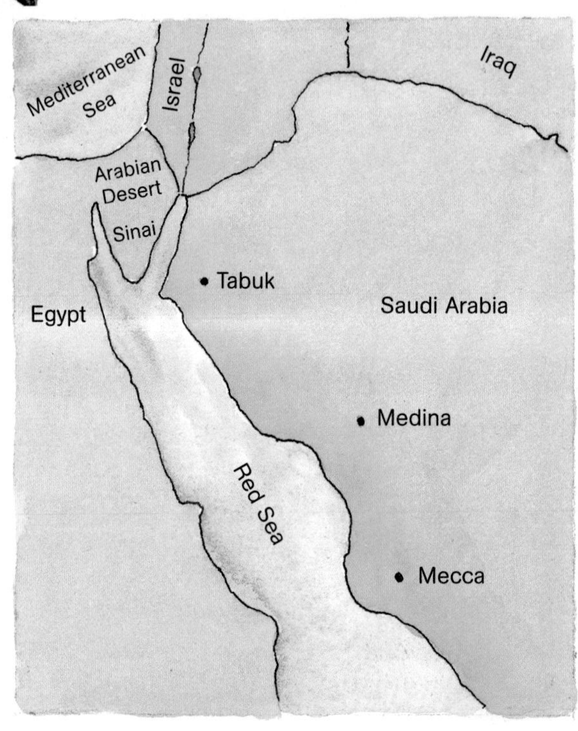

TO KNOW

REVELATION = something revealed, usually by God or a divinity.

During the years Muhammad lived in Mecca, he often went to a place called 'The Mount of Light'. This was a hill a few miles north-east of Mecca.

The Muslim religion believes it is disrespectful to have pictures of Muhammad.

REVELATION to MUHAMMAD

ALLAH

On the hill was a small cave. Muhammad would go into the cave and spend time on his own, thinking. It was here, at the age of forty, that he received a '**Revelation**' from **Allah**.

These Revelations were written down in the Holy Book of Islam.

The Qur'an (Koran)

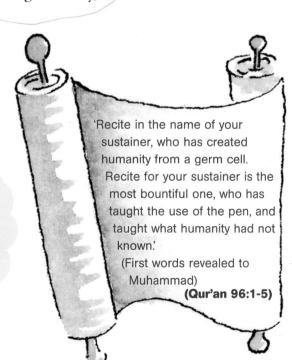

'Recite in the name of your sustainer, who has created humanity from a germ cell. Recite for your sustainer is the most bountiful one, who has taught the use of the pen, and taught what humanity had not known.'
(First words revealed to Muhammad)
(Qur'an 96:1-5)

Muhammad was given the responsibility of spreading the message of Allah.

Muhammad was to announce to all people the guidance that Allah had given him and write it down for future generations to know of it.

For you to do!

Draw the symbol for Islam.

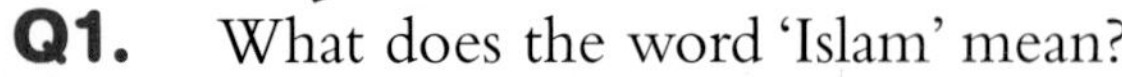

Q1. What does the word 'Islam' mean?
Q2. What is the name Muslim people use for God?
Q3. Name the man who started Islam.
Q4. What country did it start in?
Q5. Name a country that lies next to Saudi Arabia.
Q6. When was Muhammad born?
Q7. What does 'Muhammad' mean?
Q8. Who became his foster-father?
Q9. Name his uncle.
Q10. How did he help his uncle?
Q11. What age was Muhammad when he got married?
Q12. What was his wife's name?

Bubble writing to do in your copy:

'Muhammad received Revelations from Allah.'

Q. **Name the Holy Book of Islam.**

RSTUPREVELATIONSTOOKALWMUHAMMADLPSTUABSAUDIARABIASCUXPTOKFALLAHSTCAXEVULOEKHADIJAHKORANSTVULISLAMKP

When you have found the words in the word wheel use them in a sentence, here:

A. When Muhammad was growing up, what work did he do?
B. Where did he live?
C. What was it about the young Muhammad that impressed Khadijah?
D. What was the name of the hill Muhammad often went to in Mecca?
E. What does 'Revelation' mean?
F. From whom did the Revelation come?
G. Name the Holy City of Islam.

Muhammad in Mecca

Muhammad announced to the people of Mecca that they should turn away from their bad ways, especially idolatry (worshipping false gods).

They should return to their one true God, Allah. According to Muhammad . . .

. . . those who believed and obeyed the laws in the **Qur'an** would be rewarded in Paradise . . .

. . . those who rejected the message would be punished in Hell.

Some people became angry with Muhammad because of what he was saying.

Opposition against him grew until eventually he and his followers fled from **Mecca** in fear of their lives.

They escaped to **Medina**.

The Hijra

The journey from Mecca to Medina is called the Hijra and it took place in July, A.D. 622.

Muhammad became the Head of a religious community in Medina. Along with his followers, he fought against his opponents in Mecca.

Eventually, in A.D. 630, he managed to conquer the city of **Mecca** and its inhabitants. The followers of Muhammad believed:

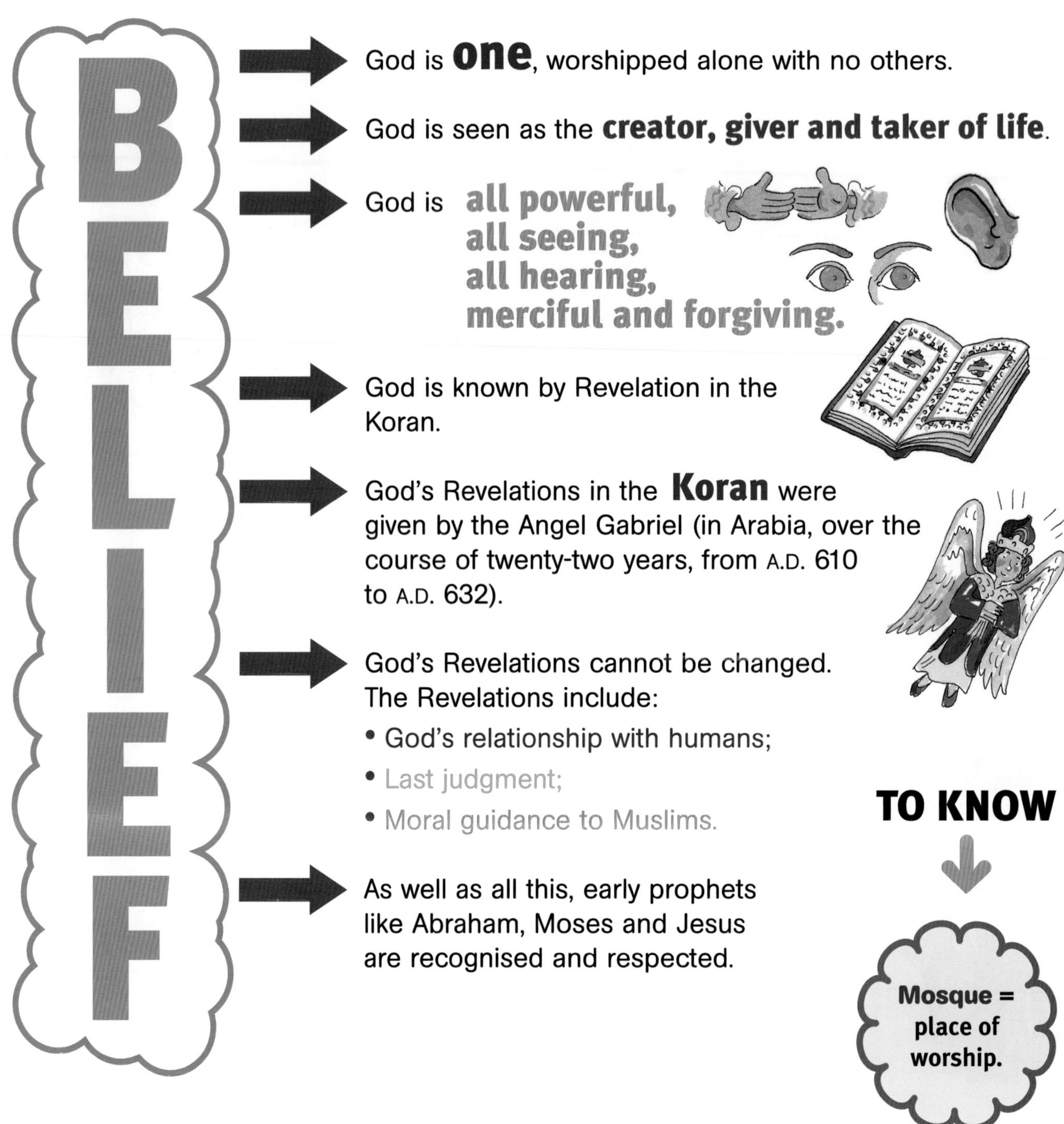

BELIEF
God is **one**, worshipped alone with no others.
God is seen as the **creator, giver and taker of life**.
God is **all powerful, all seeing, all hearing, merciful and forgiving.**
God is known by Revelation in the Koran.
God's Revelations in the **Koran** were given by the Angel Gabriel (in Arabia, over the course of twenty-two years, from A.D. 610 to A.D. 632).
God's Revelations cannot be changed. The Revelations include:
• God's relationship with humans;
• Last judgment;
• Moral guidance to Muslims.
As well as all this, early prophets like Abraham, Moses and Jesus are recognised and respected.
TO KNOW
Mosque = place of worship.

Some work to do

Q1. What did Muhammad announce to the people of Mecca?
Q2. What would happen to those who obeyed the Qur'an?
Q3. What would happen to those who rejected the Qur'an?
Q4. Why did Muhammad leave Mecca?
Q5. His journey to Medina is called what?
Q6. What happened in Medina?
Q7. When did Muhammad conquer Mecca?
Q8. What year did the Hijra take place?

A. What does idolotry mean?
B. Why were the people of Mecca annoyed with Muhammad?
C. What is the Muslim belief about Allah?
D. How does the Koran view Jesus, Moses and Abraham?
E. What do the Revelations in the Koran include, as well as God?
F. Why should the Koran Revelations not be changed?

Finish these sentences with a correct ending (in your copy)

- Muhammad told the people at Mecca to ...
- Those who obeyed and believed the Koran would...
- Opposition grew so Muhammad and his followers...
- The journey to Medina is called...
- The Hijra happened in...
- In AD 630 Muhammad...
- The Holy City of Islam is...
- According to the Koran, God is...
- Revelation was given by...
- Revelation means...
- The Revelations include...
- Jesus and Abraham are...

Exile Crossword

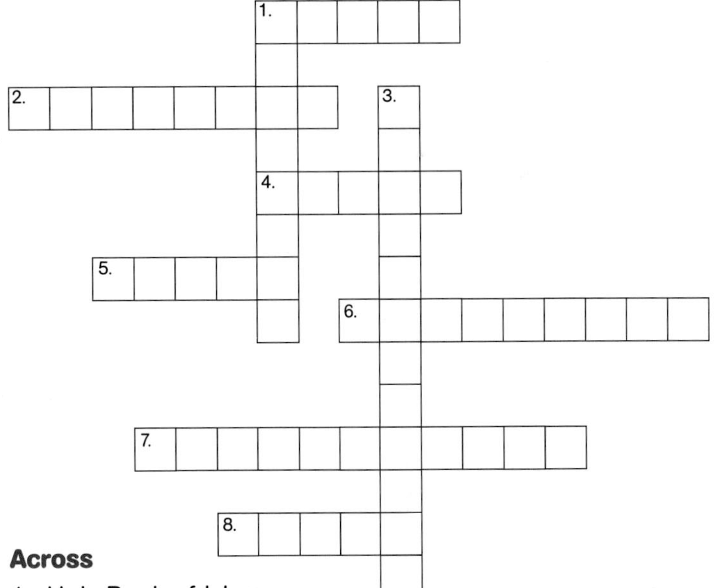

Across

1. Holy Book of Islam.
2. Prophet of Islam.
4. Name of religion.
5. Journey to Medina.
6. What Muhammad got from God.
7. Country of origin.
8. Muslim name for God.

Down

1. Wife of Muhammad.
3. Meaning of Muhammad.

Central to Muslim belief and way of life are …

The Five Pillars

TO KNOW

Ka'ba = Islam's holy site.

These are:

The statement of belief is:
'There is no god but God (Allah) and Muhammad is God's messenger!'

Muslims must pray five times a day: at dawn, midday, mid-afternoon, sunset, and before sleeping.
After washing themselves, believers face **Mecca** and pray as a group, when in the mosque, or in an appropriate place when praying alone (usually on a rug/mat). Prayer involves movements such as bowing, crossing arms, kneeling, turning one's head. Muslims recite from the **Qur'an**. Men attend prayers every Friday, at noon.

Otherwise known as **zakat**, those who can afford to do so give a yearly donation to the needy in their community.

4. Fasting

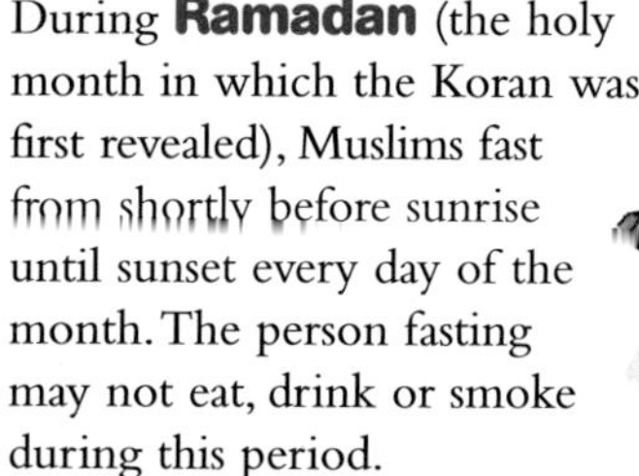

During **Ramadan** (the holy month in which the Koran was first revealed), Muslims fast from shortly before sunrise until sunset every day of the month. The person fasting may not eat, drink or smoke during this period.

5. Pilgrimage

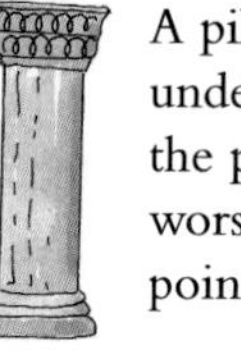

A pilgrimage, known as the Hajj, to Mecca must be undertaken at least once in life by every Muslim. At Mecca, the pilgrims walk around the **Ka'ba** ('ancient house of worship for God'), pray and offer thanks at various special points in and around the city of Mecca.

The Hajj explained!

The Hajj, as we have just seen, is the pilgrimage to Mecca.

TO KNOW

Muslims are obliged to make the pilgrimage to Mecca once in their lifetime!
The Hajj commemorates Muhammad's life!
Mecca and its surrounds are holy; a non-Muslim should not enter.
Every year 2.5 million Muslims peform the Hajj.
Pilgrims wear white robes, pray and promise to complete the Hajj.
Pilgrims walk around the Ka'ba seven times.
Then they move closer to the black stone to touch or kiss it.

NB:
Ka'ba means 'House of Allah'.

Pilgrims go to the two hills, **Safa** and **Marwo**. They run between these two hills, remembering Abraham's wife's search for water (the Old Testament).

- Pilgrims go to **Mina** and stay there for the night.
- Next day they go to the area below **Mount Arafat** and pray.
- They then go to **Mizdalifah**, gather stones, pray and sleep.

Next day they go back to Mina. Here the pilgrims throw stones at stone pillars, which represent **Satan**. When this has been done, they cut off a lock of their hair and change their clothes.

A man who completes the pilgrimage calls himself **Hajj**; a woman calls herself **Hajjah**.

Five Pillars Wordsearch

P	U	E	Y	J	P	M	J	B	H	I	C	D	H	T
R	N	Z	U	L	I	G	R	I	S	I	T	E	F	G
A	E	Q	N	D	U	H	X	Y	W	X	U	P	H	N
Y	V	Q	D	E	J	I	Z	Z	V	S	U	W	Z	I
E	E	A	N	G	N	I	V	I	G	S	M	L	A	T
R	Y	U	S	E	D	A	K	R	R	S	R	R	K	I
G	A	L	Q	E	G	A	Q	A	E	V	I	F	A	C
N	J	M	E	S	A	A	L	N	M	B	T	S	T	E
I	Y	R	A	B	O	L	M	F	H	E	G	K	K	R
W	C	A	A	D	I	M	K	I	T	E	S	N	U	S
O	T	U	R	P	A	Y	J	O	R	M	E	C	C	A
B	X	R	B	P	L	N	J	V	R	G	A	D	G	Y
X	H	C	Q	O	E	N	A	I	H	A	L	T	K	N
N	M	W	H	E	L	U	H	T	A	U	N	I	W	Y
Q	T	B	O	J	F	A	S	T	I	N	G	W	P	U

ALMSGIVING
FASTING
HOLY
MAT
MOSQUE
PRAY
RECITING
ZAKAT

BOWING
FIVE
KAABA
MECCA
PILGRIMAGE
PRAYER
SITE
CREED

HAJJ
KORAN
MIDDAY
PILLARS
RAMADAN
SUNSET

As with most other Communities of Faith, the Islamic Faith Community has religious leaders to help the believers to live good lives, worship together and move closer to their God.

Islamic Religious Leaders

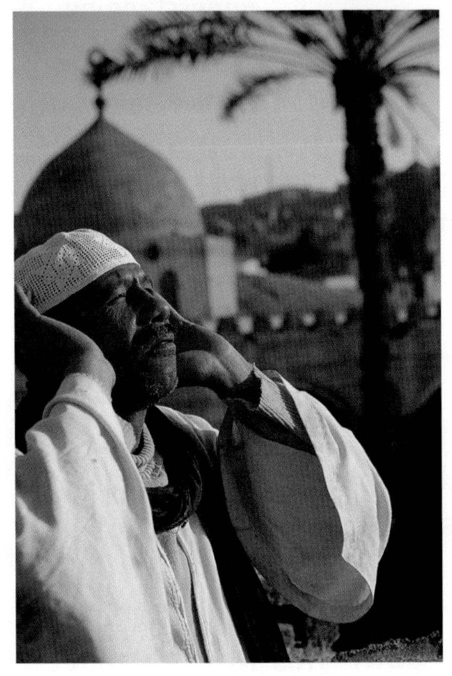

← This Muslim man is called an **Imam**; he is a religious leader in Islam. One of his most important tasks is to lead the prayers in the **mosque**. (Any man can act as an Imam, but there are usually professional Imams attached to a mosque.) Imams also preach, teach and celebrate marriages and funerals. His spiritual leadership is very important.

Ayatollah (used mostly in Iran and among Shiite leaders) is the name given to scholars of religion. These men give the religious community guidance about law and religious matters. They are important spiritual leaders, especially if there is no Imam. Another name given to a Muslim religious leader is **Mullah**. Again, this refers to a scholar of the Muslim faith and a leader of the community.

Caliph is the name usually used for the successor of Muhammad as the community leader (or Sunni leaders). Originally there were four Caliphs who immediately succeeded Muhammad: Abu Bakr, Umar, Utman and Ali; collectively called 'Rightly Guided Caliphs'.

The Islamic Community of Faith has two sects. These are …

TO KNOW

Sect =
a religious group that splits from its original Community of Faith because of belief and origin understanding.

The Sunni and The Shiite

Let's 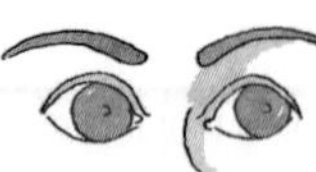 look at these sects in Islam.

Sects usually come about because of a disagreement over a religious belief, ritual, or founder of the religion. In the case of the Muslim religion, it happened because of a disagreement over who should lead the Islamic Community of Faith after Muhammad's death.

The **Shiite** (Shia) sect came about because the followers of Muhammad's son-in-law, Ali, felt he should lead the community. They gradually became known as the Shiat Ali, or party of Ali, and Ali's relatives and descendants became known as 'Imam'. The name was later reduced to Shiite and Iran is their homeland.

The **Sunni** sect, which comprises 90 per cent of the Muslim population, gets its name from Sunna, meaning '**the trodden path**'. This was the path followed by Muhammad and his first ancestors, and the Sunnis claim to continue that path. Their full name is 'the people of the Sunna and collectivity'. They follow the Caliph.

. . . even though there are two separate sects, they both believe in **Allah**, **Muhammad**, **the Koran** and **Revelation**, and **the Five Pillars**. The differences, as you can see, centre around the descendants of Muhammad and who has the right to lead the religion.

Fill in the blanks:

An I______ is a religious l______ in Islam. He l______ prayers in the m______. A p______ Imam is usually i______ to the mosque. Imams also p______, t______, and celebrate w______ and f______. A______ is the name given to religious scholars (especially in I______). The Ayatollah gives guidance on l______ and religious m______. Another name for a scholar of the Muslim Faith is M______. The name C______ is usually used for the successor to M______.

Qqs

Q1. What does 'sect' mean?
Q2. How do sects usually come about?
Q3. How did the Shiite sect of Islam come about?
Q4. Who was Ali?
Q5. What does Shiat Ali mean?
Q6. What does 'Sunna' refer to?
Q7. Who followed the 'trodden path'?
Q8. What are the Sunni Muslims properly called?
Q9. Name the different stages of the Hajj.
Q10. What does Ka'ba mean?
Q11. Why do the pilgrims throw stones at pillars?
Q12. After completing the pilgrimage, by what name can they be known?

Unmuddle these words

EQSMOU ____________________

HLALUM ____________________

TOLAHLAYA ____________________

MAIM ____________________

PHALIC ____________________

ISNUN ____________________

TEHSII ____________________

TECS ____________________

In your copy explain what the **Imam**, **Caliph** and **Sunni** are.

RESEARCH
JOURNAL IDEA

Find out about the Muslim religion in your area or region.

Interview a member of the Muslim community in your area.

Let's look at

The KORAN ...

Some of the most important elements of the Islamic Community of Faith are to be found in **The Koran**.
Here are some details:

The Koran is the sacred Book of Islam. It is believed to be the direct Word of God, given to Muhammad through the Angel Gabriel. The Word of God in the Koran cannot be changed and a person must be ritually pure before touching the book.

It is divided into 114 chapters, each of which gives instruction on different topics. Many of the early chapters concern God's oneness and identity and Muhammad as His Messenger. Later chapters are concerned with community issues, social and legal issues, family, marriage and moral teachings. For Muslims, it is the primary source of doctrine and law.

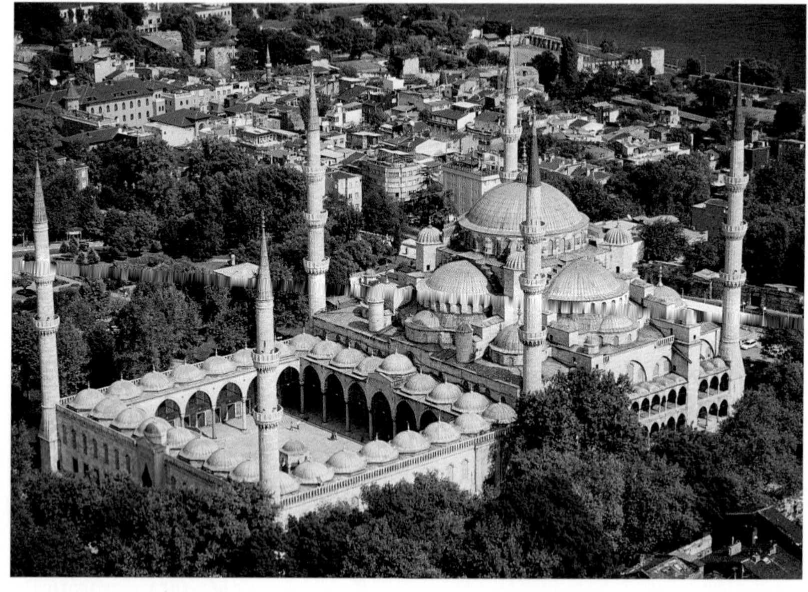

The Mosque

The mosque is the building where Muslims meet for prayer, worship, education and social discussion. The word mosque is taken from **masjid**, which means 'a place of prostration'. The first mosque was built in **Quba**, in Medina. Every mosque has space for the worshippers, an alcove or niche indicating the direction in which Mecca lies, a pulpit for preaching, a stand for the Koran and a **minaret** (tower) on the roof so people can be called to prayer.

MUSLIM MOSQUE

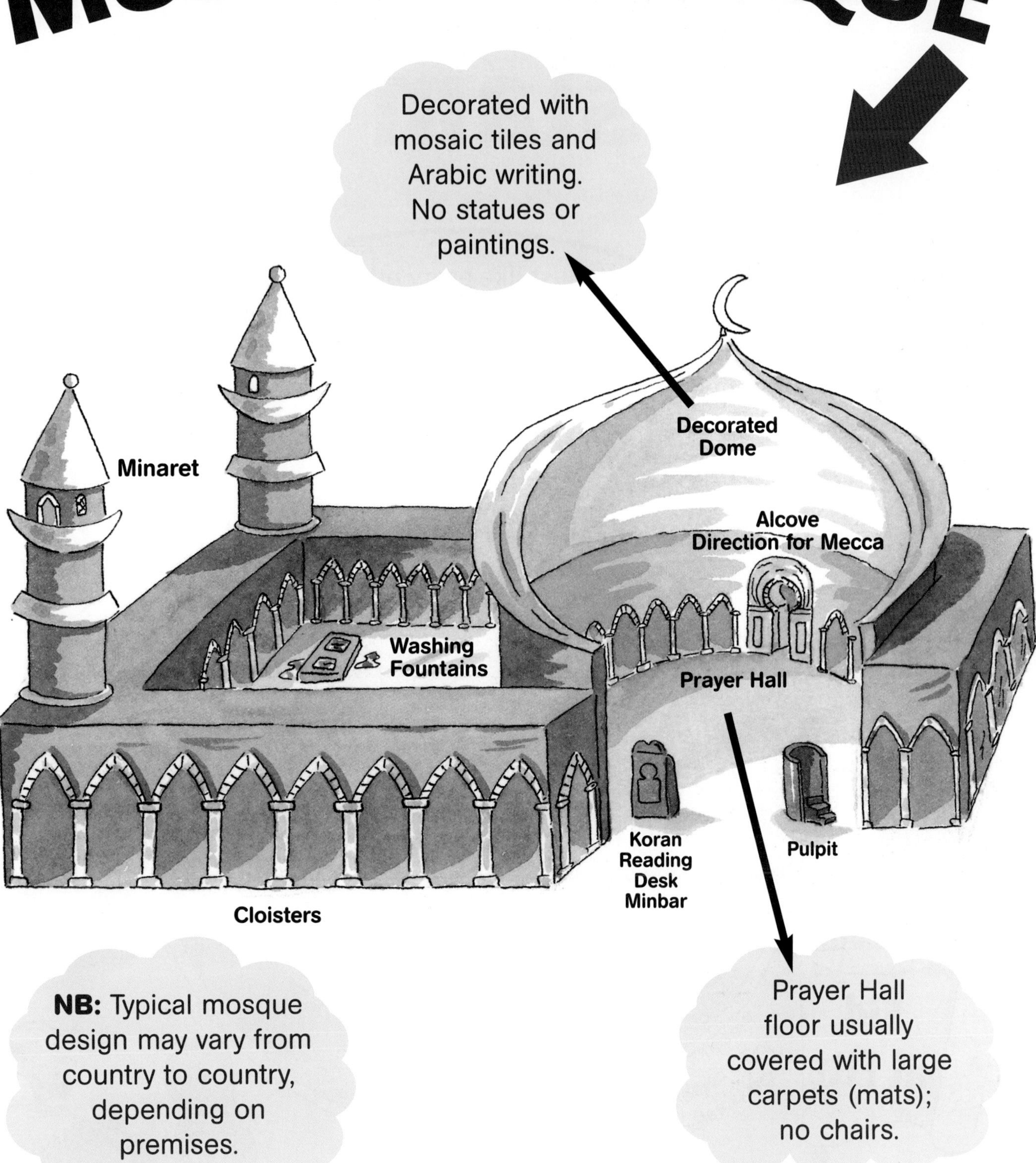

NB: Typical mosque design may vary from country to country, depending on premises.

Festivals of Islam

TO KNOW

Muslims start their calendars from A.D. 622. They use a lunar calendar of 354 days.

Just like every other **world religion**, Islam has its special times during the year! Let's have a 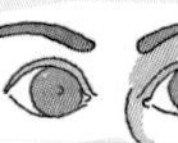 look . . .

Ramadan

This is the most important festival in Islam. It begins on the ninth month and lasts for twenty-eight/twenty-nine days. It celebrates Muhammad's receiving of the Koran. During the month, all Muslims must fast between sunrise and sunset.

Lailat al Qadr

(The Night of Power)

Celebrated over the last ten days of Ramadan: Muslims stay awake and read the Koran. This recalls the First Revelation of the Koran.

Eid al Fitr

(Festival of Fast-Breaking)

First day of the new month after Ramadan: Muslims go to the mosque to thank Allah for Ramadan. Presents and cards are given in joyful celebration and a special meal is eaten.

Foods Muslims are allowed to eat are called **Halal**.

Halal foods are:

- meat of sheep, goats, cows and poultry;
- edible plants;
- eggs (from Halal birds);
- milk (from Halal mammals);
- edible fish.

Foods which are not allowed are called **Haram**.

Haram foods are:

- all alcohol is Haram (completely forbidden);
- pig meat;
- meat from an animal that died naturally or was strangled;
- meat of carnivorous animals.

Muslim men and women are requested to dress modestly. In the case of women, this means that all of their bodies should be covered, except hands, feet and faces (although in some Muslim societies faces must be covered as well).

. . . and finally, some important points specifically about the **Muslim Community** of Faith in **Ireland** today . . .

Islam in Ireland

The history of the arrival of Islam is based on documents written by Muslim students studying there in the **1950s**.

In **1959** these students, as well as others, set up the **Dublin Islamic Society (later called Islamic Foundation of Ireland)**. At this time there was no mosque, so with money from home and financial assistance from Muslim organisations, the Society bought No. 7 Haddington Road and converted it into a mosque, which opened in 1976. In 1981 an **Imam** was appointed to the mosque. Within a few years the mosque was considered too small for the growing Muslim community, so they acquired new premises on South Circular Road, in Dublin. In 1983 the new mosque was opened for worship.

As well as Dublin, there are Islamic societies in **Galway**, **Cork**, **Ballyhaunis**, **Limerick** and **Waterford**. In 1990 the first Muslim National School was opened, in Dublin, and it is funded by the Department of Education.

At present there are an estimated **12,000** members of the Islamic faith in Ireland.

One of its most senior clerics in Ireland is **Imam Al Hussein.**

Complete this Islam fact file . . .

Some work for you to do 

Founder: ________________
Country of Origin: ________________
Name for God: ________________
Sacred Text: ________________
Holy City: ________________
Pilgrimage Journey: ________________
Mission: ________________
Holy Building: ________________
Religious Leaders: ________________
Two Sects: ________________
Five Pillars: ________________
God is: ________________

Correct the following sentences:

The Koran is the Sacred Book / least important book for Muslims.
The Koran is the Word of God / Word of Moses.
It was given to Muhammad / Khadija.
God revealed the Koran through the Angel Gabriel / Archangel Michael.
The Koran cannot / can be changed.
A person must be ritually pure / disrespectful before they can touch the Koran.
The mosque is where the Muslims eat / meet for prayer.
The word 'mosque' comes from Masjid, meaning to talk / to prostrate.
Every mosque has a stand for the Koran / Bible.

True / False?

1. Foods Muslims are allowed to eat are Haram. **T / F**
2. Edible fish is Halal. **T / F**
3. Haram means not allowed. **T / F**
4. Pig meat is Haram. **T / F**
5. Alcohol is allowed. **T / F**
6. Men and women can wear what they like. **T / F**
7. Women's hands and feet should be covered. **T / F**
8. Eggs from Halal birds may be eaten. **T / F**

Q1. Name the Holy Book of Islam.
Q2. Where does the word 'mosque' come from?
Q3. How many chapters are in the Koran?
Q4. What do the later chapters tell us?
Q5. How do worshippers in the mosque know in which direction Mecca lies?
Q6. What is usually found in the courtyard of the mosque?
Q7. What calendar do Muslims follow?
Q8. Name and explain the three main Islamic festivals.

Time To Think and Pray

I pray to God that . . .

'In the name of God, the Compassionate, the Merciful.' (Koran, Sura 1)

I will believe in Him and His goodness. **Amen**.

I will do good things in God's name. **Amen**.

I will reach out to others and show God's love to them. **Amen**.

I will spend time thinking about God. **Amen**.

I will look on my life as a spiritual journey. **Amen**.

My Journey

Travel through life, it's a pilgrimage. Stop along the way to pray and reflect. Reach out to those in need. Thank God you can journey. All the time be happy with what you have, love those you meet. Love, be loved. Reach your dreams.

'We are companions on a journey, praying to God and sharing life and in the love we share is the hope we bear, for we believe in the love of our God, we believe in the love of our God.'

Section

Expressing our Faith

- Communicating with God!
- Hard to pray?
- Praying Believers
- People of Prayer

The Experience of Worship

- What is worship?
- Places of worship
- Participating in worship
- The Mass
- The Elements of a Catholic Church
- Celebration of the Eucharist
- Participation in worship

Sign and Symbol

- What are signs and symbols?
- Religious symbols
- Christian symbols
- The Sacraments of the Catholic Church
- Baptism
- Confirmation
- Eucharist

Places of Significance

- Places of pilgrimage in Ireland
- European places of sacredness
- The Holy Land

Significant Times

- During the year
- Christian sacred times
- The liturgical year
- Advent
- Christmas
- Lent
- Easter
- Ordinary Time

Faith Begins

- Mysteries of life
- Questions asked
- Finding meaning
- Faith and meaning

The Growth of Faith

- Childhood – Adulthood
- Image of God
- Worship and mystery

The Situation of Faith Today

- Ireland in the past
- Devotions
- Catholic Ireland
- The beginnings of change
- Faith celebration
- Decline
- Influences in young people
- Helping young people
- Decline in Europe

Challenges to Faith

- The Enlightenment
- Copernicus
- Galileo
- Newton
- Creation
- Darwin/Evolution
- Communism
- No God or religion
- Atheism etc.

Science and Religion

- A relationship
- Second Vatican Council

People who are members of a Community of Faith are committed to that community. They follow its rules and guidelines and live a good life according to its holy writings and the teachings of its leaders. They also **express their faith**!

EXPRESSING OUR FAITH

What does **'express our faith'** mean?

- To express our faith means to make an action, or take on something, or to go somewhere that we believe will bring us closer to God.
- By expressing our faith we show to people around us that we are part of a religion, part of a believing community.
- Expressing our faith shows that we have a relationship with God.

People who believe in and are part of a Community of Faith express their faith by:

- **prayer;**
- **worship;**
- **the way they live.**

PRAYER

We all know that people pray – we have seen them pray and we may have done it ourselves. But what exactly is prayer? Let's have a look.

Finish this sentence:

Prayer is . . .

. . . Communicating with God!

People pray so that they can **communicate with God**. Speaking to God is a very important part of expressing faith.
There are many different types of prayer and ways to pray:

Prayers of Thanks!

Saying thanks to God for the good things in life and all that we have!

Prayers of Asking!

Asking God for something to help other people, or to help yourself. Asking for good things!

Prayers of Praise!

Praising God for His creation and for all the good things in this world! Praising His mystery!

Prayers of Forgiveness!

Asking God for forgiveness for wrongs we have committed against ourselves or against others!

As you can see, most of the time people pray using words. Sometimes, however, people don't pray out loud. Instead they choose to pray in the silence of their  hearts!

This way of praying can be achieved through . . .

MEDITATION

Meditation means taking time out to focus quietly on God (through Jesus in Christian meditation). Sometimes people create a special area in which they meditate, with candles and soft music. During meditation, people focus on and think about God and all His works.

CONTEMPLATION

Contemplation is slightly different from meditation. In contemplation we sit in God's presence with an open mind and contemplate all the religious thoughts we have.

Let's try some

Q1. If people are committed to their **Community of Faith**, what do they do?

Q2. What does 'expressing your faith' mean?

Q3. In what ways can believers express their faith?

Q4. From your experience, how do people look when they pray?

Q5. Name the four ways in which prayers can be expressed?

Q6. What does '**contemplation**' mean?

True / False?

- Members of religions express their faith! **T / F**
- Worship is expressing your faith! **T / F**
- Expressing faith brings people closer to God! **T / F**
- Prayers of thanks are about asking God for something. **T / F**
- Prayers of forgiveness are about being in awe of God! **T / F**
- Sometimes people pray in silence. **T / F**
- Prayer is communicating with God! **T / F**
- Contemplation is prayer out loud with others. **T / F**
- Prayers of praise are about praising God! **T / F**
- When meditating, people think about God! **T / F**

- Make up a Prayer of Thanks to God. Think about all the good things you have and have experienced and say thanks to God for them!
- Make up a Prayer of Asking to God. Think about what you need in your life and what others need and ask God to give them help, strength and courage!

With the help of your teacher, go about trying to take time to pray with music and a piece from the Gospels.

. . . so people of faith pray,
but why do people pray?

For many things to do with themselves or others, and issues of peace/justice/love.

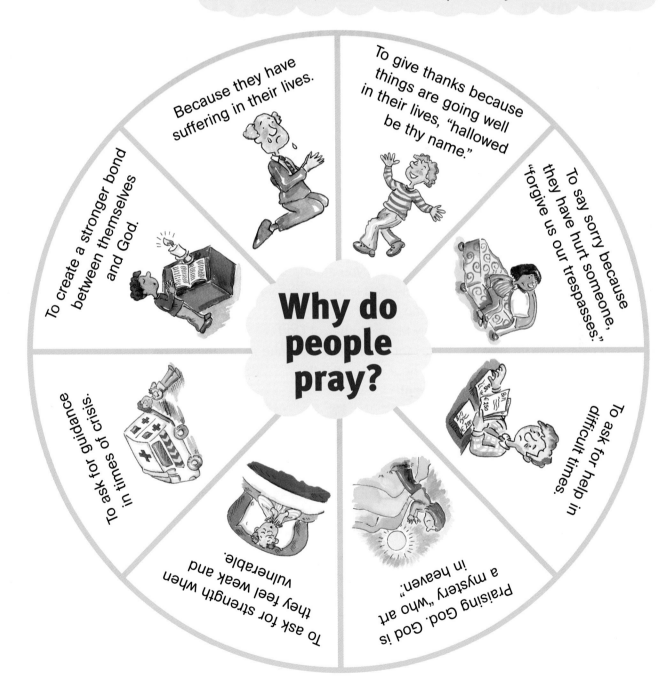

Why do people pray?

- Because they have suffering in their lives.
- To give thanks because things are going well in their lives, "hallowed be thy name."
- To say sorry because they have hurt someone, "forgive us our trespasses."
- To ask for help in difficult times.
- Praising God. God is a mystery "who art in heaven."
- To ask for strength when they feel weak and vulnerable.
- To ask for guidance in times of crisis.
- To create a stronger bond between themselves and God.

Ways to Pray

Praying can be done in different ways!

1. Praying on your own

2. Praying as a group ...

with the other members of your religion.

3. Praying in silence

4. Praying using your own words ...

this means talking to God in your own way – just like having a conversation!

5. Praying using Formal Prayers ...

... these are prayers we have learned and which were created by our Community of Faith!

The 'Hail Mary'

Hail Mary full of Grace,
the Lord is with you.
Blessed are you among women
and blessed is the fruit of your
womb, Jesus.
Holy Mary, Mother of God.
Pray for us sinners, now and at
the hour of our death.
Amen!

This is a special prayer to the Virgin Mary, Mother of God. It is based on the proclamation of Elizabeth, Mary's cousin, when she was told that Mary was pregnant.

The 'Our Father'

Our Father, who art in Heaven,
Hallowed be thy name.
Thy kingdom come,
thy will be done,
on Earth as it is in Heaven.
Give us this day our daily bread
and forgive us our trespasses
as we forgive those who
trespass against us
and lead us not into temptation but
deliver us from all evil.
Amen!

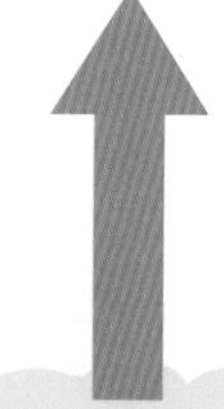

This is a prayer of: praise; thanks; asking; forgiveness.

NB:
The 'Our Father' (or 'Lord's Prayer') was given by Jesus to his followers to show them how to pray! (Lk 11:2-4) (Mt 6:7-16)

Over to you ...

A bit of artwork for you to do!

In your copy draw a picture for each of the following:

- a person praying out loud;
- a person praying with other people;
- a person praying on his or her own.

Fill in the blanks:

People _____ because things are going _____ in their lives. Some people pray to say _____ for hurting _____ or doing something _____. Others pray to ask God for _____ because things may be difficult. Because God is great, people pray to _____ Him. Some people might feel _____ and _____ and pray to ask God for _____. Others just want to create a strong _____ between themselves and God.

List six reasons why people pray:

1. ______________________________
2. ______________________________
3. ______________________________
4. ______________________________
5. ______________________________
6. ______________________________

Q1. Give two reasons why people pray.
Q2. Why would a person praise God?
Q3. Name two ways in which people can pray.
Q4. What are Formal Prayers?
Q5. What is important about the 'Our Father'?
Q6. How is it a prayer of praise and of thanks?
Q7. What is the 'Hail Mary' about?
Q8. When and where do you pray?

In your own words explain why . . .

- a person might pray on his or her own!
- a person might pray using his or her own words!
- a person might join with others to pray!
- a person might pray the 'Our Father'!

RESEARCH

JOURNAL IDEA

Interview a person you know who prays. Ask them nicely:

- to whom do they pray?
- why do they pray?
- when do they pray?
- how do they pray?

Make sure you ask someone you know well!

Hard to Pray?

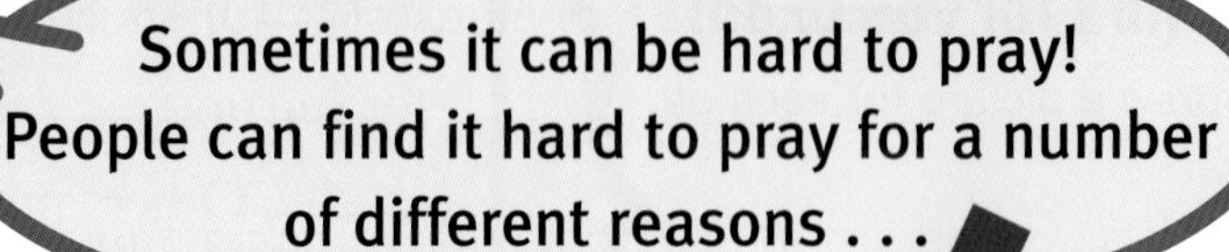

Sometimes it can be hard to pray! People can find it hard to pray for a number of different reasons . . .

They might be upset and annoyed about something and it prevents them from being able to concentrate on prayer or trying to communicate with God!

They may not truly understand what prayer is: they may feel that God never answers them and therefore they give up praying!

They may have too many distractions in their lives, such as money worries, shopping, children, etc. and cannot focus on prayer.

They may not be able to make a quiet place where they can step away from noise, talk, music, etc. to begin praying!

They may have a hectic schedule and be too busy to stop and pray!

- They need to remember that God works through them and they must play a part in the request, the forgiveness, or the praise. If they fail to realise this, they may find it hard to pray.
- God works and speaks through the people around them.
- Sometimes what we ask for may not really be good for us or for the good of others, therefore we may not receive it.

Praying Believers

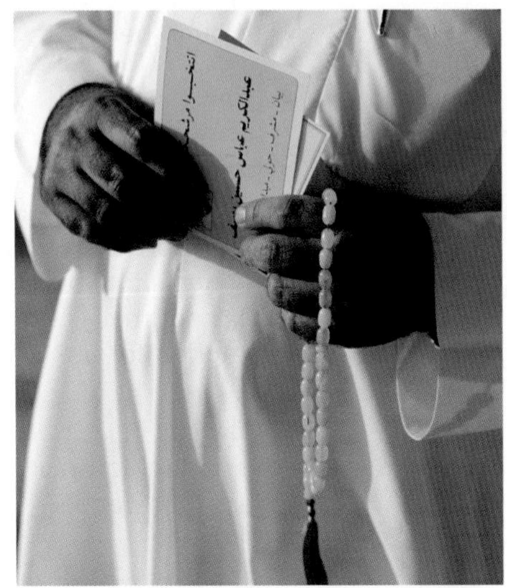

The **Salat** requires **Muslim believers** to pray five times a day. This must be done while facing Mecca and kneeling on a prayer mat. They pray using the **Ra'ku** prayer movements. Muslim prayer beads, or **Subha** (meaning 'to exalt'), help believers to pray to Allah. The **Subha** has ninety-nine beads, each representing the ninety-nine names for Allah and broken into thirty-three sections of prayer. Muslims use the **Tahmid** and **Tahlit** prayers to Allah to ask for evil spirits to be banished and for forgiveness to be bestowed on them.

Jewish believers gather together to pray in the **synagogue** on the Sabbath (Saturday). The most important part of the ceremony is reading from the Torah.

Monks use the **Aum** – 'the voice of God' – in their prayers and meditations. They chant **Aum** before they pray in the temple.

Catholic believers sometimes kneel in front of the **Blessed Sacrament** (the Sacrament of Jesus' body) while praying in a church.

Rosary beads are used by Catholic believers to pray to God and Mary, the Mother of God. The beads represent a repeated pattern of prayer: recite the 'Our Father' once, the 'Hail Mary' ten times and finish with 'Glory Be'. Each set of prayers is associated with various events in Jesus' life.

Some work to do!

Prayer Wordsearch

M N F A I T H A R B

U O P R A Y E R U Q

S I H C R U H C C M

L S R E V E I L E B

I S Y N A G O G U E

M E D I T A T I O N

G R C I L O H T A C

O P Z T E M P L E I

D X U D N I H I R H

G E F J K T O F O I

AUM	BELIEVERS	FAITH
CHURCH	EXPRESSION	MEDITATION
GOD	HINDU	SYNAGOGUE
MUSLIM	PRAYER	
TEMPLE	CATHOLIC	

Research

Find out about:

- Muslim **Salat**.
- Catholic Blessed Sacrament.
- Jewish Sabbath prayer.
- Hindu chanting.

More Qs

A Why do you think some people believe God doesn't listen when they pray?

B How do you think God works through people?

C How might God answer our prayers?

D What sort of requests to God may not really be good for us?

E Why is it important to pray for other people?

Qqs

Q1. Name three reasons why people may find it hard to pray.

Q2. Why might it be hard to find a quiet place to pray?

Q3. What distractions might people have that keep them from praying?

Q4. When do Hindus use the Aum?

Q5. Explain how Rosary beads are used.

Q6. Describe the Muslim Subha beads.

CATHOLICUPRAYERZACDFAITHHIJKBEADSMPRSCOMMUNITYVXYFORMALBLSTCOMMUNICATIONUNRSTEXPRESSING

Find the words in the word wheel

Put each word you find into a proper sentence in your copies!

People of Prayer

As you can see, prayer is a very important part of life for a person who is a member of a **Community of Faith**. However, the way a person lives his or her life also shows the world his or her commitment to his or her faith. Here are three people whose actions showed the world that God was at work in their lives!

Matt Talbot

Matt Talbot was a man from Dublin. He lived between 1856 and 1925. He was born into a poor family. The family had nothing and relied on charity. At the age of twelve, Matt began drinking alcohol. Eventually he became a chronic alcoholic and his life was in a terrible mess. Finally, in his twenties, he realised he had to do something to change his ways. He became friendly with the local priest and with the priest's help he began to turn his life around. Through a programme of prayer and rehabilitation he started on the path to normality. This path wasn't easy. Matt struggled, but he relied on prayer and God to give him the strength and courage he needed to achieve his aim.

Matt finally reached that aim – to be sober – and remained so until he died, forty years later. With his priest friend he led a life of prayer and charity **(like a monk)**. Every day he would pray to God a number of times and attend Mass. He gave most of his wages to the poor and always tried to help people less well-off than himself. He lived his life as an example of God's love for him and for all people. He communicated with God through prayer and his life was changed forever. Matt Talbot will be made a saint **(Canonised)** by the Vatican very soon.

Mother Teresa

Teresa was born in Macedonia in 1910. She grew up in a very devout and religious family. They all prayed together every day and went to Mass every morning. By the age of twelve, little Teresa knew she wanted to give her life to God, especially to helping the poor people she saw all around her. She joined the Sisters of Loreto and went to **Calcutta**, in India, as a **missionary sister**. While there, she continually asked God to help the poor. She set up her own school for the poor children of Calcutta.

Sister Teresa also set up her own group of nuns to help the poor. They were called the **Missionaries of Charity**. She then set up a home for people who were dying, so they could die with dignity and God's love. Her order soon began to spread and orphanages and leper homes were opened all over India, all in the name of Jesus.

Mother Teresa became a symbol for consistent love and care for the poor, needy and dying. She was a woman who was holy and prayerful and she had a very close relationship with God. In 1979 she received the **Nobel Peace Prize** in recognition of all her good works. Thanks to her example and her followers, today there are 570 missions all around the world. There are over 4,000 nuns, 400 brothers and over 100,000 lay volunteers working with the poor, the dying, orphans, AIDS sufferers, children, family groups, and setting up soup kitchens and homes for the homeless. Mother Teresa is an example of a person who expressed her belief and faith through her actions, expressing the love and compassion of God for all people through her life's work. She will soon be made a saint **(Canonised)** by the Vatican.

People of Prayer Crossword

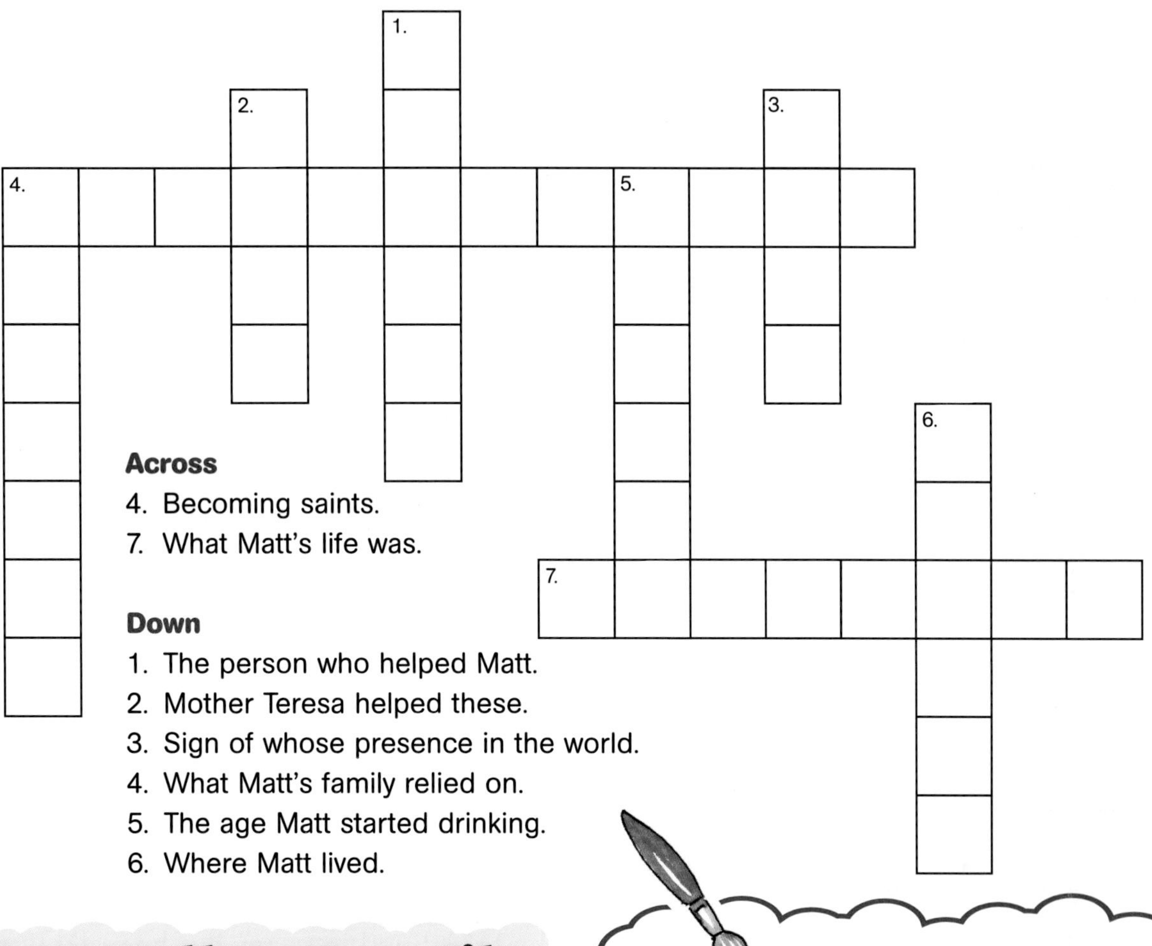

Across

4. Becoming saints.
7. What Matt's life was.

Down

1. The person who helped Matt.
2. Mother Teresa helped these.
3. Sign of whose presence in the world.
4. What Matt's family relied on.
5. The age Matt started drinking.
6. Where Matt lived.

Matt Talbot Fact File

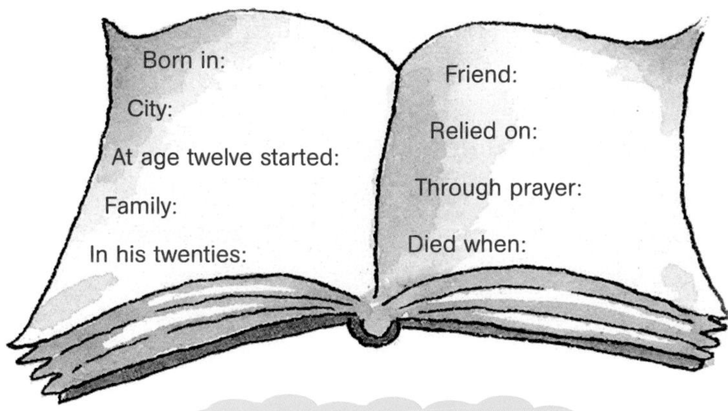

Born in:
City:
At age twelve started:
Family:
In his twenties:
Friend:
Relied on:
Through prayer:
Died when:

RESEARCH

Find out how a holy person becomes a saint in the Catholic Church.

Artwork to do!

Using about eight boxes, draw a cartoon strip describing Matt Talbot's life!

Q1. What helped Matt Talbot to get back to a normal life?
Q2. Who did Matt rely on?
Q3. What type of life did he live when he was sober?
Q4. Who did he reach out to?
Q5. How was his life an expression of his faith?
Q6. What type of family did Teresa grow up in?
Q7. Who did she want to give her life to?
Q8. What did she set up?
Q9. What type of symbol did she become?
Q10. How was she expressing her faith?

John Paul II

Before he became Pope, his name was **Karol Wojtyla**. Karol was born in Poland in 1920. His family were not well-off; they relied on his father's Army pension for all that they needed. Sadly, when Karol was nine, his mother died. Later his brother, who was a doctor, also died. This meant that Karol and his father became very close. Having suffered these tragic losses, Karol began to pray a lot for his loved ones who had passed away. Karol and his father were very religious, and Karol served as an altar boy in his local church. When Karol was eighteen years of age, he and his father moved to the city of Krakow and Karol went to university there. He was a bright student. But then the Second World War broke out and all the universities were closed down. Karol got work on a quarry, which meant he avoided being sent to a concentration camp.

The Nazis were persecuting the Jews in Poland, so Karol and his father secretly helped to rescue Jewish families and hide them in underground tunnels. Throughout this difficult time, Karol felt the strength and closeness of God. As a result, he decided to become a priest. He had to study for the priesthood in secret, but he really wanted to devote his life to God and to doing God's work so he was not afraid of what he had to do. But then, tragedy struck again: his father died. Karol knew that relying on God was now more necessary than ever.

As a priest he reached out to all his parishioners with compassion and love. When the war ended and he was allowed to minister to all the poor and needy who came his way, he became a living symbol of God's presence in the Church. He later became a great teacher and eventually was made a bishop. He was seen as a holy and loved man. He became Pope in 1978 and was regarded as a new shining light for the Church. He travelled the world to show God's love, prayed continuously, reached out to the needy and brought peace to troubled areas. He was truly the 'servant of the servants of God'. John Paul II died in 2005, but he will soon be made a saint **(Canonised)** by the Vatican.

Do a bit!

Unmuddle each of the clue words

Copy the letters in the numbered boxes to the other, blank cells with the same number.

POEP HONJ APUL II

RONB NI OLDANP

BAEMEC A HIBPOS

SWA REYV GULIEROSI

SAW VYER PYFLUREAR

HELDEP THE NEYED

SAEVD MESO SJWE

REARYP ROF WDLOR CEPAE

WILL CEMEOB A SIATN

1 2 3 4 5 6 7 8 9 10 11

Fill in the blanks:

John _____ II. Before being _____, his name was Karol _____. He was born in _____, in _____. His family were not _____-_____. His father had an Army _____. When he was _____ years old his mother _____. Later his _____ died. Karol _____ a lot, looking for _____ from God. He and his father were very _____. At eighteen he moved to _____ and went to study in the _____. Then the S_____ W_____ W_____ broke out. He helped _____ hide from the _____. Throughout all this he felt _____ to God. Because of all this he decided to become a _____ and studied for the _____hood. He wanted to do _____ work. As a priest he reached out to the _____ and _____. As Pope he brought _____ to some countries and spoke out for all the needy. Soon, he will be made a _____!

Q Explain how John Paul II's life was an expression of his faith.

Unmuddle each word and in your copy put each one into a sentence about John Paul II:

- ALUP II HNJO
- LOKAR JOYLTAW
- LOPNDA
- ISEPRT
- RAW II ROWLD
- RPYERA
- PHSOPIB
- OEPP
- VERASNT
- TAINS
- ONAIEDENOS

THE EXPERIENCE OF WORSHIP

NB: The word 'Worship' comes from the Old English word **Weorthscipe**, which means something is recognised as being worthful!

TO KNOW

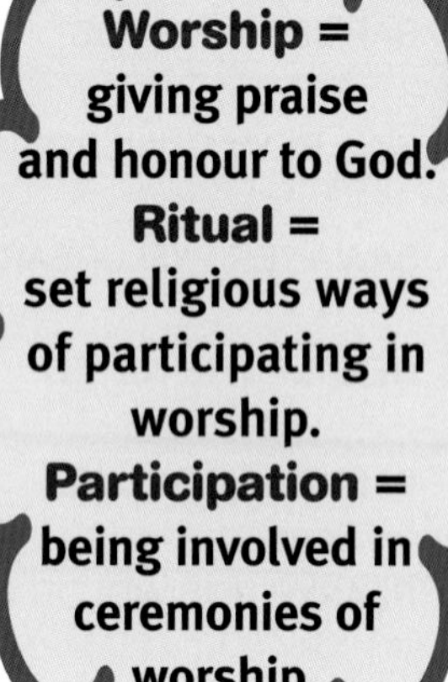

Worship =
giving praise and honour to God.
Ritual =
set religious ways of participating in worship.
Participation =
being involved in ceremonies of worship.

'What is worship?'
you might ask. Let's have a  look!

If you were to ask a religious person what worship was for them, you might hear . .

- Coming together with my community to pray!
- Gathering in a holy building to focus on God!
- Offering my life and prayer to God!
- Doing special things in praise of God!
- Taking time to be with God!

Worship is about all these things. Let's put it this way:

Worship is ...

the action of giving praise and honour to God in religious ceremonies, rituals and actions and in private and communal prayer!

Christians, Jews and Muslims believe that only God is worthy of worship.

. . . In WORSHIP we can pinpoint that there are certain COMMON CHARACTERISTICS that people share, such as...

People of faith gather together in holy places.
People of faith are involved.
They gather to worship at certain times (Church seasons).
They come closer to God in their lives.
People of faith take part in 'ritual', i.e. set ways of doing things.

Remember that people of faith can worship in private or in their own homes, but for the most part they go to a holy place to worship with other believers.

Worshipping Christians go to a . . .	Worshipping Jews go to a . . .	Worshipping Muslims go to a . . .
CHURCH	**SYNAGOGUE**	**MOSQUE**

Do a Bit!

Q1. Where does the word 'worship' come from?

Q2. What would a religious person say about worship?

Q3. Give a definition of worship.

Q4. What do Christians, Muslims and Jews believe about God?

Q5. Name three common characteristics of worship.

Q6. Where do Christians, Jews and Muslims go to worship?

Complete these T / F sentences in your copy:

The word 'worship' comes from Italian. **T / F**

Worship can mean gathering in a holy place. **T / F**

Worship is the action of giving praise to God. **T / F**

Only Jews believe God is worthy of worship. **T / F**

People of faith don't gather together. **T / F**

Worshipping people come close to God. **T / F**

Muslims worship in the synagogue. **T / F**

Christians worship in the mosque. **T / F**

Artwork

Draw a poster with the definition of worship written in the centre and drawings of worship characteristics around the edge.

Finish each sentence in your copy:

- Coming together with my community to ______.
- Offering my life and ______.
- Taking time to ______.
- Worship is the action of ______.
- Christians believe that ______.
- People of faith gather ______.
- Religious people take part in ______.

More Qs to do!

A. Why do religious people come together to pray?

B. Why do Christians, Muslims and Jews believe that only God is worthy of worship?

C. What do you think 'rituals' are?

D. How do worshippers come closer to God?

E. How do you think people worship in private?

PLACES OF WORSHIP

Going to their **places of worship** helps believers to focus their thoughts on God, allows them to meet others of their faith and share their worship and encourages them to participate together in the rituals of worship and to recognise their holy place as a house of God, where people connect spiritually with God and with each other!

These places of worship come alive when the worshippers gather together there and praise God. Let's have a look inside a church.

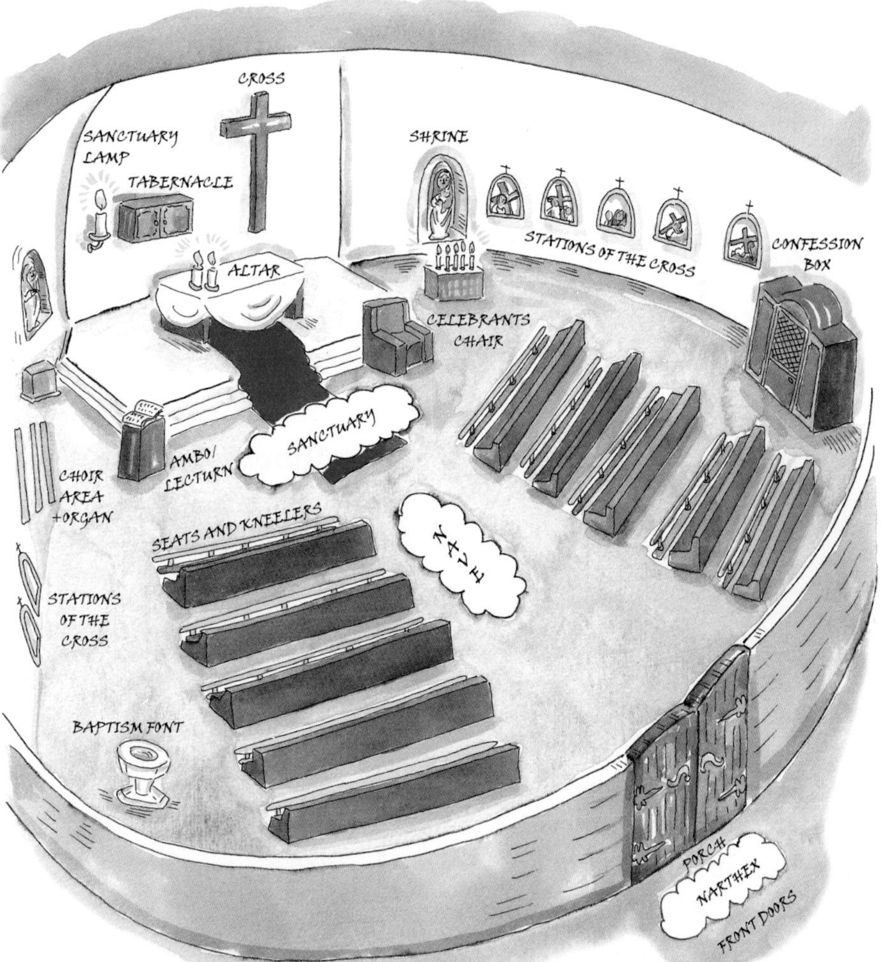

This is a typical Roman Catholic church. Not all Roman Catholic churches are built exactly like this, but it gives us a good basic idea.

Other **Christian Denominations**, such as Protestant/Orthodox, also have churches in which to worship together. They follow this basic design:

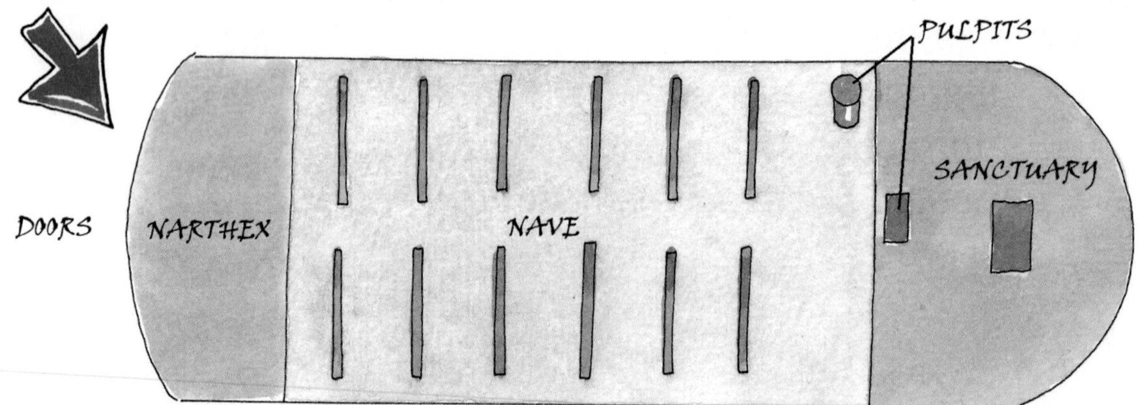

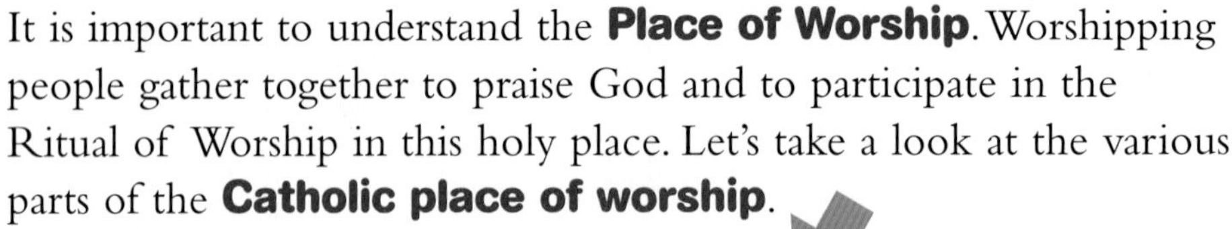

Protestant churches usually have fewer statues and less decoration, and they do not have confession boxes or Stations of the Cross. **Orthodox churches** have much more elaborate decoration, with many candles, strong-smelling incense, holy icons and shrines.

It is important to understand the **Place of Worship**. Worshipping people gather together to praise God and to participate in the Ritual of Worship in this holy place. Let's take a look at the various parts of the **Catholic place of worship**.

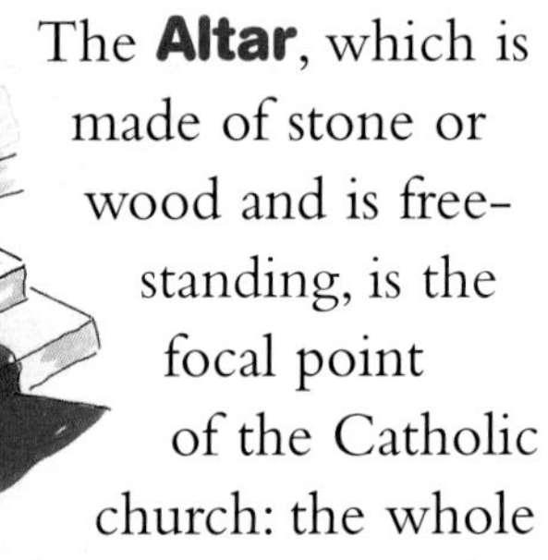

The **Altar**, which is made of stone or wood and is free-standing, is the focal point of the Catholic church: the whole congregation can see it. On the altar the priest celebrates and remembers the life, death and Resurrection of Jesus through the Liturgy of the Word and praying the Eucharistic Prayer.

The Tabernacle is a sacred box made from solid metal or wood. It is placed and secured in an appropriate area of the church, usually the sanctuary. Inside it is placed the Blessed Sacrament – the body of Christ – either in a monstrance or a **ciborium**.

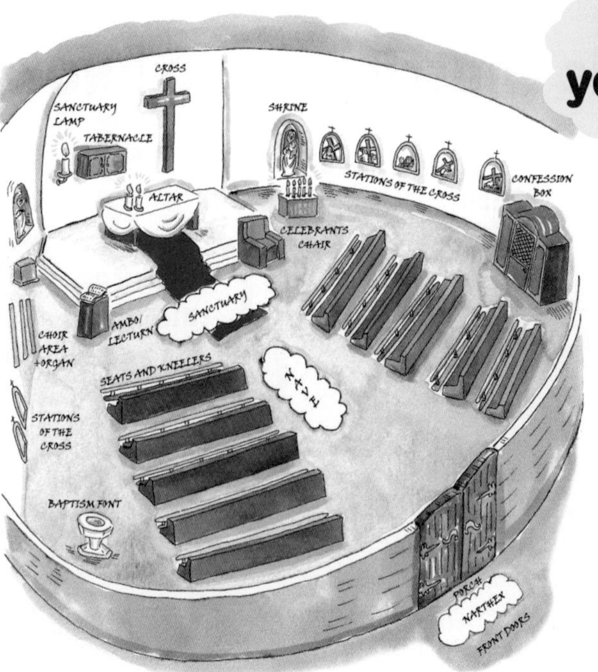

Over to you again!

Put the correct name on each church item

- Sanctuary lamp
- Altar
- Shrine
- Narthex
- Seats
- Organ
- Stations of the Cross
- Tabernacle
- Baptism font

Fill in the blanks in your copy:

Going to their _____ of _____ helps believers to _____ their _____ on _____, to meet others of their _____ and to share their _____. They also _____ together in the _____ of _____ and recognise the place as a _____ of _____ in which people connect with _____ and each other.

To Do In your copy draw the basic design of all Christian places of worship. Beside it, list the differences between this basic design and that of a Catholic church.

Think and Answer

Q. Why is it important to have a place of worship?

Q. Why, do you think, do people want to worship and participate in the rituals?

Q1. What does going to their places of worship help believers to do?

Q2. With whom do people connect when they pray?

Q3. Name the items in the sanctuary area of a Catholic church.

Q4. How might Protestant churches differ from Catholic churches?

Q5. In your own words explain the 'altar'.

Draw and design the interior of a Catholic church, including all the basic elements.

The Elements of a Catholic church

The **Ambo** or **Lectern** is the place from where Scripture is read – the Old Testament and the New Testament – in the **Liturgy of the Word**. Priest and people proclaim God's Word. The priest delivers his homily from here. The Prayers of the Faithful are read.

The **Celebrant's Chair** is a symbol of the priest's role as leader of the Celebration of the Mass, and all the worshippers can see it.

TO KNOW

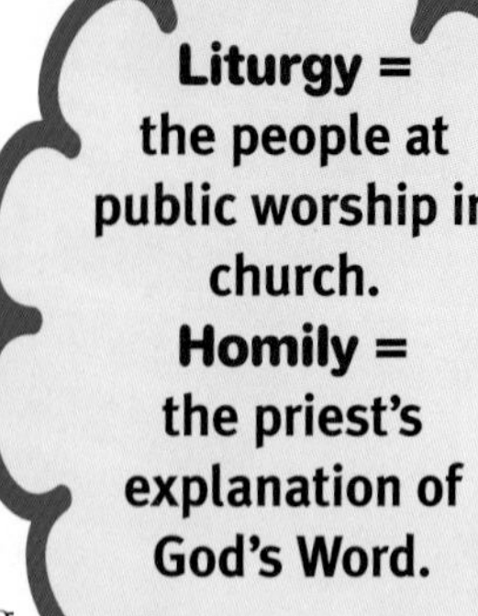

Liturgy =
the people at public worship in church.
Homily =
the priest's explanation of God's Word.

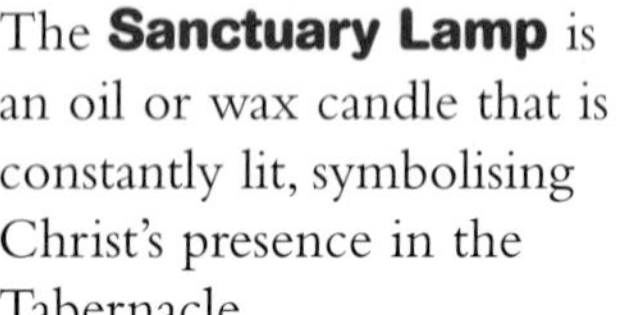

The **Sanctuary Lamp** is an oil or wax candle that is constantly lit, symbolising Christ's presence in the Tabernacle.

The **Baptism Font** is used to baptise people (usually babies) in the Sacrament of Baptism, during which they enter the family of God as Christians. It holds the water that is poured on the person's head in baptism.

The **Stations of the Cross** tell the story of Christ's journey from Pilate's palace to Calvary to be crucified. There are fourteen stations placed around the church's nave. People pray to the stations, especially on Good Friday.

The **confession box or Reconciliation Room** is where worshippers go to receive the Sacrament of Reconciliation, to receive God's forgiveness for their sins and wrongdoings. The priest, acting on God's behalf, listens to and forgives sins. He receives the worshippers in the confession box and is usually seated behind a grill.

The three sections of a Catholic church

The Sanctuary, as we can see from the earlier picture, is an area that is usually raised up so all the worshippers can see it while they pray. The **altar**, the **ambo** and the **celebrant's chair** are always kept in the Sanctuary. Usually you will see the **Tabernacle**, the **sanctuary lamp** and the **crucifix** here as well.

The **Nave** is where the worshippers congregate to participate in the ritual of worship. It usually contains chairs, or pews, and kneelers for the worshippers to sit, kneel and stand while praying.

The **Narthex** is basically a porch. It symbolises the worshippers' movement from everyday life to the sacred place of God: once they step through the porch, their minds should be clear and ready to worship God. Sometimes the people are welcomed by church helpers in the Narthex, and during baptism the family of the child gather here for the ceremony.

SYNAGOGUE SACRED PLACE

. . . This is where Jewish people go to worship, have a look at THE SYNAGOGUE

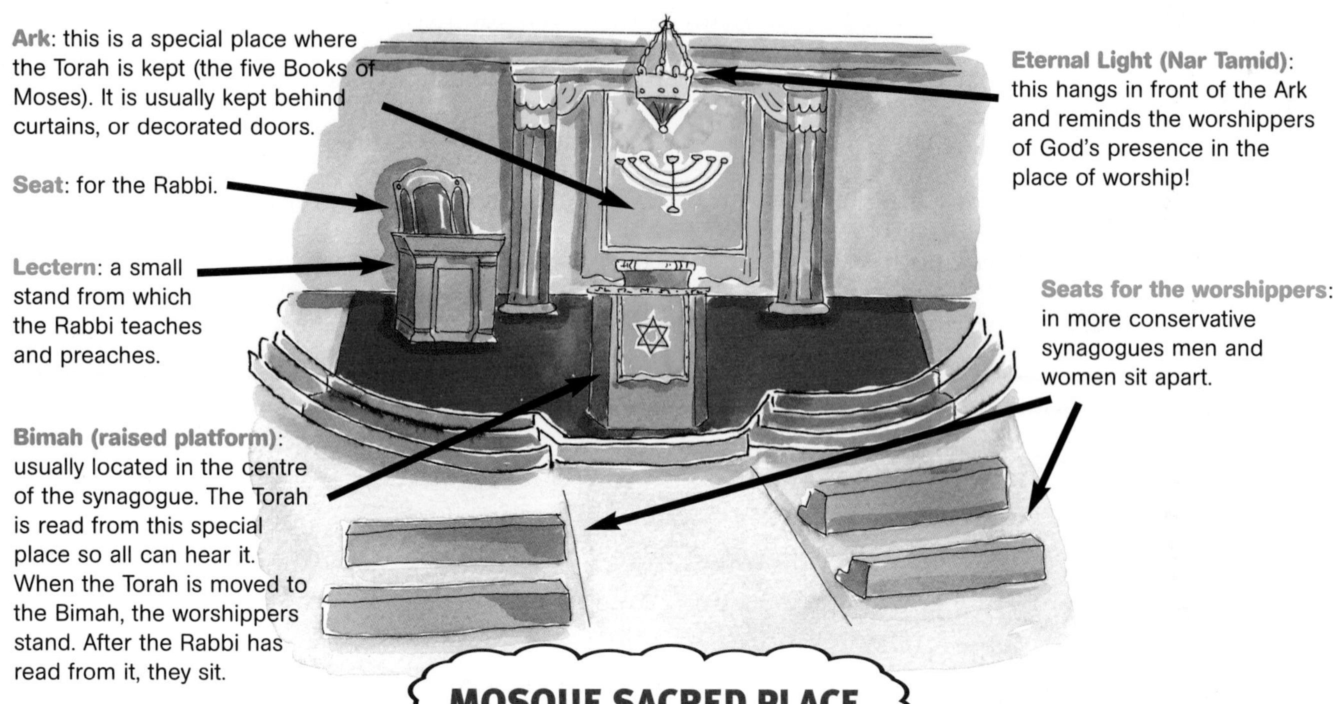

Ark: this is a special place where the Torah is kept (the five Books of Moses). It is usually kept behind curtains, or decorated doors.
Eternal Light (Nar Tamid): this hangs in front of the Ark and reminds the worshippers of God's presence in the place of worship!
Seat: for the Rabbi.
Lectern: a small stand from which the Rabbi teaches and preaches.
Seats for the worshippers: in more conservative synagogues men and women sit apart.
Bimah (raised platform): usually located in the centre of the synagogue. The Torah is read from this special place so all can hear it. When the Torah is moved to the Bimah, the worshippers stand. After the Rabbi has read from it, they sit.

MOSQUE SACRED PLACE

. . . This is where Muslim people go to worship, have a look at THE MOSQUE

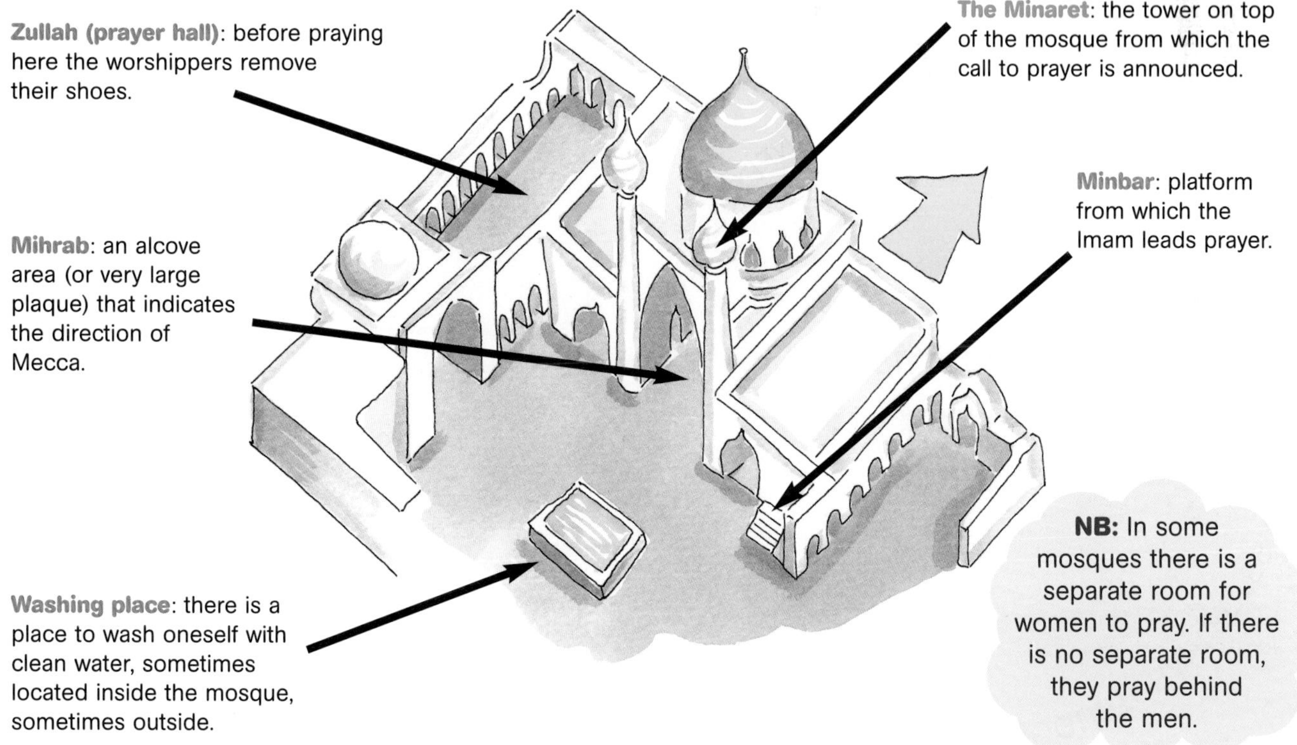

Zullah (prayer hall): before praying here the worshippers remove their shoes.
The Minaret: the tower on top of the mosque from which the call to prayer is announced.
Minbar: platform from which the Imam leads prayer.
Mihrab: an alcove area (or very large plaque) that indicates the direction of Mecca.
Washing place: there is a place to wash oneself with clean water, sometimes located inside the mosque, sometimes outside.

NB: In some mosques there is a separate room for women to pray. If there is no separate room, they pray behind the men.

Qqs

Q1. Give a name for the stand from which the priest reads the Old Testament.

Q2. What is the name for the candle that is constantly lit at the altar?

Q3. How many Stations of the Cross are there?

Q4. What is the name given to the place where the congregation sit or stand?

Q5. Give another name for the chairs the congregation sit on.

Q6. Give another name for the church porch.

More Qs to do

A. What is the difference between the Sanctuary and the rest of the church and what does the Sanctuary contain?

B. The word 'reconciliation' means the giving of God's forgiveness: where and why would you go for reconciliation?

C. Can you name any similarities between a church, a synagogue and a mosque?

D. Why is it important to have the sanctuary lamp lit all the time? What is a similar light called in a synagogue?

E. What is the symbolic connection between the Tabernacle and the Ark?

LITURGYAMBOCHAIRBAPTISMFONTCONFESSIONBOXARKBIMAHMIHRABZULLAHMOSQUESYNAGOGUETORAHLECTERNPEWSNARTHEX

Find the words and put each word into a sentence.

Artwork

Pick four items found inside a Catholic church, draw them and explain them in your own words!

RESEARCH

JOURNAL IDEA

Go to your local Catholic church and draw exactly what you see inside – include everything!

That was a look at Places of Worship, now let's have a look at **those who worship: the believers . . .**

BELIEVERS PARTICIPATING IN WORSHIP

TO KNOW

***Eucharist* = Greek for 'Thanksgiving' and Christ's presence is the bread and wine.**

All members of the world religions participate in special religious ceremonies connected to their religion. They **participate** in the 'rituals' that are central to the worship.

For worshippers, participating in worship means that they:

- gain spiritual strength for their religious lives;
- come together as a religious community;
- come closer to God through prayer and ritual;
- have a deeper understanding of their beliefs.

Focus on Catholic worship

For worshippers in the Roman Catholic Church the primary religious celebration is **The Mass**. As with all Christians, Sunday is the most important day for Catholic worship.

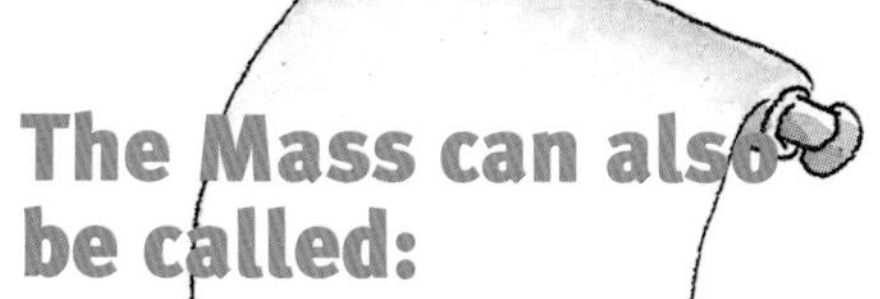

The Mass can also be called:

The Celebration of the Eucharist;

The Breaking of Bread;

The Holy Sacrifice of the Mass.

NB: 'Mass' comes from the Latin, **'Missa Est'**, which the priest says at the end of Mass and which means, 'You are sent'.

So the Mass, or Eucharist, is the primary religious celebration of the Catholic Church. Members of the religion go to church on Sundays – the Day of Resurrection. They also attend Mass on holy days, during liturgical seasons and indeed every day of the week, if they wish.

The Celebration of the Eucharist has its origins in the **'Last Supper'** that Jesus celebrated with His Apostles on Holy Thursday night, the night before He was crucified, died, buried and rose from the dead!

At this meal Jesus said, **'Do this in memory of me'** … He took the bread and said, 'This is my body, given up for you.' He took the cup of wine and said, 'This is my blood, the blood of the new **covenant**, poured out for you.'

From that moment the Apostles made sure that this Eucharist was celebrated throughout the centuries as Jesus asked!

NB: A **covenant** is a bond/agreement between people.

Over the centuries the celebration changed and became two distinct parts: **Liturgy of the Word**, which focuses on God's presence in his Word, the words of worship and Holy Scripture, and **Liturgy of the Eucharist**, which focuses on Christ's presence in the bread and wine: His body and His blood. During the Middle Ages the worshippers participated less in the celebration and the priest did everything. But it changed later …

Try these ...

Find the two phrases:

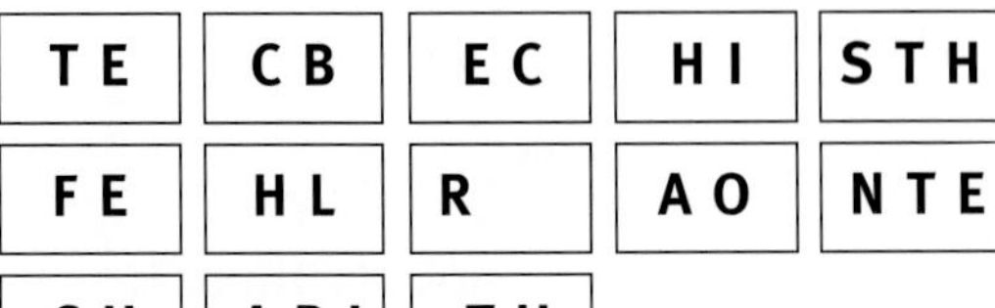

BOA	RFD	ET	AH
KE	IB	NR	GE

____

____

____

Qqs

Q1. Give two meanings for '*Eucharist*'.
Q2. What do worshippers participate in?
Q3. What do the worshippers gain by participating in worship?
Q4. By participating in worship, what do they have a deeper understanding of?
Q5. What is the primary day of worship for Christians?
Q6. Why is it this day?
Q7. Give two other names for the Mass.
Q8. Where does the word 'Mass' come from?
Q9. What are the origins of the celebration of the Eucharist?

The Celebration of the Eucharist

COPY AND COLOUR

WORSHIPXUPSAMASSXKPUEUCHARISTIWNBREADMUSCATHOLICFYMEMORYPIRESURRECTIONYIPSUPPERWSLITURGYWEF

Find each word and put into a proper sentence.

Artwork

Draw a poster with the words of Jesus in the centre and around the edges all the elements of a Catholic Mass.

To Read and Reflect

Read the Gospels Matt 26:26; MK 14:22; LK 22:14; JN13. What's the same? What's different?

More Qs to do

A. At the Last Supper, what did Jesus ask the Apostles to do?
B. What did He mean by 'New Covenant'?
C. Why did this happen at the Last Supper?
D. What happened over the centuries?
E. Why, do you think, did it change during the Middle Ages?

RESEARCH
JOURNAL IDEA

Go to a Celebration of the Eucharist. Observe and write down all that happens and report back to the class!

The Mass changed to **five distinct**, yet connected parts

. . . let's take a closer look at the

Celebration of the Eucharist.

Keep an eye out for the various rituals!

TO KNOW

Lay =
not ordained to priesthood.
Holy Orders =
the sacrament of ordination to priesthood.
Second Vatican Council =
Council held between 1962 and 1965 in the Vatican to examine the role of the Church and how it responds to the world.

Worshippers are the people of God.

The priest leads the celebration; he has received Holy Orders (ordination).

Gathering Rites

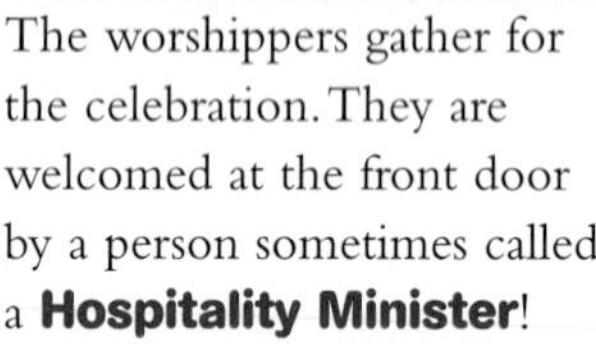

The worshippers gather for the celebration. They are welcomed at the front door by a person sometimes called a **Hospitality Minister**! People take their seats. A bell rings to indicate the priest is arriving. People stand and sing a hymn. The priest arrives and kisses the altar. He begins the Mass with the Sign of the Cross, prayer and repentance.

Liturgy of the Word

This is when worshippers hear the Word of God. A layperson **reads the First Reading and the Second Reading**. In between the **Psalm is either sung or recited**. Then the priest reads the Gospel. Afterwards, the priest gives his homily, explaining the words of the Gospel. All the people proclaim the Creed. A layperson reads the **Prayers of the Faithful**.

Liturgy of Eucharist

The bread and wine are brought to the altar. The priest receives them. He proclaims the **Eucharistic Prayer**. The bread and wine are consecrated to Christ's body and blood through the Holy Spirit. The whole Church – people, priests, bishops and Pope – are prayed for during this great **Prayer of Thanksgiving**. The bread is broken!

Communion Rite

This part begins with the **'Our Father'** and all stand to recite it. Next is the **Sign of Peace**, when people shake hands before receiving the Body of Christ. Then **Holy Communion** is given to all worshippers. (Sometimes the wine is received, too.)

Blessing and Dismissal

The priest stands and says the **final prayer**. He blesses all and says, 'Go in peace to love and serve the Lord'.

… As you can see, a lot happens during the Celebration of the Eucharist. The priest and the worshippers are involved in a ritual that is very sacred and full of symbol and meaning!

The Mass is the memorial of Christ's actions at **the Last Supper**: 'Do this in memory of me.'

The Mass is the sacrifice that Christ made on the cross! Jesus offered himself on the cross for our sins and this happens again each time on the altar at Mass. The sacrifice is made a reality each time the Eucharist is celebrated.

The Mass is a celebration of all that Jesus did to save us! The worshippers come together to celebrate that Jesus is the way to God, the Father. Through Jesus' life, death and Resurrection people return to God.

The Mass is a moment of unity between all the worshippers gathered together! The people come together and are strengthened by each other in their spirituality. They participate, listen and act in the uniting rituals of the Mass.

T / F? Decide which statement is **true** and which statement is **false** and put a circle around T or F in each case:

1. When a bell rings at the start of Mass the whole congregation sit down. **T / F**
2. The time when people hear the Word of God is called the Liturgy of the Word. **T / F**
3. The Liturgy of the Eucharist is when the bread and wine are consecrated to Christ's body and blood. **T / F**
4. The Communion rite begins by all saying the 'Hail Mary'. **T / F**
5. At the blessing, when Mass is over, the priest tells people, 'the Mass is ended'. **T / F**

To Do

Finish the sentences

a. The Mass is the memorial of _____ actions at the _____ _____!

b. The _____ is the _____ that Christ made on the _____!

c. The Mass is a moment of _____ between all _____ gathered!

d. The _____ and _____ are consecrated to Christ's _____ and _____!

Liturgy of the Word

COPY AND COLOUR

Unscramble the tiles to reveal a message

LO	IF	TH	UE	RE
CU	Y C	HI	AS	RT

WI	OT	RU	DR
OG	F Y	TL	HE

Qqs

Q1. Name the five parts of the Mass.

Q2. What happens during the Liturgy of the Word?

Q3. What happens during the Communion rite?

Q4. What was the Second Vatican Council?

Q5. How is the Mass 'the sacrifice that Christ made on the Cross'?

From all this we realise that the worshippers participate in the rituals of the Celebration of the Eucharist. **Participation** is the only way to experience fully all that the Celebration of the Eucharist has to offer, both spiritually and physically! The Eucharist is essentially an act of the community, with the priest leading the celebration.

The worshippers participate by

Presence

Being present in the church as part of the gathered community. **'The Body of Christ'** ('Where two or three are gathered in my name, there I am').

Responding

Many times during the Mass worshippers respond loudly to the prayers and acclamations, for instance:

- in thanks for the readings;
- responding to the Psalm;
- saying **'Amen'** (so be it);
- singing hymns;
- responding to prayers and blessings;
- in prayer – the **'Our Father'**.

Listening

Active listening to all that is proclaimed during the Mass – the prayers, the readings, the hymns, the blessings, the homily. By **actively listening**, the worshippers open their hearts and minds to the Word of God.

Ministering

In the Catholic Church baptised laypeople can minister to each other. At Mass laypeople can be:

- a Minister of the Word (reader);
- a Minister of the Eucharist;
- a singer, or musician;
- a hospitality member (welcome);
- an altar server;
- a collector;
- a member of the altar preparation team.

Movement

Worshippers use certain ritual movements during the celebration, especially:

- **Standing** – sign of a resurrected people and of unity.
- **Kneeling** – in awe and worship of the presence of God.
- **Blessing** – the Sign of the Cross on our person, using the Trinity.
- **Shaking Hands** – making peace at the table of the Lord.

Communion

Full participation in the Mass means receiving the **Blessed Sacrament**, Christ's body (and blood), at Communion. All the gathered worshippers receive the Eucharist and are nourished by it, an act that helps them to bring Christ to the World.

Members of all the world's religions participate in worship and its rituals. It brings them closer to God and to each other and strengthens their faith.

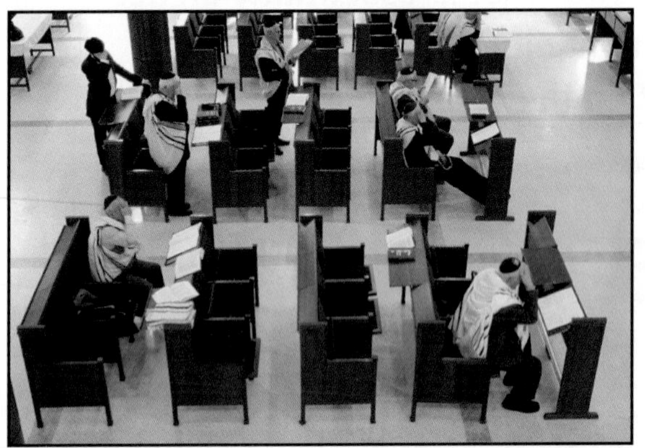

Jews

Jews involve themselves in worship by going to the **synagogue** on Saturday mornings. They gather together for prayer, reading and singing. They listen to readings from the **Torah** (Sacred Scriptures), sing psalms (from the Book of Psalms), listen to a sermon from the Rabbi and pray prayers of thanks to God. Men usually wear their prayer cap and the shawl called a **Tallith**.

Muslims

Muslims involve themselves in worship by going to the mosque, where they gather each Friday for their ritual prayer. They wash themselves before prayer, remove their shoes, kneel on prayer mats and face the direction of Mecca. They perform the Ra'ku prayer movement, which uses particular hand and body gestures to worship God.

Christian Denominations

Christian Denominations involve themselves in worship by going to church on Sunday to pray, sing, listen to readings and the preaching of the priest, vicar, rector, minister, etc. Members of the Anglican Community receive the bread and wine as symbols of Christ's Last Supper. All worshippers gather to be nourished by word and action and to create a better world for all.

LET'S DO THESE

Fill in the blanks:

Participation is the way to _____ fully all that the _____ of the _____ has to offer both spiritually and _____. The _____ is essentially a _____ action, with the _____ leading the celebration. Worshippers _____ by: _____, _____, _____, _____, _____ and ministering.

Finish each sentence:

- Being present in the church is part of _____.
- 'Where two or three are _____.'
- Many times during the Mass worshippers _____.
- Active listening to all _____.
- Opening their hearts and _____.
- Worshippers use certain ritual _____.
- Full participation in the Mass means _____.
- Laypeople, because of their baptism, can _____.

Unmuddle the words and put each one in a sentence:

TCHIAREUS
RCNPESEE
ONUCMIMON
GITMESRNNII
NTSEIGLIN
DRSONPENIG

Give five examples of worshippers responding during worship.

Name and draw the ritual movements that worshippers use.

Answer This During the celebration, how do worshippers minister to each other?

Q1. Where do Jews go to worship?
Q2. What do they listen to?
Q3. Who says the sermon?
Q4. What do men wear?
Q5. Where do Muslims go to pray?
Q6. When do they gather for prayer?
Q7. What is the Ra'ku?
Q8. What does 'receiving the Eucharist' mean?

To THINK and PRAY

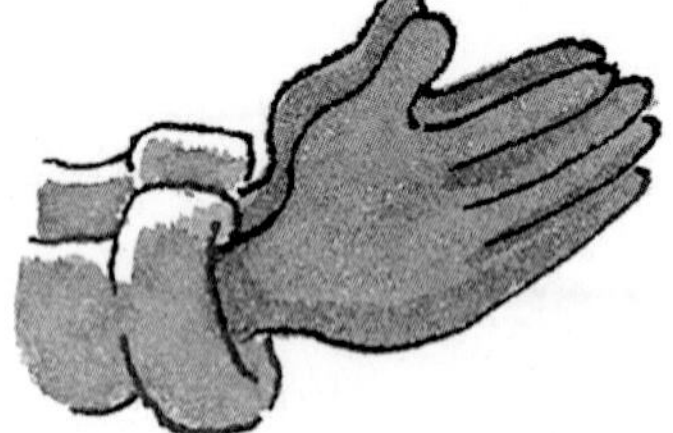

Matthew 26:17-34

As a class community we pray . . .

- For peace and quiet, so that we can take time to pray. Amen.
- For the ability to quieten and hear God speaking in our hearts. Amen.
- To be able to join our religious community and participate in worship. Amen.
- For all our friends and family, that God will keep them close to His heart. Amen.

I see Jesus in the poor on the street!
I see Jesus in my neighbour!
I hear Jesus in his Holy Word!
I hear Jesus in his priesthood!
I know Jesus in the Mass!
I know Jesus in the bread and wine!

As members of the worshipping community we offer our lives to God so that good work will be evident to all. We offer our prayers so that God will know we are people who believe. We offer our bread and wine at Mass so that Christ's presence in the Eucharist will be with us forever.

Amen.

Members of Communities of Faith involve themselves in prayer, in worship, in ritual, in expressing their faith, in connecting and communicating with God and each other. As part of all these religious ceremonies and religious life they will encounter **SYMBOLS**!

TO KNOW

Sign =
points to one meaning or item.
Symbol =
points beyond itself to multiple meanings.
Icon =
sacred picture of Jesus or the saints used by Orthodox Christians.

SIGN AND SYMBOL

What exactly is a symbol?

A symbol points to something beyond itself! It can have more than one meaning and imparts a deeper understanding or explanation of something!

A symbol is different from a sign because . . .

a sign points to only one message or meaning and is self-explanatory – there is one meaning and no confusion!

Some symbols

Some signs

In everyday life we communicate with each other through words, gestures, body and language. We use telephones, post, email, etc. to communicate. In religious ceremonies and life, communication can happen through **'symbol and sign'**.

Have a look . . .

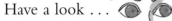

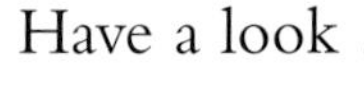

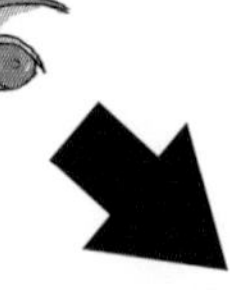

Every day we see signs that tell us something specific ...

The bus stops here!

Motorway ahead!

No Smoking!

Signs give us information about a certain thing or action to direct and help us in our daily routines.

However, it can sometimes happen that words, gestures and signs are not enough to communicate something. Sometimes we need a **'symbol'** that points to a deeper meaning. Have a look

We see symbols that tell us something is important and has many meanings

Wedding rings can symbolise love, marriage, eternity, sacredness!

The Irish flag can symbolise national identity, unity, politics, history, relationships!

Easter eggs can symbolise the end of Lent, new life, Resurrection, good time, treats!

Water can symbolise cleanliness, purity, freshness, power, quietness!

Q1. What is a symbol?

Q2. What is the difference between a symbol and a sign?

Q3. Name five symbols and five signs and draw pictures of them in your copy.

Q4. What do signs do for us?

Q5. What do symbols do for us?

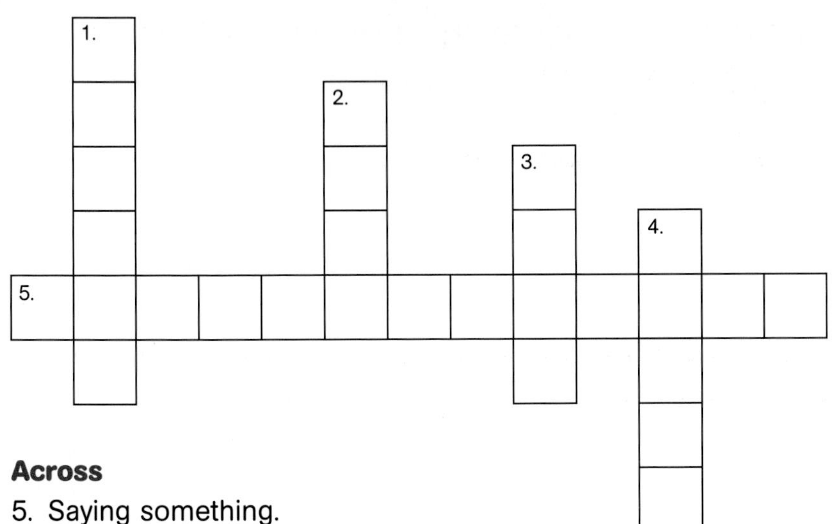

Across

5. Saying something.

Down

1. Explains something deeper.
2. Points to one meaning.
3. Symbol of Identity.
4. Symbol of Marriage.

When you finish the crossword, put the five words into sentences.

FILL IN THE BLANKS:

Members of Communities of Faith involve themselves in prayer, in worship, in ______, in expressing their faith, in ______ and ______ with God and each other. Throughout all these parts of ______ ______ and life, they will encounter _____.

More Qs to do!

A. In your opinion, what would be the difference between a symbol and a sign?

B. How would you go about making your own symbol, which means something to you?

C. Why did you choose this and what does it mean to you?

D. Why do you think it can be that words, gestures and signs are sometimes not enough to communicate something?

E. What other meanings can you think of for the following: wedding rings, Easter eggs, Christmas tree, harp, MacDonalds, Nike?

Of course, let's not forget such symbols, or symbolic gestures, as …

… giving a bunch of flowers to say, 'I love you', 'I am sorry', 'Thanks!'

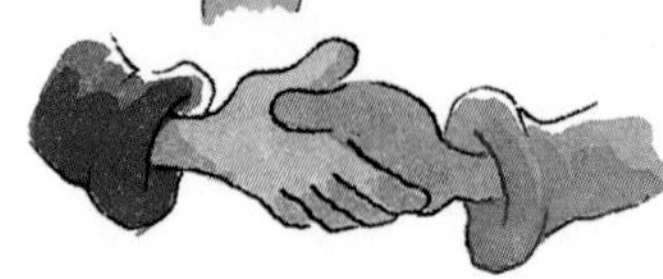

… shaking hands to say, 'Well done', 'Nice to meet you', 'Goodbye'.

Symbols and symbolic gestures are really important in our everyday lives because they help us to communicate a deeper message or meaning, often one that we cannot put into words!

BECAUSE

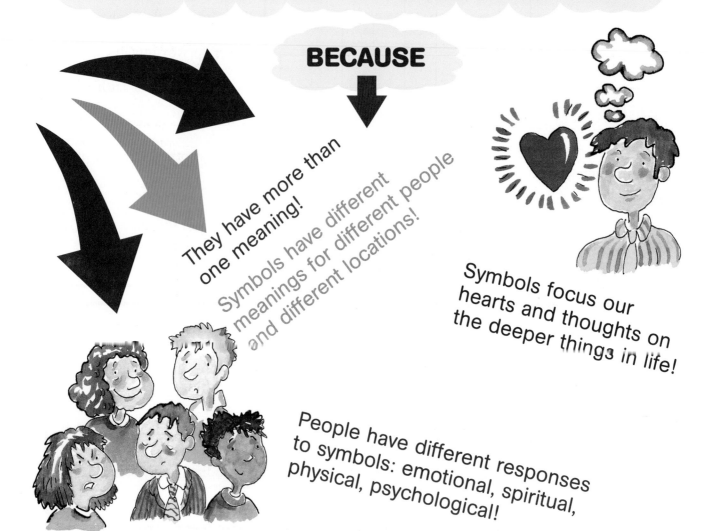

They have more than one meaning!

Symbols have different meanings for different people and different locations!

Symbols focus our hearts and thoughts on the deeper things in life!

People have different responses to symbols: emotional, spiritual, physical, psychological!

All world religions deal with the sacred things in people's lives. All religions help people to connect with God through different ways of worship and various rituals. Central to all the world's religions are symbols, because symbols help to make the '**sacred**' a reality. 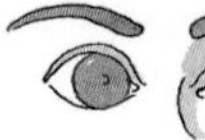 Let's see . . .

Symbols of the world's religions express a 'sacred reality'

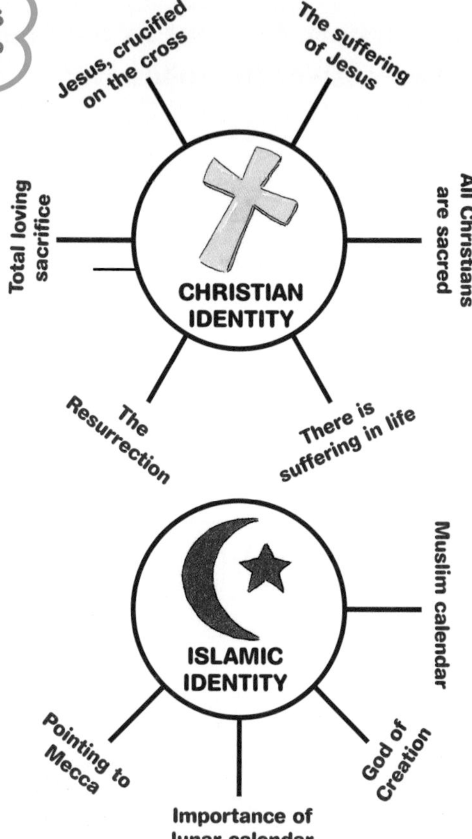

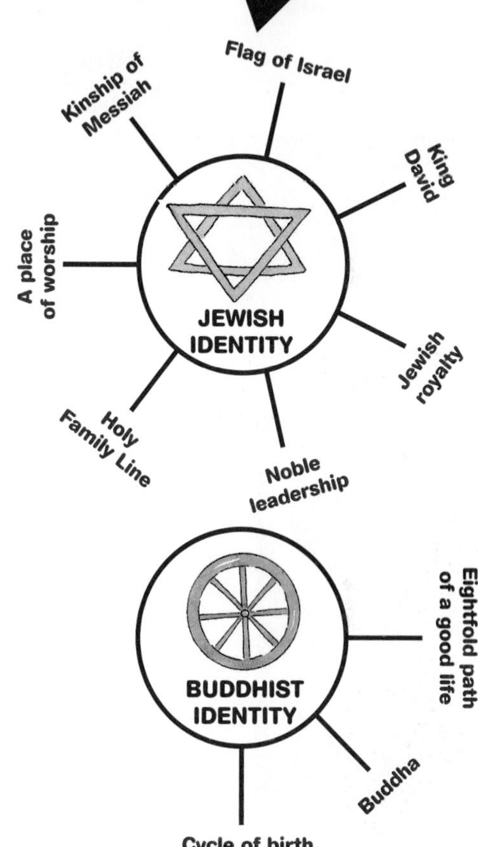

. . . and many of these world religions have symbols in common (although Muslims don't use symbols in worship and ritual). Examples of common symbols are:

Water

- Entering into the life of Christ at baptism.
- Purification – before prayer in the mosque, and Allah's presence.
- Purification before prayer in the synagogue and a symbol of freedom to Jews.

Light/Fire

- The light of Christ in the world.
- The flames of the Holy Spirit.
- Day of Judgment for Muslims, fires of hell.
- Presence of God in Scriptures and in the synagogues.
- Candles for the Jewish Sabbath.

Food

- The Eucharist, bread and wine, Christ's body and blood.
- **Halal** foods, permitted to be eaten by Muslims.
- **Heram** foods, not permitted to be eaten by Muslims.
- Worship God in preparing **kosher** food for Jews.

Figure out the two word tiles

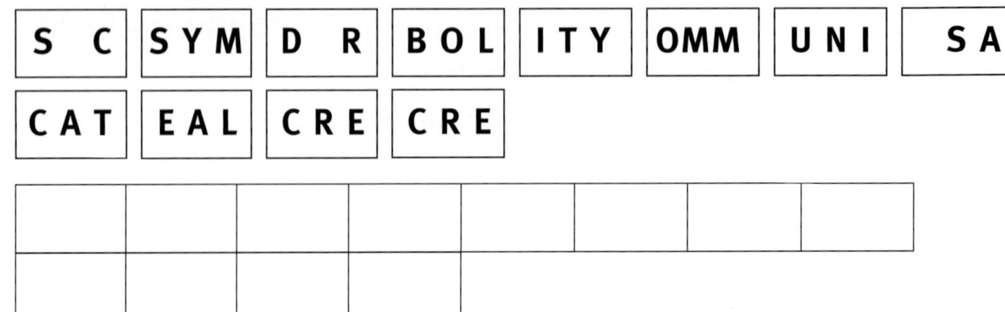

Garda symbol

Study these three symbols. Find out as much as possible about them and then answer the following:

Symbol of Justice

Q1. What do these symbols mean to people? What are they saying? And why?

Q2. What is the origin of these symbols?

Q3. Do the smallest details on these symbols mean anything? And if so, why?

Q4. Out of these three symbols, which stands out the most? Why did this one catch your eye?

Q5. Are symbols an effective way of communicating? Explain.

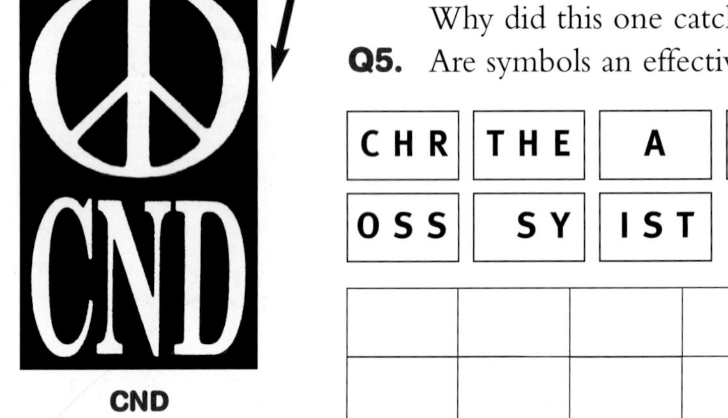

CND

Fill in the blanks:

All religions around the world deal with the _____ things in people's lives.
All religions help people to _____ with God in different _____ _____ and _____.
Central to all the world's religions are _____, because these symbols help to make the '_____' a reality for them.

More Qs for you!

1. What do all religions around the world deal with?

2. What is a central point of these world religions?

3. Give some meanings for the symbol of a cross.

4. Name three symbols the world religions have in common.

5. What is the symbolic meaning of water in Christianity, Judaism, Islam?

A. How do religious symbols communicate a sacred reality?

B. Why do you think people want to communicate with God through worship and ritual?

C. Why do you think that, in some cases, words and gestures are not enough?

D. How can symbols communicate something that words and gestures cannot?

Symbols are a very important part of the ceremonies and worship of the world religions, none more so than in **Christianity**. The religion of Christianity is rich with symbols. Here are some of them.

CHRISTIAN SYMBOLS!

The Cross

This is the primary symbol of Christianity. It focuses people's thoughts on Jesus Christ, on His death and Resurrection.

The Crucifix

This is also a very prominent symbol in Christianity and helps worshippers to focus on the suffering Jesus willingly endured for His people.

INRI

These letters were inscribed at the top of Jesus' cross. They stand for the Latin words, **Iesus Nazarenus Rex Iudaeorum**, which translate as: Jesus of Nazareth, King of the Jews.

IHS

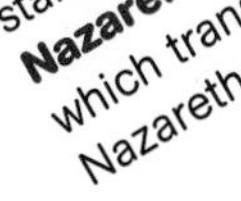

The monogram for the Greek version of Jesus' name.

The Paschal Candle

This is a special candle that is lit at the celebration of Christ's Resurrection at the Easter Vigil. It is the light of Christ for yesterday, today and tomorrow, for all time, the **Alpha** and **Omega** – the beginning and the end.

The Chi-Rho

In the Greek language Christ is spelt: **Xpistos**. The 'XP' of this word make up the Chi **(X)** and Rho **(P)**.

The Ichthus

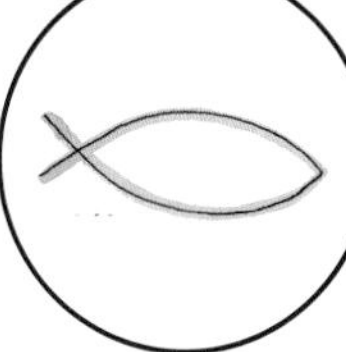

The Greek word for fish is *Ichthys*. Each letter of this corresponds to a title for Jesus Christ.

I = *Iesos* = Jesus
C}
H} = *Christos* = Christ
T}
H} = *Theou* = of God
V = *Vios* = Son
S = *Soter* = Saviour

When followers of Christ were persecuted and forced to hide their religious beliefs, they used this symbol instead of the cross.

Try these ...

Qqs

Q1. What is Christianity rich in?

Q2. What is the primary symbol of Christianity?

Q3. What does the cross help people to focus on?

Q4. What is the difference between a cross and a crucifix?

Q5. What does INRI mean in English and in Latin?

Q6. Explain the Chi-Rho.

To do in your copy:

True / False?

- The cross focuses people's thoughts on Our Lady. **T / F**
- The figure of Christ is on the 'cross'. **T / F**
- 'INRI' was placed at the foot of the cross. **T / F**
- The Paschal Candle is lit at Christmas. **T / F**
- In Greek, Christ is spelt Xpistos. **T / F**
- IHS is Greek for fish. **T / F**
- The Ichthys is the symbol of a fish. **T / F**

Art to do

Draw a poster of all the Christian symbols discussed here and write on the poster: The Symbols of Christianity.

Fill in the blanks:

Symbols are a very important part of the _____ and _____ of the world religions, none more so than in _________.Christianity is _____ with _____. The _____ is the primary symbol of Christianity. It focuses people's _____ on _____. The crucifix has the figure of _____ on it. The _____ is Greek for fish. Each letter corresponds to a _____ for _____ _____. The IHS is a _____ for the name of Jesus in _____.

Which one is which?

- It is the primary symbol of Christianity; it is the
- It means 'Jesus of Nazareth, King of the Jews'; it is the _____.
- It is lit at the Easter Vigil; it is the _____.
- It looks like this [XP]; it is the _____.
- Each letter is an initial for a title for Jesus; it is the _____.
- It is the monogram for Jesus in Greek; it is the _____.
- It has the figure of Jesus on it; it is the _____.

. . . Remember that 'symbols' always point to something beyond themselves, to a deeper meaning about a sacred moment or a sacred reality. This is especially true when we look at

the Sacraments of the Catholic Church!

The Sacraments are special, sacred moments in the life of the religious community. The Sacraments are '**Sacred Mysteries**' or '**Holy Mysteries**' and were given to the Church by Jesus.

In the Sacraments Catholics worship together and celebrate Jesus' presence with them at special moments in life.

The Seven Sacraments celebrate Christ's love and grace being given to Catholics at sacred moments in their lives. They are an outward, visible sign of an inward, invisible grace!

NB:
Grace = God's favour bestowed on His people so that they will be saved and may enter Heaven.

Baptism!

Confirmation!

Eucharist!

Reconciliation!

Marriage!

Holy Orders!

Anointing of the Sick!

SACRAMENTS ...

... of Initiation!

BAPTISM

CONFIRMATION

EUCHARIST

Initiation means to start something. These are the Sacraments that start you into the Catholic faith. Infants are **baptised**; at seven or eight years of age **Eucharist** is received; and at twelve or thirteen years of age the young person is **confirmed**.

... of Vocation!

MARRIAGE

HOLY ORDERS

These Sacraments signify the choice we make in our loving commitment to God and to each other for the rest of our lives. One is **Marriage**, the joining of people and the recognition of God's love between them. The other is **Holy Orders**, where a person gives his life to God and becomes a priest.

... of Healing!

RECONCILIATION

ANOINTING OF THE SICK

These Sacraments give healing to people, both spiritual and psychological. **Reconciliation** helps us to develop our relationship with God and with each other by recognising when we do wrong and saying sorry. The **anointing of the sick** gives us the strength to endure suffering and death to reach God's Kingdom.

Finish the Sentences in your copy

1. Symbols always point to _____.
2. In the Sacraments Catholics worship together and celebrate _____.
3. The Seven Sacraments are _____.
4. Initiation means to start something. These are the Sacraments that _____.
5. These Sacraments symbolise the choice we made in our loving _____.

Unmuddle these words and explain what they are:

PTABMSI

____

FNCOIRAMTNIO

____

ECHUITSAR

____

CILNOCRELLONAT

____

RARAIGEM

____

OYHL RODSER

____

AOFNOIINNGT SCIK THE

____

More Qs

A. What do the Seven Sacraments celebrate?

B. What is the symbolic meaning of the Seven Sacraments?

C. Why is it important that Christ's love and grace be given to us at special moments in our lives?

D. What do you think 'receiving grace' really means?

E. Why do you think it is important that Jesus is present at these sacred moments?

There are times in our lives when really special things happen and we want to mark them with a celebration. In Christianity there are times when Jesus is with us and we receive his grace! These moments are celebrated in the

SACRAMENTS.

TO KNOW

Baptism = from Greek, *Baptizion*, meaning 'to dip'.

This is the first Sacrament all Christians receive. Baptism is about entering into the family of Jesus, the people of God and the Church community, and is received only once in a lifetime.

Let's SEE

BAPTISM

as an infant

- The family gathers in the church to baptise their child into the Christian community!
- They listen to God's Word, read to them from the Old Testament and the New Testament. The priest explains what Baptism is all about!
- The parents and godparents say they will bring up the child as a Christian and pray for themselves and for the baby!
- The priest anoints the baby with oil and blesses the water of Baptism!
- The baby is baptised with water poured on the head!
- A white shawl is wrapped around the baby and the family holds a candle!
- The congregation prays the 'Our Father' and all are blessed by the priest!

Important
SYMBOLS
in Baptism

The baptismal water symbolises purity, washing away an old way of life and entering into the Christian way of living. Entering into the new life of Jesus. Becoming a resurrected person!

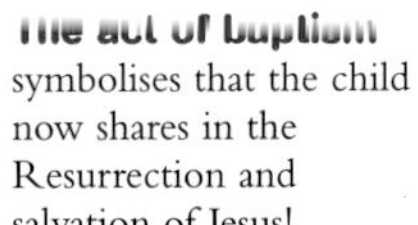

The act of baptism symbolises that the child now shares in the Resurrection and salvation of Jesus!

The Oil of Catechumens is used to symbolise the beginning of the Christian journey. A journey of mission to the world. The Oil of Chrism is used to show witness to being called a Christian and to give strength for the continuing mission.

The candle the family holds symbolises the Light of Christ and that Jesus dispels the darkness for the child. 'Receive the Light of Christ.'

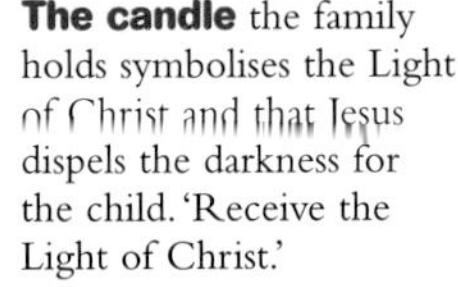

Words and gestures used by the priest in Baptism are significant, especially, 'I baptise you in the name of the Father and of the Son and of the Holy Spirit,' while pouring the water three times over the baby's head.

Over to you!

What is the meaning of each of these symbols?

Q1. What do the sacraments do to special moments?

Q2. What do sacraments focus people's thoughts on?

Q3. What does the Greek word Baptizein mean?

Q4. What is baptism all about?

Q5. What is the first part of Baptism?

Q6. What does the priest say to baptise the child?

Unmuddle each word and then put each in a sentence about Baptism:

PMBATIS
ARSECHAMT
MOUIYTCMN
LOI
TWREA
LSWHA
DRWO

You are at a baptism celebration – say what is happening and explain all that you see!

'I baptise you in the name of the Father, and of the Son, and of the Holy Spirit!'

Copy this bubble writing into your copy and colour.

More Qs

A. How important is the symbolism of water? Why is it used in Baptism?

B. Two oils are used in Baptism: name them. Why are they used?

C. What does the white shawl symbolise? What does it actually mean?

D. Name some of the ritual words and gestures and explain them.

E. What is the role of the godparents? How important are they?

RESEARCH
JOURNAL IDEA

Interview a person you know who has been to a Baptism recently. Ask them:

- What it meant?
- What symbols did they see?
- How was it a celebration?

TO KNOW

CONFIRMATION
at the age of twelve/thirteen

This Sacrament strengthens the believers on their journey as followers of Jesus. It confirms their belief in God and their decision to follow Jesus.

Confirmation = from the Latin *Confirmare*, meaning 'to strengthen'.

- The family, friends and child gather in the church for the Sacrament of Confirmation!
- It usually takes place during the Mass (although sometimes it is a separate ceremony)!
- All the children say that they believe in Jesus and ask for Jesus' help in their lives!
- At a special moment all the children process to the Bishop with their '**sponsor**' (this person cares for the faith of the child).
- The Bishop stretches his hands over the children and lays his hands on their heads! He says: '**Be sealed with the gift of the Holy Spirit**'!
- The Bishop anoints each child with the Oil of Chrism!
- Each child has a candle and it is lit!

Important SYMBOLS

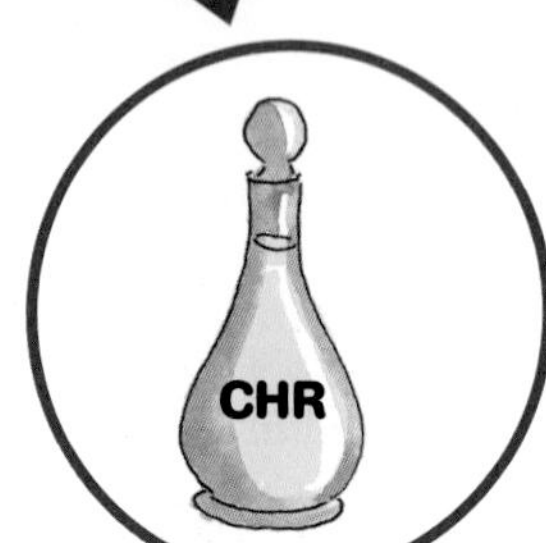

The Oil of Chrism symbolises the giving of Christ's strength for the journey to be a dedicated Christian!

The words and gestures used by the Bishop during the sacrament are significant: 'Be sealed with the gift of the Holy Spirit!' and laying on of hands – a symbol of responsibility.

The candle each child holds symbolises the Light of Christ present within the Church and for the Christian life!

The dove is the symbol of the Holy Spirit. In Mk 1:10 the dove is used as God's spirit descending on Jesus during his baptism.

In Confirmation we receive the Seven Gifts of the Holy Spirit

- WISDOM
- KNOWLEDGE
- RIGHT JUDGMENT
- COURAGE
- UNDERSTANDING
- REVERENCE
- WONDER AND AWE

Do a bit!

Explain what each picture is about:

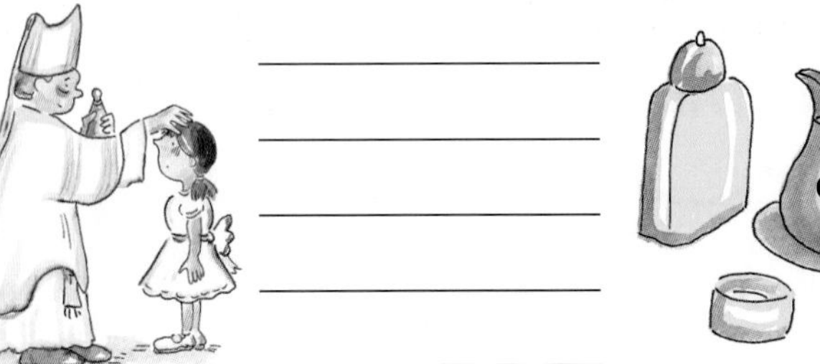

____

____

____

____

____

____

Put these in the correct order

- The children process to the Bishop with their sponsors.
- The Bishop anoints the children.
- Children, family and friends gather in the church.
- The Bishop stretches his hands over the children.
- He says, 'Be sealed with the gift of the Holy Spirit.'
- The children declare their belief in God.

Q1. What is the meaning of the Sacrament of Confirmation?

Q2. What is the usual age for one to receive the Sacrament of Confirmation?

Q3. Where does Confirmation usually take place?

Q4. What is the role of the sponsor?

Q5. Why does the Bishop stretch his hands over the child's head?

Q6. What does he say when he anoints the child?

Q What is the meaning of each of these symbols of Confirmation?

To Do Pick four of the gifts of the Holy Spirit! What does it mean to have each of these gifts in your daily life?

More Qs

A. How important is the '**sponsor**', do you think?

B. Why is the dove used as a symbol of the **Holy Spirit**?

C. Name some of the symbolic **gestures** and **words** of Confirmation.

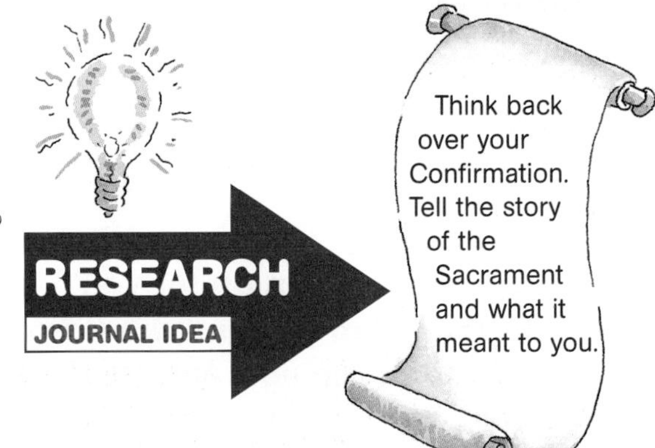

RESEARCH
JOURNAL IDEA
Think back over your Confirmation. Tell the story of the Sacrament and what it meant to you.

THE MASS EUCHARIST

at the age of seven (First Holy Communion)

This Sacrament allows the child to receive Jesus' body and blood. It is the celebration and thanksgiving for all that Jesus did through his life, death and Resurrection. The child now joins all believers at the table of the Lord!

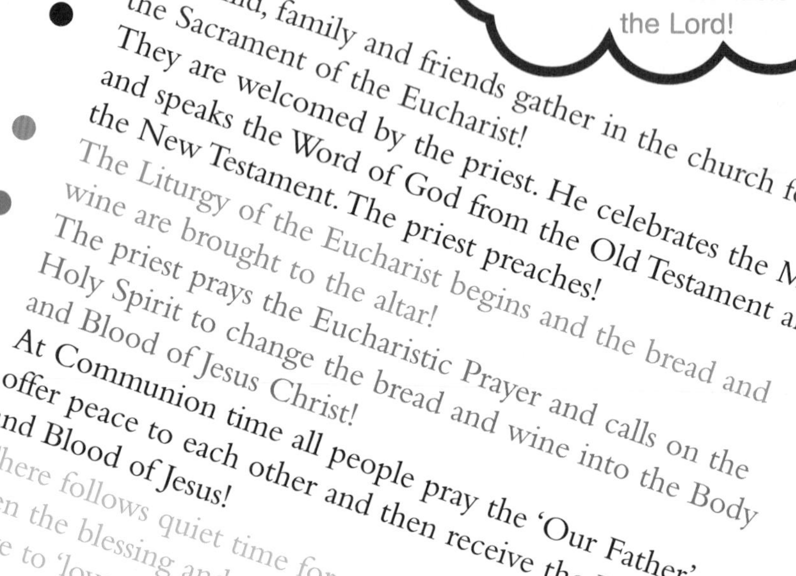

The child, family and friends gather in the church for the Sacrament of the Eucharist!
They are welcomed by the priest. He celebrates the Mass and speaks the Word of God from the Old Testament and the New Testament. The priest preaches!
The Liturgy of the Eucharist begins and the bread and wine are brought to the altar!
The priest prays the Eucharistic Prayer and calls on the Holy Spirit to change the bread and wine into the Body and Blood of Jesus Christ!
At Communion time all people pray the 'Our Father', offer peace to each other and then receive the Body and Blood of Jesus!
There follows quiet time for personal prayer, then the blessing and the people leave to 'love and serve the Lord'.

The bread and wine are offered from all the gathered believers. They will become the Body and Blood of Jesus, which all people will receive in Communion!

ALTAR
This is the table of the Lord. The table of the sacrifice of Jesus on the cross. We celebrate the Last Supper and remember Jesus' command!

The Liturgy of the Word is when the people hear the Old Testament and the New Testament and are nourished by God's Word!

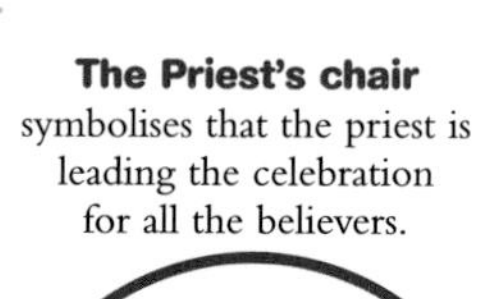
The Priest's chair symbolises that the priest is leading the celebration for all the believers.

The words and gestures used by the priest are significant: blessing, hand movements and stretching out hands over the bread and wine, saying: 'Lord you are holy indeed… Let your Spirit come upon these gifts to make them holy.'

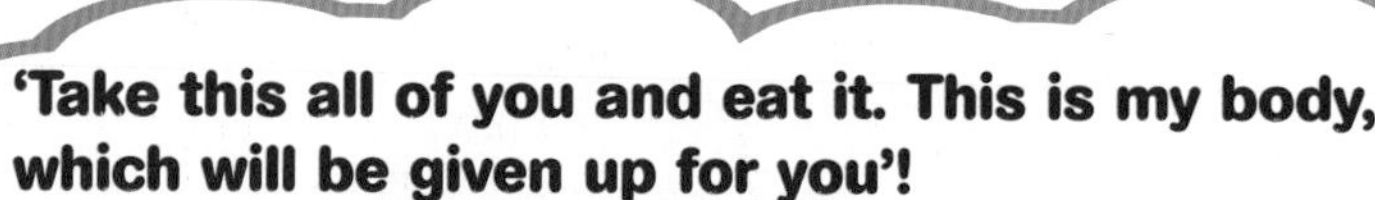

'Take this all of you and eat it. This is my body, which will be given up for you'!
'Take this all of you and drink from it. This is my blood, the blood of the new and everlasting covenant. It will be shed for you and for all. Do this in memory of me'.

Lifting the bread and wine.

Some work to do

RESEARCH
JOURNAL IDEA

Attend a celebration of Mass. How are the symbols used? How do the believers participate?

Find the hidden words and use each one in a proper sentence.

QSVALTAREUCHARISTACPGHCOMMUNIONYLOPBREADRSUNNWINEXYZBODYLTOBLOOD

Fill in the blanks:

The _____ allows the child to receive _____ Body and _____. It is the celebration and _____ for all that _____ did through His life _____ and _____. The child now joins all _____ at the table of the _____. The _____ of the Eucharist is celebrated at the age of _____ and is also called First _____ _____.

AN	THI	LL	IT"	D E	OF	AT	YOU
KE	"TA	S A					

THE	SUS	OOD	JE	BL	AND	OF	DY
BO							

Qqs

Q1. At what age is the Eucharist first celebrated?

Q2. What is the Sacrament of the Eucharist about?

Q3. What begins the Liturgy of the Eucharist?

Q4. What happens at Communion time?

Q5. What are the important words that the priest uses?

Rewrite these correctly:

- The priest /nun celebrates the Sacrament of the Eucharist.
- The altar /chair is the table of the Lord /Mary.
- The Bread and Wine /Bible become the Body and Blood of Jesus.
- People receive Jesus /the saints in Holy Communion.
- Do this in memory of me /don't do this was Jesus' command.

More Qs to answer

A. Why does the Sacrament of Eucharist take place mainly around the altar?
B. How important is God's Word in the celebration, do you think?
C. The priest uses certain words over the bread and wine: why are these words used?
D. How important is it that Catholics go to Mass?

. . . in the other sacraments there are also . . .

Important Symbols

Marriage!

The couple exchange rings as a sign of eternal love to each other and of Christ's presence in their love (takes place during a Mass)!

The priest witnesses the promises that the couple make to each other. He blesses the rings and blesses the married couple and celebrates Mass.

Holy Orders! (Ordination)

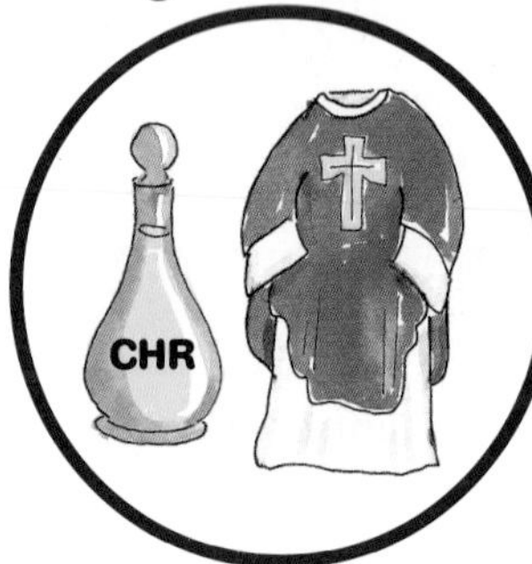

A man gives over his life to Jesus and to the Church. He promises to be the helper of all worshippers and to celebrate the Sacraments. The Oil of Chrism is used to symbolise strength, and he receives his priestly vestments!

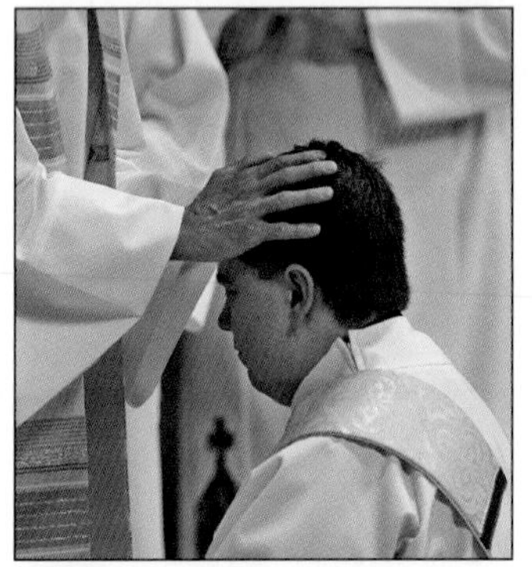

The Bishop lays his hands on the man. He anoints the man's hands with the Oil of Chrism.

Reconciliation! (Confession)

Believers receive the Sacrament of Reconciliation for all the wrongs they have committed. The priest wears a purple stole as a sign of penance!

In Confession, the priest stretches his hand over the person and asks for forgiveness! 'I absolve you of your sins, in the name of the Father, the Son and of the Holy Spirit.'

Anointing of the Sick!

The Oil is used so that the sick person will gain strength from Christ during this difficult time!

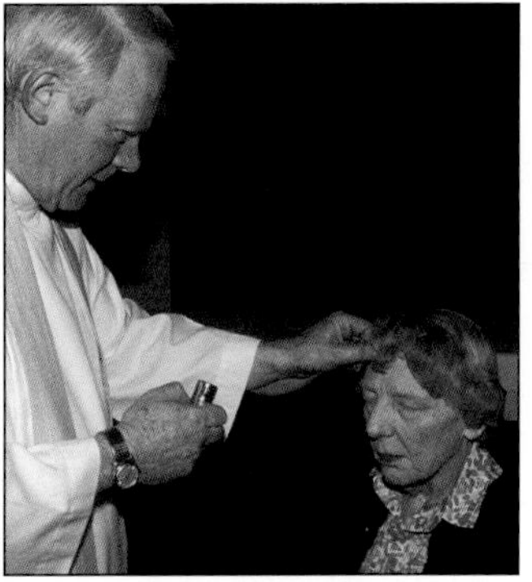

The priest anoints the person with the holy oil. He prays with outstretched hands over the sick person for God's strength!

The other Christian denominations celebrate the sacraments. In the Anglican Church they celebrate two sacraments **BAPTISM** and **THE LORD'S SUPPER**. These are seen as being instituted by Jesus. The other five recognised by the Catholic Church are called **RITES**. These **RITES** come from the tradition and practices of the Early Church but were not necessarily instituted by Christ.

BAPTISM and **THE LORD'S SUPPER** are the sacraments generally necessary to salvation and are the only ones contained in the gospels. In **BAPTISM** God's love and grace are bestowed on the recipient by the Holy Spirit to create anew. It must be responded to and committed to by the person. **THE LORD'S SUPPER** is seen as the one perfect sufficient sacrifice for the sins of the world. **THE LORD'S SUPPER** is a calling into the present of that perfect sacrifice. It makes that sacrifice effective and relevant to Christians now!

Sacraments in the Orthodox Church

Members of the Orthodox Church celebrate the Seven Sacraments and believe they were instituted by Jesus. All three initiation Sacraments are celebrated together when a child is eight days old, and the same symbols are used.

The use of symbol is very important in their celebrations and worship, especially during the Liturgy of the Eucharist.

Icons are used – pictures of Jesus and the saints – to lead people to God and to help focus prayers.

A bit more to do

Looking at each of the sacramental symbols, explain each one. Which Sacrament is associated with each?

Think back to when you last received the Sacrament of Reconciliation (Confession).

- What exactly happened?
- How did you feel?
- What, in your opinion, was it all about?

Q Name the Sacraments in which the Oil of Chrism is used.

Q Why is it used so much, do you think?

Complete this chart in your copy:

	Number of Sacraments	Two symbols of Baptism	Instituted by Jesus
CATHOLIC CHURCH			
CHURCH OF IRELAND			
ORTHODOX CHURCH			

Q1. What is the role of the priest during a marriage ceremony?

Q2. Why do Catholic people go to the Sacrament of Reconciliation?

Q3. What happens in Ordination?

Q4. Why is a sick person anointed?

Q5. How is Christ present in the Sacraments, do you think?

Q. When we say that **grace** is given to believers in the Sacraments, what do you think that means?

So far we've seen that worship, prayer, sign and symbol are extremely important to religious people, to their religion and to their relationship with God. What is also important is '**place**'.

TO KNOW

Pilgrimage = to go to a holy place.
Apparition = appearance of a holy person.

Places of Significance

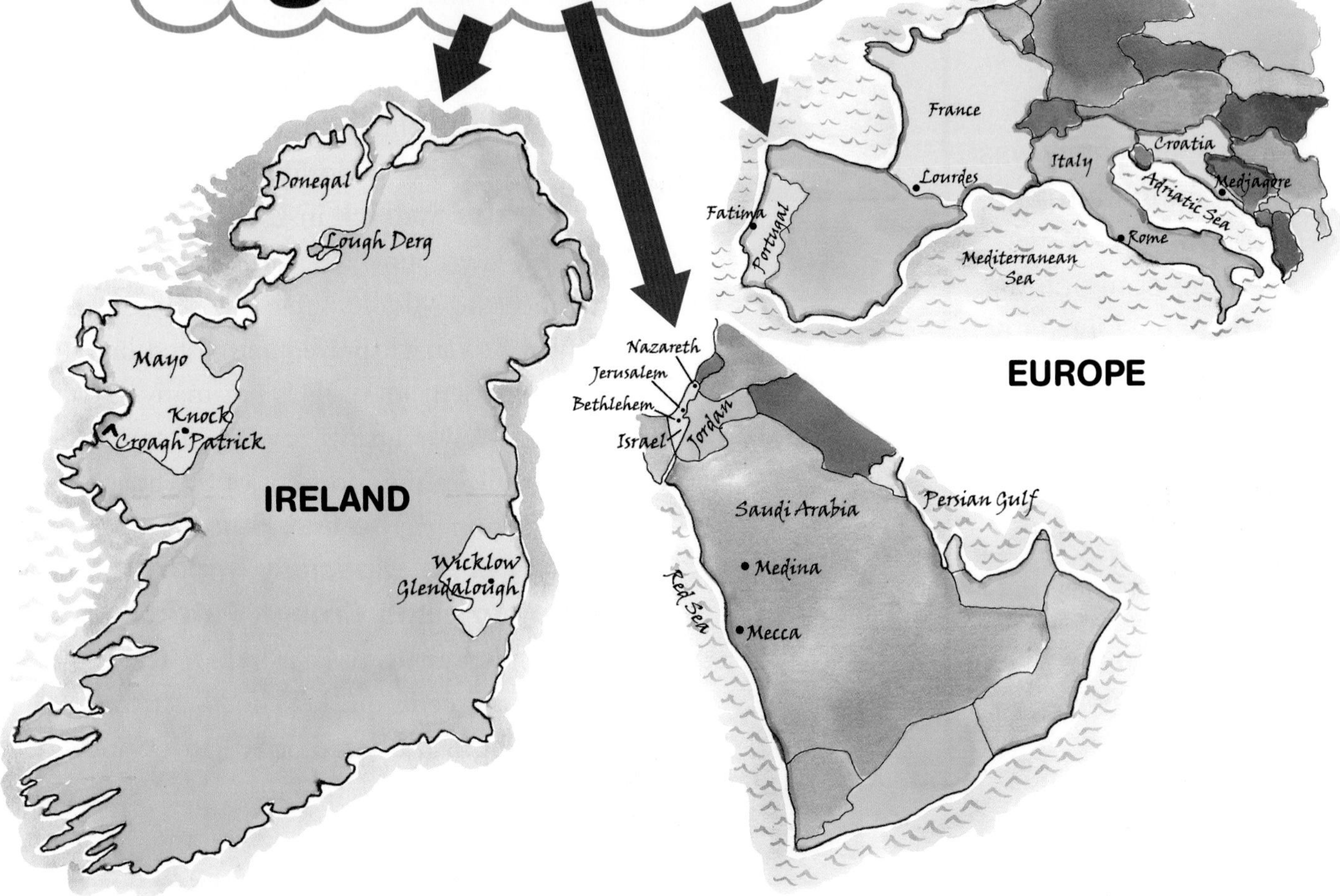

To the members of the different world religions all these places above are holy for a number of reasons …

- they are connected with the life of Jesus!
- they are connected with the life of a saint!
- they are connected with the founder of a religion!
- they could be the burial place of a holy person!
- they are places of '**Apparition**'!
- they are pilgrimage destinations!
- they are places of positive atmosphere, prayer and meditation!

Irish Holy Places

Over the centuries, when Christianity was developing in Ireland, a number of places became connected with Jesus, Our Lady and holy men and women. These places became destinations for sacred **pilgrimage**.

A pilgrimage is a journey taken by a religious person to a place he or she considers holy and sacred!

Knock in Co. Mayo is the holy site connected with the Apparition of the **Virgin Mary** on 21 August 1879. It was reported that a group of people saw an apparition of Our Lady, St Joseph and St John on the side of the local church. Also in the apparition was an altar and a lamb. No words were spoken, it was just visual. The Church investigated it and found it to be a genuine apparition. Knock is now a site of world pilgrimage!

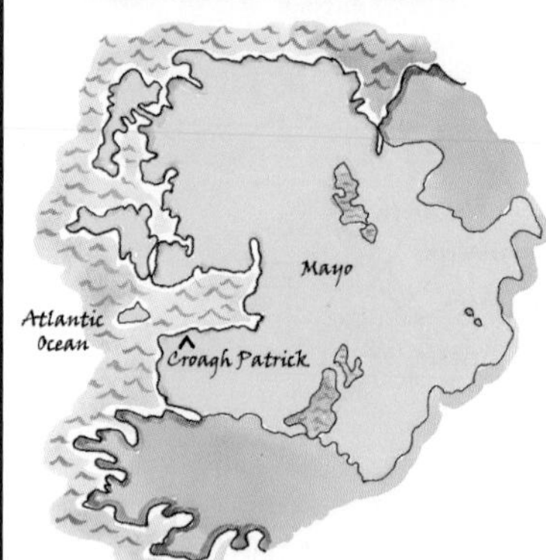

Croagh Patrick in Co. Mayo is a holy site connected with **St Patrick** since the Middle Ages. It is believed that St Patrick prayed and fasted here during lent in AD 441. For many years now pilgrims have been coming to walk in the footsteps of St Patrick, and to pray. **The last Sunday of July is an especially important day to climb Croagh Patrick.** Some pilgrims walk it in bare feet, others ascend on their knees. At the top there is a statue of St Patrick and a small church.

People go on pilgrimage because they want ...

- to strengthen their faith and their lives.
- to ask for God's forgiveness.
- to seek guidance in their lives.
- to pray with other pilgrims.
- to ask God for help.
- to help people around them and to do good works.

Q1. What is a pilgrimage?

Q2. Name one sacred site in Ireland.

Q3. Why would someone go on pilgrimage?

Q4. Explain what an apparition is.

Q5. Where would you find other world religious pilgrimage sites?

Ilpmigragae

Ppaaiirton

Pstacirkj

Giounace

Gvienoressne

Unmuddle each word and then use it in a sentence in your copy.

True / False?

1. Croagh Patrick is located in Knock. **T / F**
2. People go on pilgrimage because they want guidance in their lives. **T / F**
3. In 1879 the Virgin Mary appeared in Knock, Co. Mayo. **T / F**
4. Most religions have pilgrimage sites. **T / F**
5. It was reported that a group of people saw Jesus in Knock. **T / F**

A. Some places are holy because …

B. What do you think pilgrims expect to get by going on a pilgrimage?

C. Why do you think pilgrimage is an important part of religion?

D. What do people get from believing in apparitions?

Fill in the blanks:

Knock, in __ ____, is the holy site connected with the ________ ______. She appeared on ______ ______ ______.

It was reported that a group of people saw an apparition of ______, St _______ and St ____ at the side of the local church. Also in the apparition was an ______ and a ______. No words were ______. It was just visual.

European Holy Places

TO KNOW

Marian Shrine = site related to the Virgin Mary.

As well as Ireland, there are sacred sites in Europe. Let's see

Lourdes, in France, is a holy site connected with the **Virgin Mary**. Our Lady appeared there to a young girl called **Bernadette Soubirous (St Bernadette)** on 11 February 1858. From then there was a number of apparitions to Bernadette. Our Lady appeared in a grotto. She told Bernadette to dig a hole in the grotto and from this sprang holy water. Today people can receive the water and visit the Basilica at Lourdes. Thousands of pilgrims visit Lourdes each year.

Rome, in Italy, is a holy site connected with the Catholic Church. It was here that both St Peter and St Paul set up Christian communities and died. From then on the leader of Catholicism has been based here: **the Pope**. Pilgrims come to see the Pope in the Vatican and to receive his blessing. They also visit the tomb of St Peter, St Peter's Basilica, the Sistine Chapel and other holy sites in Rome.

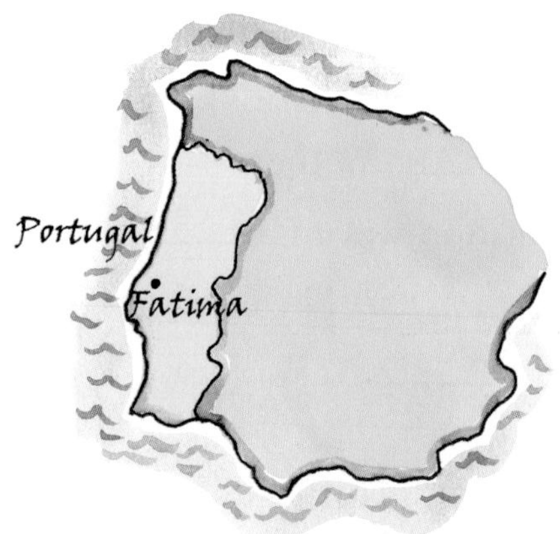

Fatima, in Portugal, is a holy site connected with Our Lady. It was here, in 1917, that Our Lady appeared to three children on six different occasions between 6 May and 13 October. The children received messages to share with the world. By 1930 the Catholic Church had accepted it to be genuine. As in Lourdes, there is a water spring. Thousands of pilgrims come here all through the year.

The Holy Land

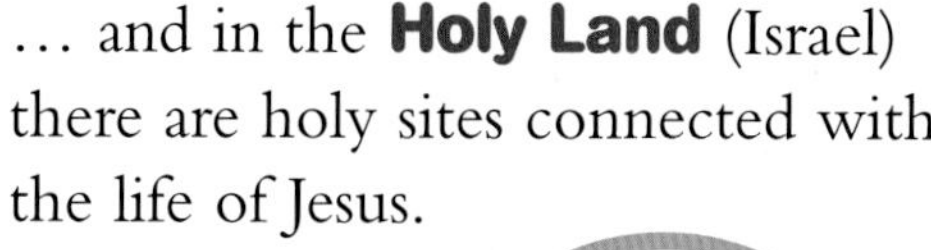

… and in the **Holy Land** (Israel) there are holy sites connected with the life of Jesus.

Nazareth!

Here Jesus grew up with his family as a young boy. On this spot are churches dedicated to Mary, Jesus' mother and the Holy Family.

Bethlehem!

The site of the birth of Jesus, as detailed in the Gospels. The pilgrims visit the Church of the Nativity.

River Jordan!

The river in which Jesus was baptised by John the Baptist. From that moment he started his public ministry.

Jerusalem!

Here Jesus preached and spent his last days before his Crucifixion and Resurrection. Pilgrims come here to remember the last days of Jesus, especially during Easter, and to retrace Jesus' steps to Calvary, the site of His Crucifixion. There are many churches here connected with the life of Jesus.

Thousands of Christians go on pilgrimages to these sacred sites every year!

… for the Jews

Jerusalem is also a sacred site. It was here that their great temple stood which housed the Ten Commandments. **The Western Wall (Wailing Wall)** is all that is left of the great Temple of King Herod. Jews came here to pray and ask God's forgiveness.

Jerusalem is also a sacred site for the Islamic faith. In fact, it is their third Holy Site. It is sacred for them because it is believed that it was from the Rock on this site that Muhammad was taken up to heaven by Allah and given instructions about prayer and how to preach to the people. A mosque was built on the rock.

Other Islamic sacred sites are ...

Mecca is the holiest City of Islam. It was here that Muhammad was born in AD 370. In Mecca is the shrine of the Ka'ba, built by the prophet Abraham and his son, Ishmael. Inside the Ka'ba is the 'Black Stone' believed to have been given to Adam by God. During the **Hajj** pilgrimage pilgrims try to touch this sacred stone!

TO KNOW

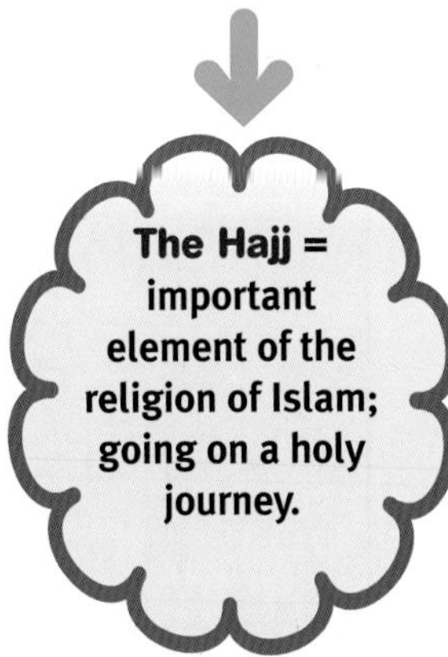

The Hajj = important element of the religion of Islam; going on a holy journey.

Medina (meaning City of the Prophet) is the second holiest City of Islam. When Muhammad began preaching in Mecca people didn't like it and began to persecute him. He decided that he and his followers should leave for a while. In AD 622 he left Mecca (the **Birth of Islam**) for Medina. In **Medina** he meditated and prayed and the number of his followers grew, as did the religion of Islam. He then returned to take the City of Mecca from the Pagans!

Fill in the blank spaces on the chart below, writing in where they are and why they are a place of interest.

Holy Places

Christianity	Where	Why
Rome	Italy	
Islam	**Where**	**Why**
Judaism	**Where**	**Why**

True / False?

1. Fatima is in the centre of Rome. **T / F**
2. Our Lady appeared to Bernadette. **T / F**
3. Jesus was born in Nazareth. **T / F**
4. The Western Wall is in Germany. **T / F**
5. Medina is the second holiest city in Islam. **T / F**

Q1. What appeared to Bernadette Soubirous?
Q2. Why is Fatima important?
Q3. How many times did Our Lady appear to the three children in Fatima?
Q4. Why are these places important to Christians: Bethlehem, Nazareth, River Jordan, Jerusalem?
Q5. What is the Western Wall?

RGI	IN	VI	ES	LO	THE	AP	N M
ARY	URD	RED	PEA				

RESEARCH
JOURNAL IDEA

Pick two of the sacred sites mentioned. Carry out an indepth study of them, finding out and presenting as much information as you can.

Fill in the blanks:

Fatima, in ______, is a holy site connected with ______. It was here in ______ Our Lady appeared. She appeared to ______ children, ______ times between ______ and ______. The children received messages to share with the world. By ______ the Catholic church saw it to be ______. As in Lourdes, there is a ______. Thousands of pilgrims come here all through the year.

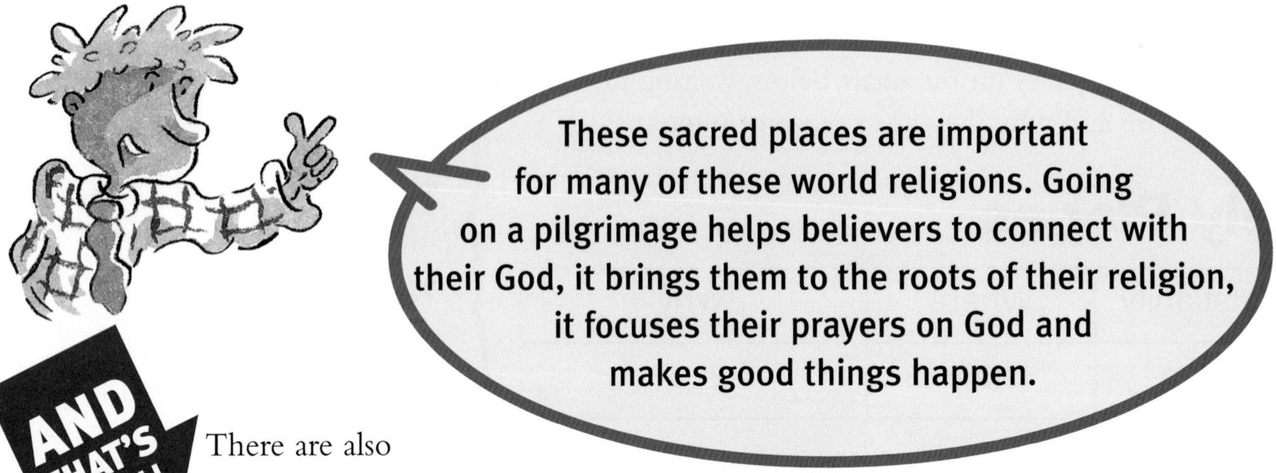

These sacred places are important for many of these world religions. Going on a pilgrimage helps believers to connect with their God, it brings them to the roots of their religion, it focuses their prayers on God and makes good things happen.

AND THAT'S NOT ALL

There are also

'SIGNIFICANT TIMES' (Sacred Times)

during the year to help worshippers come close to God and celebrate their beliefs.

During the year in our family or school, on our road, with our friends, in the club we're in, etc. there are times to celebrate!

TIMES OF SADNESS AND GRIEF

WINNING SOMETHING

CELEBRATING A MOMENT TO REMEMBER

SHARING A ROMANTIC MEAL

We celebrate the good things and the not-so-good things that are happening now, or have happened in the past, or, indeed, which may happen in the future!

During the year there are days set aside to celebrate and remember a particular thing.

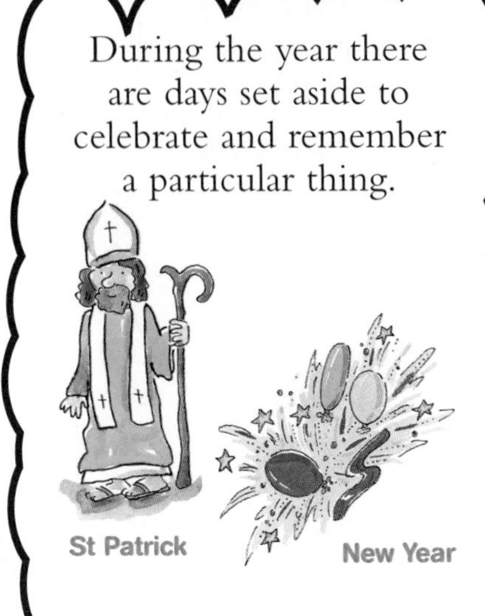

Groups and clubs organise themselves to a specific yearly timetable.

Schools have a set timetable for the academic year.

So, for everyone there are things that are happening across the year to be remembered, prepared for and celebrated.

The world religions are no different. The members of the religions involve themselves in 'Sacred Times' during the year, celebrating a particular part of their religion, their belief and their God.

TRY THIS!

Q1. What does 'significant times' mean?

Q2. What times do families celebrate during the year?

Q3. What are the good times and what are the not-so-good times that you might celebrate?

Q4. How does a school organise its special times?

Q5. Name a few sporting events during the year.

Q6. What do religious sacred times celebrate?

Art to do

Draw a poster showing four significant times across the year, naming each and saying why it is important.

True / False?

- Significant times are times to remember. **T / F**
- Schools celebrate special times during the year. **T / F**
- Families ignore special times during the year. **T / F**
- Winning a match is a special time during the year. **T / F**
- St Patrick's Day is a significant day during the year. **T / F**
- Members of religions ignore sacred times. **T / F**

Explain in your own words:

- Significant times
- Sacred times
- Celebrating family moments
- Celebrating belief in God

Fill in the blanks:

There are ______ times during the year to help ______ come close to ______ and ______ their beliefs. During the year is our ______, our ______ and with our friends, there are times to ______. Religions across the ______ are no.

More Qs

A. Why do families celebrate special moments?

B. Why is it important to remember significant times in our lives?

C. What are the significant times in your life?

D. Why do members of religions involve themselves in sacred times?

CHRISTIAN SACRED TIMES

TO KNOW

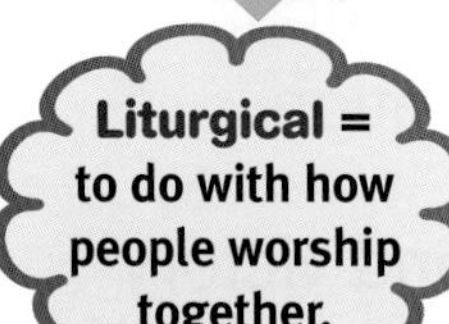

Liturgical = to do with how people worship together.

Christianity has the LITURGICAL YEAR!

ADVENT — The time of waiting for Jesus

CHRISTMAS — The time of Jesus' birth

ORDINARY TIMES — The time of Jesus' public ministry

The liturgical year is all about marking the life of Jesus, his death and Resurrection, to make it real for us every day of our lives. Over the liturgical year the past, present and future are celebrated because Christ is with us today and He will come again.

PREACHING

IN THE DESERT

LENT — The time of preparing and fasting

EASTER — The time of Crucifixion and Resurrection

ORDINARY TIME — The time of public ministry

MIRACLES

Throughout the liturgical year special times in the life of Jesus are celebrated by Christians.

Special colours are used during the liturgical year to focus on a theme of the season.

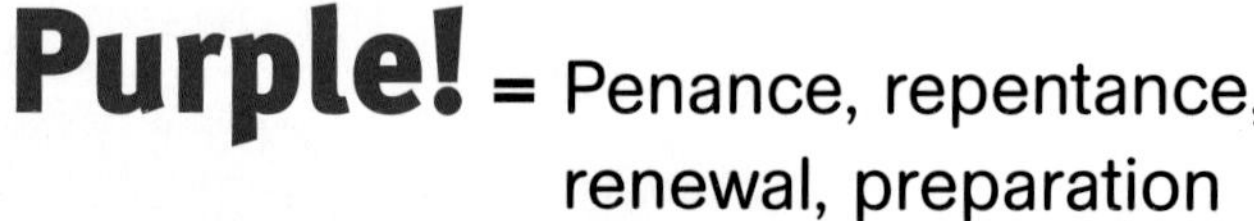

Purple! = Penance, repentance, renewal, preparation

Gold/White! = Joy and victory

Green! = New life, hope

Red! = Fire/courage.

The ritual clothes the priest wears – **the vestments** – also change colour according to the season or the celebration, as do the altar cloth and the church banners.

ADVENT

The liturgical year of the Church **begins** on the **First Sunday of Advent** (Nov./Dec.). The Advent season is the four weeks before Christmas. The word Advent means **'Coming'**. During this season Christians prepare themselves for the coming of Christ…

- on Christmas Day!
- in their hearts and souls!
- at the end of time!

Purple is the colour of the Advent season, symbolising preparation and repentance.

The **Advent wreath** is an important symbol used during Advent. It is made of evergreen leaves, three purple candles and one pink candle. Each candle is lit, one at a time, each Sunday. The pink candle is lit on the third Sunday of Advent to symbolise joy, that the time is now close! (Gaudete Sunday)

The **Jesse tree** is another symbol of Advent. This is a family tree/timeline of Jesus' family and Jesus' descendants and people mentioned in the Old and New Testaments.

CHRISTMAS

The Christmas season is next in the liturgical calendar and it celebrates the Birth and early years of Jesus. The important day is **the feast of the Birth of Jesus, Christmas Day, 25 December**.

The celebrations begin with the Vigil Mass on Christmas Eve, to welcome Christ into the world.

The Feast of the Epiphany (6 January) is also celebrated during the Christmas season. It is the celebration to mark the arrival of the Magi (the three wise men) to visit the baby Jesus. (Epiphany means 'to show'.)

LENT

The season of Lent is the **forty days before Easter** (except Sundays). It is the time when we remember Jesus praying in the wilderness of Judea before beginning his public ministry. There are six Sundays in Lent. The day before Lent begins is called **Shrove Tuesday** (or Pancake Tuesday). Tradition has it that families wanted to get rid of all their rich foods, including eggs and butter, before Lenten fasting began, which is why they made and ate pancakes. The first day of Lent is **Ash Wednesday**. This is the day we celebrate the start of Lent by wearing ashes on our foreheads and not eating meat.

This is a symbol of dying and rising with Jesus.

During the Lenten season our thoughts focus on Jesus and His message.
We are asked to do positive things for the needy in our society. Some people give things up and the money saved is given to charity. Some people go to Mass everyday.

EASTER

The liturgical season of Easter is the most important in the Christian year. Easter Sunday is the most important celebration of the year. It is the celebration of Christ's victory over death and His **Resurrection from the dead through God's power**. The week before Easter Sunday is **Holy Week**.

Holy Week remembers the last days of Jesus in Jerusalem.

Palm Sunday – Jesus enters Jerusalem.

Holy Thursday – Jesus has the Last Supper.

Good Friday – Jesus is crucified and dies.

Holy Saturday – Jesus lies in the tomb.

Easter Sunday – Jesus rises from the dead!

Easter Sunday is celebrated on the first Sunday after the first full moon after the spring equinox.

ORDINARY TIME

The season of ordinary time is split in two. The first period of ordinary time is between Christmas and Lent; the second period of ordinary time is between Easter and Advent.

There are thirty-three/thirty-four Sundays in ordinary time. This time focuses on the life of Jesus, his preaching and miracles. The Readings in the Sunday Masses in ordinary time are taken from the Gospels of Matthew, Mark and Luke, so that worshippers can listen to accounts of the main events and moments in Jesus' life.

ASCENSION

Ascension Sunday is celebrated on the seventh Sunday of Easter (this used to be forty days after Easter, on a Thursday). It celebrates the ascension of Jesus to His Father in Heaven – the destination of all believers.

PENTECOST

Pentecost Sunday is the last day of the Easter season. It is seen as the birthday of the Church, when the Apostles received the Spirit of Christ!

Rewrite and re-draw this chart and then fill in the blanks.

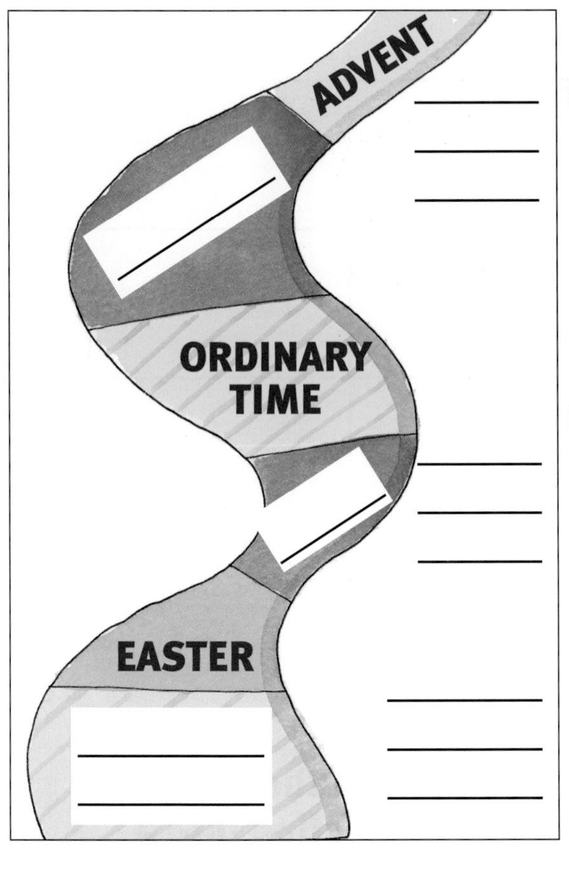

Put these in the correct order:

- The time of Jesus' birth.
- The time of preparing and feasting.
- The time of public ministry.
- The time of waiting for Jesus.
- The time of Crucifixion and Resurrection.
- The time of Jesus' public ministry.

Q

- Name the colours of the liturgical year.
- Explain the meaning of each colour.
- What items change with the colour of the season?

Q1. What is the liturgical year?

Q2. What does 'liturgical' mean?

Q3. What is remembered during the liturgical year?

Q4. What is the first sacred season of the liturgical year?

Q5. What does 'ordinary time' focus on?

Q6. What is Easter all about?

More questions...

A. When does the liturgical year begin?

B. How long does Advent last?

C. What is the purpose of the Advent season?

D. Why is purple the liturgical colour of Lent?

E. Draw the Advent wreath and explain each of its items.

RESEARCH

JOURNAL IDEA

Find out about the Jesse tree. Explain what it is, name all the symbols on it and explain them.

Season	Liturgical colour	Explanation of season	Important Days	Symbol Used	Drawing of Symbol
CHRISTMAS					
LENT					
EASTER					
ORDINARY TIME					

Liturgical Year Crossword

Across

3. The giving of the Holy Spirit.
4. Symbol of Advent.

Down

1. First season of the liturgical year.
2. Begins Lent.
5. Celebrates the Resurrection.

ASHUSBCDWEDNESDAYCEREASTERCQRSTVCHRISTMASVRTVWXEATCEAGHORDINARYJKLMOPSTIMELPSOTURVPENTECOSTEBCDA

Put the words you find into a sentence about the liturgical year.

1. Explain the Feast of the Epiphany.
2. What is the season of Lent based on?
3. What is the origin of Shrove Tuesday?
4. Name the days of Holy Week.
5. How many Sundays are there in ordinary time?
6. What happened at Pentecost?
7. When is Ascension celebrated? What is it?

FAITH BEGINS

Think for a moment about some of the big mysteries of life:

Love!
Death!
Joy!
Sorrow!
God!
Faith!

Throughout history humanity has been asking questions about these mysteries.

If we go back a few thousand years, we see that early man was looking around the world and trying to figure out its mysteries for himself: **the sun, the moon, nature, death and life …** these were all mysteries to be questioned and answered!

TO KNOW

Polytheistic = belief in many gods.
Monotheistic = belief in one god.

It was at this point that primal religions began … humans made a leap of belief to accept that there was something greater than them at work… early man saw the sun, moon and nature as gods and began to try and connect with these gods.

Over time man's understanding changed to see that there were gods behind these mysteries.

Humanity's relationship with these gods developed.

Faith was emerging …
Belief and trust in God!

These early primal religions were polytheistic, but over time monotheistic religions developed as humanity evolved and gained a greater understanding of God. In time, God revealed himself to humanity.

Today religions still deal with the mysteries of life. Questions like:

Does God exist?

What does my future hold?

What is life all about?

Why do bad things happen?

What happens when I die?

How can I be happy?

What is true love?

OVER TO YOU!

Figure out these life questions:

APP	I D	T H	ENS	WH	WHA	IE ?	EN

HAP	PEN	WHY	?	GS	BA	DO	HIN
D T							

Q1. What are some of the big questions of life?
Q2. How did early man try to deal with the mysteries of life?
Q3. Explain polytheism.
Q4. Explain monotheism.
Q5. Explain how faith was developing among humans.
Q6. Name three monotheistic religions.

ART TO DO!

Draw a poster of four of the big questions of life and give it a heading.

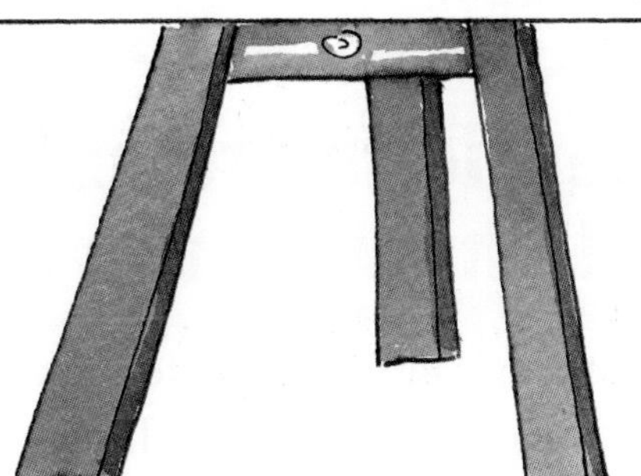

True / False?

- Love is a big mystery of life. **T / F**
- Early man saw the sun as a god. **T / F**
- The Romans didn't have gods. **T / F**
- Faith is belief and trust in God. **T / F**
- Judaism is polytheistic. **T / F**
- Religions deal with the big questions of life. **T / F**
- 'Does God exist?' is easy to answer. **T / F**

More questions ...

A. Why did early man see the world as a mystery?
B. What do you think are the mysteries of life today?
C. How, over human history, did faith emerge?
D. Name some differences between polytheism and monotheism.

Human beings, by their very nature, are questioners. They want answers and religions try to provide these answers.

Having faith means we reflect on our lives, but it also means accepting there are mysteries we cannot understand. We look at our God in wonder and awe because in this world we can never fully understand God.

From Childhood **To Adulthood**

The Mysteries exist and questions are asked

Qs

- What is love?
- Does God exist?
- Why am I in this relationship?
- What does my future hold?
- Why do people get sick?
- Why are there 'Acts of God'?
- What is religion all about?

Qs

- Where did I come from?
- Do Mam and Dad know everything?
- Am I safe?
- Will I live forever?
- Who am I?

Qs

- Am I in love?
- How do I express my sexuality?
- Where will I get money?
- Why do people die?
- Why do adults treat me this way?

Questions are asked across the years of our lives and answers are sought!

People from all walks of life look for **meaning** in a number of things and ways in this world, for example …

Music!

Magazines!

Nature!

And ...

In relationships!

In politics!

In writing!

... People listen to the words and lyrics of songs to see what they say to them about the world and life!

... People flick through the pages of magazines to see what answers they hold for them, how they should look, how they should behave, what life has in store for them!

... People go to the countryside for peace and quiet and hope that answers will come to them through nature!

... People look to their loved ones to be the answers to all their questions and to share their lives!

... People involve themselves in politics to try and make a difference in their lives and the lives of others around them!

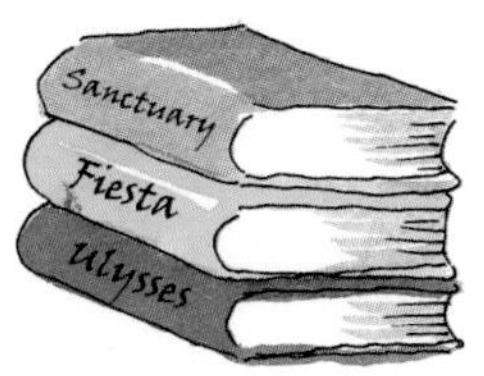

... People delve into literature and the wisdom of poetry to find answers to life's questions: love, death, relationships, God!

Fill in the blanks:

Human ______, by their very ______, are ______. They want ______ and religions try to ______ those ______! Being involved in ______ is ______ on our lives, accepting there are ______ that we can't ______. Looking at our God is ______ and ______, because we can never fully ______ God and His ______.

- Give three examples of the questions a child might ask.
- Give three examples of the questions a teenager might ask.
- Give three examples of the questions an adult might ask.

Q1. Where do people try to find meaning in their lives?
Q2. How might politics bring meaning to a person's life?
Q3. How might magazines bring meaning to a person's life?
Q4. How might relationships bring meaning to a person's life?
Q5. Why do people ask questions?

RESEARCH
JOURNAL IDEA

Pick something from music, magazines, literature, etc. What does it say about life mysteries? What answers to life does it have?

Q. Name one big question that a person might ask all the way through their lives.

A. Do the questions of life change from childhood to adulthood?
B. Where do you find meaning to life's mysteries? Explain.
C. Name some songs that might give meaning to life.
D. How do magazines influence people and their lives?

When we look at our society today we see people constantly searching for meaning. Some of the main ways they do this are through …

Many people find meaning in their lives through their family. Becoming parents gives a couple an exceptional responsibility to bring up their children as best they can. The love they have for each other is shown in their daily lives. Everyday the family makes a difference to each other and gives each other meaning, an aim and a purpose.

Many people find meaning in the work they do. Being able to constantly better themselves in their daily lives and make a difference to the people they come in contact with gives them an aim and a purpose.

Many people find meaning in their lives by being successful. No matter what they turn their hands to they are successful and can help people along the way. This gives them an aim and a purpose in life.

Of course, for some people these mean nothing, none of those things above gives them meaning, all that is 'meaningless'. For others, they may see all these things as giving some meaning, but above all that their **FAITH** gives the most meaning to their lives.

Their faith, their belief in God gives ultimate meaning in their lives!

This belief is expressed through their religion!

Just like early man, people who find meaning in their faith realise there is something greater than themselves that is the source of all Truth and Love.

Answers to these Questions of Life

Most people of faith belong to the religions of the world, which try to give meaning to people's lives ...

Love!

- God is love.
- Love is patient and kind.

Death!

- Be raised to Heaven.
- Enter God's Kingdom.

Suffering!

- The brokenness of our world leads to suffering.
- Create a better world.

Sin!

- A rift between us and God bridged by our love for each other and by penance.

Life!

- Love your neighbour as yourself.
- Treat others as you wish to be treated.
- Create the Kingdom of God.

God!

- Loving Father.
- Creator of all.
- Sustainer of all.
- Is love.
- Reveals himself.

Future!

- A world that is the Kingdom of God.
- A place of love, justice and peace.
- The Kingdom of Heaven.

1. 2. 3. 4. 5.

Across

3. Gives ultimate meaning.
4. Not having any meaning.

Down

1. Meaning from doing well in life.
2. Brokenness between us and God.
3. Parents and children together.
5. Creator of all, loving Father.

Complete each sentence in your copy:

- Throughout their lives people try to …
- People find meaning in family because …
- People find meaning in success because …
- Other people find meaning through …
- Through faith and religion they can …
- Some of the issues that religions deal with are …

Qqs

Q1. Name the three main ways a person might try to find meaning in his or her life.

Q2. How does work give meaning to a person's life?

Q3. What does success mean? How does it give meaning?

Q4. What other thing gives meaning to people's lives?

Q5. Name the important issues that faith tries to deal with.

Q6. What does faith make people realise?

What does religion have to say about:

Love	
Life	
God	
Sin	
Death	
Suffering	

THE GROWTH OF FAITH

Faith is like a seed that needs time and nourishment to grow.

Have a look at these two 'faith growth' charts. They are basically the same, but one is more psychological and the other more practical. Together they give us an excellent picture of the growth of faith within us.

The growth of faith in a person is a journey to a mature understanding for oneself and a mature understanding of God.

Childhood

Time of total trust in parents and special adults ● Accepting faith of adults ● Beginning of faith appreciation ● Simple view of world ● Later on the child makes the parents' faith personal ● Learns stories of faith ● Begins to vocalise belief in 'Holy God'!

Teenage/early adult

Peers become important ● Parents' views take a back seat ● Conforms to group's ideas ● Able to think abstractly, uncritical faith ● Personal faith begins! ● Later, critical thinking begins ● Values are examined and criticised ● Acceptance/rejection of ideas ● Choices are made.

Adult/mature adult

Becoming comfortable with accepting mysteries and paradoxes of life ● Balance between views of the world ● Open to theories, questions and answers ● Later on there is acceptance of life mysteries ● Good and evil in the world, image of God developed ● Knows what to believe and how to live it.

Childhood

Attitudes to and appreciation of faith from parents will form the basis of future faith acceptance and development.

School/indoctrination

Formal education begins ● Stories of faith are read and heard ● Religious ways of life are seen ● Faith presented ● Participates in rituals of faith ● Teachers express faith.

Socialisation/practice

From school to the world ● Conformity begins ● Do what the others are doing ● Following and unity ● Rituals are habitual.

Commitment/internalising

Becoming personally interested in developing faith ● Want to know more about faith ● Making faith their own ● Relationship with God developing.

Active faith

Making a choice to give time/life to faith, to God ● Work for the good of others ● Faith is alive!

Holiness

Giving life totally to God ● Spirituality a course for living ● Wisdom and truth are part of life!

GIVE THESE A SHOT!

Summarise the meaning for each faith development stage:

TEENAGE / EARLY ADULT

Growth of Faith Wordsearch

C	0	M	M	I	T	M	E	N	T
H	T	F	Y	T	L	Z	C	P	H
I	E	A	I	L	A	P	N	E	T
L	E	I	H	U	C	A	A	E	U
D	N	T	T	D	I	R	T	R	R
H	A	H	W	A	T	E	P	S	T
O	G	H	O	L	I	N	E	S	S
O	E	M	R	B	R	T	C	C	Z
D	R	A	G	R	C	S	C	B	I
T	C	A	R	T	S	B	A	Y	S

ABSTRACT, ACCEPTANCE, CRITICAL, CHILDHOOD, COMMITMENT, HOLINESS, FAITH, GROWTH, TEENAGE, PARENTS, PEERS, TRUTH, ADULT

1. Why do you think some young people are apathetic about faith?
2. Explain why, in your opinion, some people are stuck in the socialisation/ practice stage.

A. Why is faith like a seed that needs to be nurtured?

B. How are faith and God connected, do you think?

C. What is 'abstract thinking'?

D. Explain the stage 'Active faith'.

E. What role does formal education have to play?

F. Name some people who you think have reached the Holiness stage.

Speaking honestly, unfortunately it seems that around 'late teenage' and before 'practice' stages on those charts some teenagers are becoming apathetic. They don't begin to make critical choices or ask critical questions about faith or religion! (More on this later ...)

TO KNOW

To grow apathetic = not bothered one way or the other. **Internalising =** to make something your own; to live something.

Many studies also suggest that people of faith are stuck in the **socialisation/practice** stage. Doing what they are supposed to do and never making the leap to **'internalising' their faith**!

NB: closely connected to the development of faith is our...

Image of God!

What do we mean?

Just as a person's faith matures (or not) over time, so too does their image of God. The image of God a person has is always influenced by the world around them: their parents, their relationships, what they have seen and heard about religion and God, teaching and the experience of religion that a person has!

It may also happen that a person's image of God does not mature and develop. It may remain stagnant and underdeveloped because their faith has become stagnant and underdeveloped.

Have a look at some of these common images of God a person might have

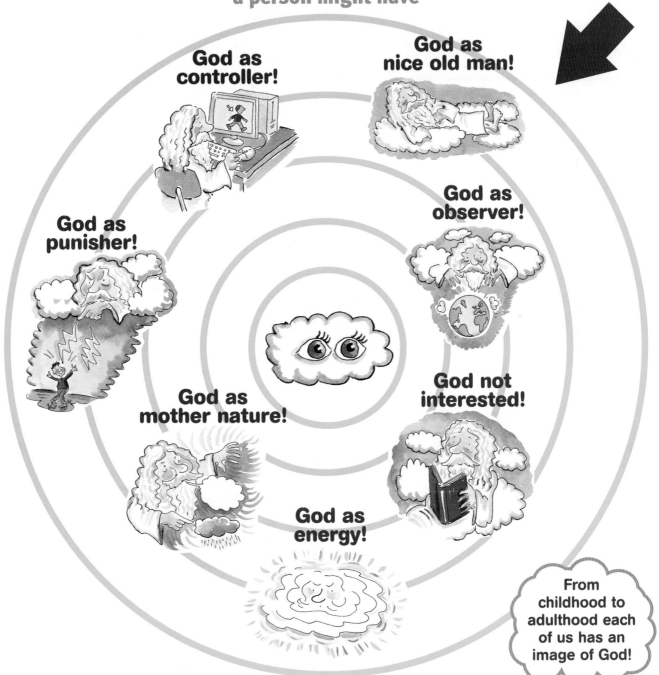

God as controller!

God as nice old man!

God as observer!

God as punisher!

God not interested!

God as mother nature!

God as energy!

From childhood to adulthood each of us has an image of God!

Try these ...

Qqs

Q1. What influences a person's image of God?

Q2. Name three common images of God.

Q3. Explain 'God is energy'.

Complete this art chart! Draw a picture for each one and explain each image.

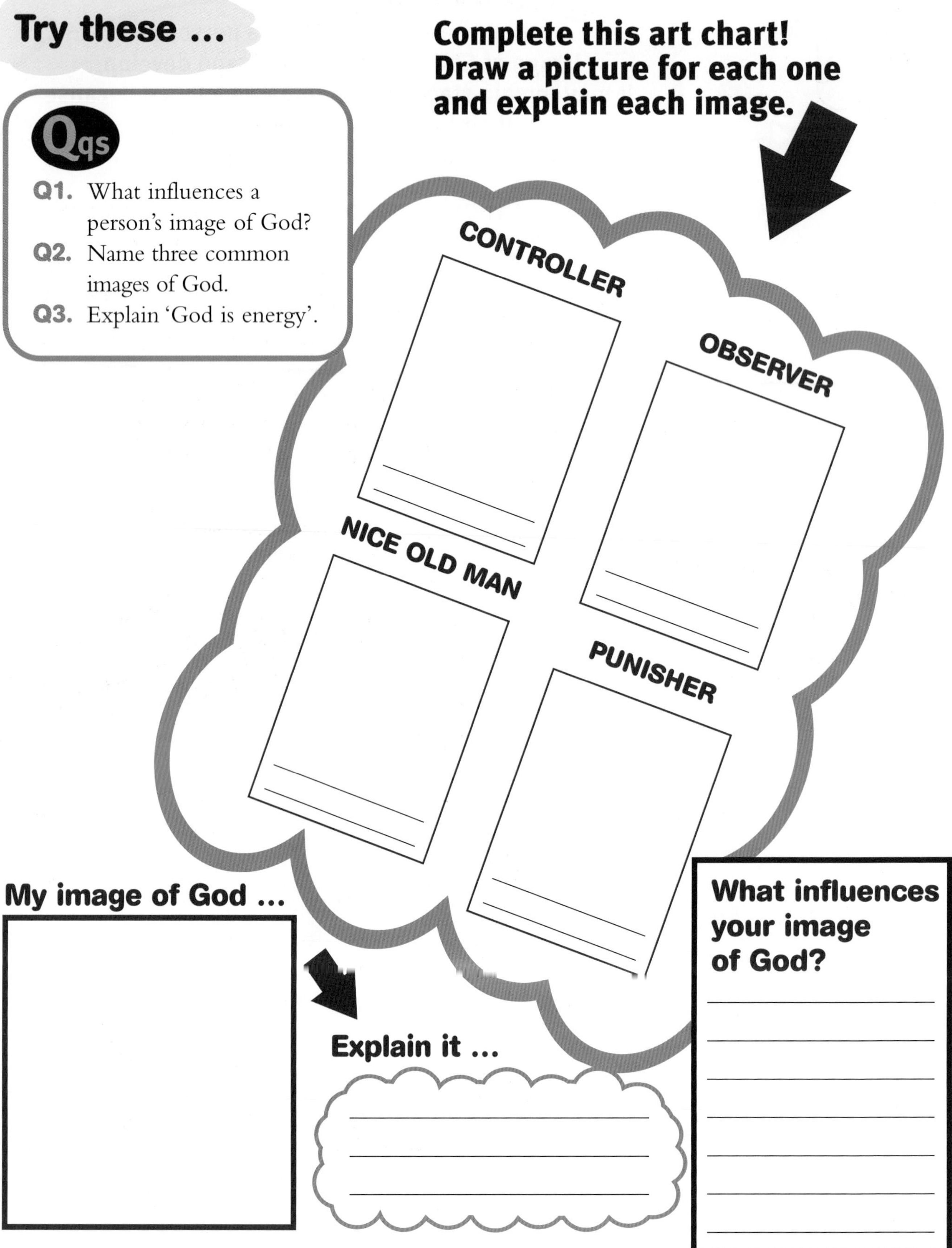

My image of God ...

Explain it ...

What influences your image of God?

These images of God come from the experiences of and attitudes towards God that people have. Some people have positive images of God, some people have negative images of God. Their image could be one of those mentioned, or it could be a mix of these, or it could be different from them.

TO KNOW

Islam never presents an image or artwork of Allah or Muhammed

All the world religions present an image of God to help believers focus on God!

It is hard to give an image of God because God is an ultimate '**mystery**' and any attempts to give an image will always fall short of the truth of God!

Islam!

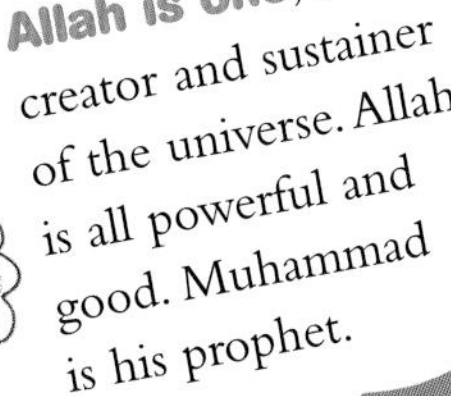

Allah is one, the creator and sustainer of the universe. Allah is all powerful and good. Muhammad is his prophet.

In the name of Allah, the merciful, the compassionate ... Lord of all being ... the All merciful, all compassionate. (The Koran)

Judaism!

Yahweh is one god.

God as mother (Isaiah 66:12-13)

God as father (Malachi 2:10)

God as king (Psalm 42:5-8)

God as fire (Exodus 13:21-22)

These images are in the Old Testament and therefore are used by Christians as well.

CHRISTIANITY!

New Testament images of God.

(Luke 15:4-7)

God, the Good Shepherd

(Luke 15:11-32)

God, the loving Father

(John 8:12)

God, the light of the world

(Luke 15:8-10)

God, who searched for the lost

(John 14:15-17)

God, the spirit of Truth and Love

Jesus himself taught his followers to call God 'Father', he also spoke about having a relationship with God the Father through prayer. Another name he used to speak about God, His Father, was '**ABBA**' ('Dad' in Hebrew). Jesus was constantly giving an example that all people could have a personal, loving relationship with God.

The images of the New Testament and the world religions present a God that is approachable, loving, compassionate, caring, accepting, a creator and sustainer – an image that allows us to have a mature and developed relationship with God, a God that we can trust.

NB:
Read the 'Our Father' again.

Fill in the blanks:

These images come from the ______ and ______ that people have to ______. Some people have ______ images, some have ______ images. All world ______ present an ______ of ______. It's hard to give an ______ of ______ because God is an ultimate ______, any attempts to give an ______ will always fall ______ of a ______ image!

Qqs

Q1. Why is it hard to give a true image for God?

Q2. What does Islam never present in art or drawing?

Q3. Give three titles for 'Allah', according to Islam.

Q4. Where do we read the names for 'Allah'?

Q5. Give two images of God taken from the Old Testament.

Q6. Give two images of God taken from the New Testament.

Q7. What did Jesus teach us about God?

Q8. What does the 'Lord's Prayer' tell us about God?

Find the words in the word wheel!

Put each word you find into a sentence about this section.

ZSPIRITLMOPFIRETSLUKEUXIMAGEFGHIGODKLALLAHSTUWEABBAFUXMERCIFULHOPMOTHERQSTUFATHERUXY

Q

- Explain why God is presented as '**FIRE**' in the Old Testament.
- What image is it trying to present?

It's clear from all of this that our faith is a gift, a gift that should be nurtured and cherished and lived. Faith is also a journey, and that journey eventually leads to a mature image of God, together with a mature faith in God.

Throughout history God has revealed himself to humanity, finally and ultimately revealing himself in Jesus Christ. **A journey of revelation**!

Revelation is God revealing himself to humanity.

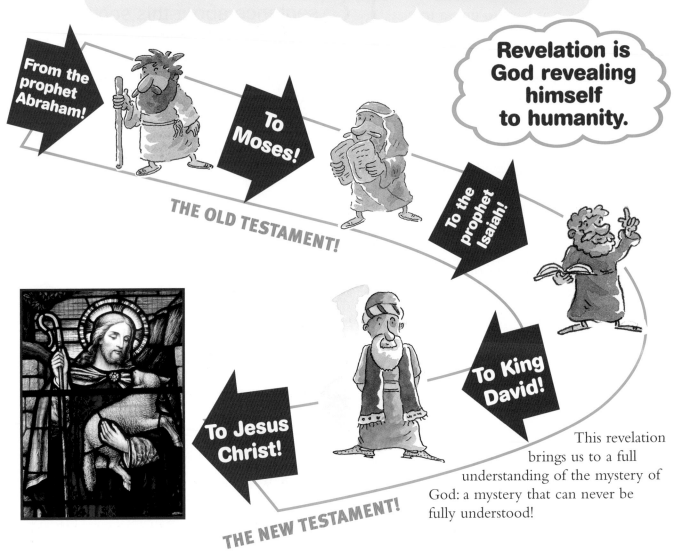

From the prophet Abraham!

To Moses!

To the prophet Isaiah!

To King David!

To Jesus Christ!

THE OLD TESTAMENT!

THE NEW TESTAMENT!

This revelation brings us to a full understanding of the mystery of God: a mystery that can never be fully understood!

Some people on their faith journey need proof that God exists. But really, as God is an ultimate mystery, can real proof ever be given?

Thomas Aquinas (1225–1274)

He was a famous Italian theologian and philosopher. He was a member of the Dominican order. He wrote many books about God and Christ, one of which is especially famous, the **Summa Theologiae**. In this he presents some indirect proofs of God's existence. Here three are condensed and summarised. See what you think!

God: The Beginning!

No event happens on its own; something must cause it, something starts it at the beginning. Aquinas believed that God caused things, God was the Beginning.

God: The Designer!

Looking at the world around us – the seas, the flowers, snow, the seasons – life is extremely complex. Aquinas believed that all this was designed, and that the designer is God.

God: Ultimate Good!

We all have the ability to know what is good, what is bad, what is right, what is wrong. This we call our 'conscience'. If we know good, then there must be ultimate goodness. This, according to Aquinas, is God.

Think these over, do they make sense to you? What do you feel about them?

Put these in the correct order:

- A Journey of Revelation.
- To the Prophet Isaiah.
- To Jesus Christ.
- From the Prophet Abraham.
- To King David.
- To Moses.
- Full revelation.

Explain...

- How God caused all things.
- How God is the Designer of all things.
- How God is Ultimate Good … according to Aquinas?

Q1. What is Revelation?
Q2. What does Revelation do?
Q3. Who is the Complete Revelation of God?
Q4. Complete this quick fact file for Thomas Aquinas

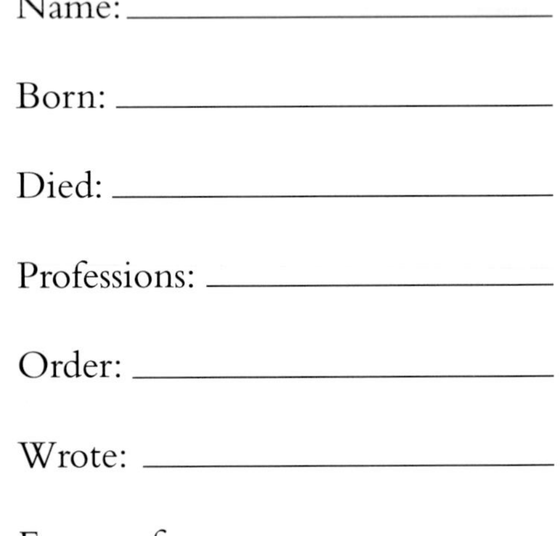

Name: ________________

Born: ________________

Died: ________________

Professions: ________________

Order: ________________

Wrote: ________________

Famous for: ________________

Q5. What is 'conscience'?
Q6. How can we see that the world is complex?
Q7. Name Thomas Aquinas' most famous book.
Q8. What would you disagree with / agree with in his proofs for God?

COPY AND COLOUR

God: The Beginning!
The Designer!
Ultimate Goodness!

Through all the questions and imagery something is dawning on us, this something is really **MYSTERY**. We are beginning to come to terms and appreciate **MYSTERY**.

When people encounter mystery they might:

Ignore it!
Are not interested!
Put it on the long finger!
Are afraid!
Find it too difficult!
Make no effort to understand!
Do something else!

Other people **'Embrace the mystery'**

Embracing the **MYSTERY** means really appreciating that there are things in this world that we don't fully understand. There is also a dawning of the notion that Religions can help with this understanding of **MYSTERY**.

Religious people use their

WORSHIP AS A RESPONSE TO MYSTERY

Through worship members of the world religions are responding to the mystery of their faith.

As we saw earlier, worship is prayers, rituals, words, gestures all directed to God.

Throughout all of this is an attempt to

Encounter the mystery of God,

to grasp as best as we can the meaning of our faith and, our image of God!

Through prayer, meditation, contemplation and Scripture } we **reflect** on our understanding and see God at work in the world!

Behind our worship is wonder, **wonder** at the marvels of our existence and our world and an expression of this wonder in our **celebrations**.

As a religious person, and through our worship, we are **encountering God**. We use our words and rituals to attempt to connect with our God in the community.

WORK TO DO!

Complete each sentence in your copy:

When they encounter mystery some people …

Find it ____________________

Make no ____________________

Put it ____________________

Are not ____________________

Embrace ____________________

Write an explanation for each of the following:

- Reflect
- Wonder
- Encountering God
- Encountering the mystery

Unmuddle each word

POSRWHI FRELCTE
YMTSREY CEVOTNRNE
MERBCAE

Fill in the blanks:

Some people, when they encounter ______, put it on the _____ _______, or do something else. Religious people use their ______ as a ______ to mystery. Throughout all of this is an attempt to _____ the ______. To grasp the meaning of our ______ and image of ______. Through ______ and meditation people ______ on their understanding and see _____ at work in the ______.

Q1. What is it that we can never truly comprehend?
Q2. Name six ways in which people deal with mystery.
Q3. What do religious people do?
Q4. How do worshippers 'reflect' on their understanding of God?
Q5. What do people 'wonder' at?
Q6. Where do people encounter God?

More Questions

A. Why do some people ignore a mystery when they come across it?
B. Why are some people afraid?
C. How do religious people use worship as a response to mystery?
D. How do we encounter God through religion and in what ways?
E. What does it mean 'to reflect on this world, our faith, our God'?

THE SITUATION of Faith Today

NB: The way faith is lived and expressed has changed over the years.

Let's travel back in time about 100 years. What will you learn about Ireland and faith?

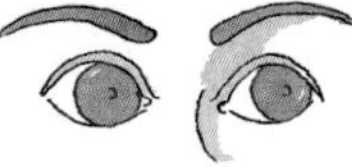 **Ireland seen as very much a Catholic country.**

 **People attend Mass on Sundays and/or every day.**

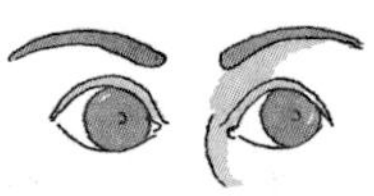 **Young people/adults receive the Sacraments.**

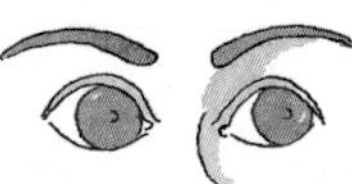 **Religion was important in people's lives**

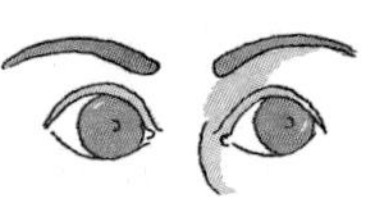 **Men join the priesthood. Priests are important in communities.**

Ireland was seen as a very religious country, to the extent that is was sometimes called **'Catholic Ireland'**.

Over the century Irish people expressed their faith and beliefs through **'devotions'**, as well as by attending Mass. These devotions were part of the worship of the community (and still are today, albeit to a lesser degree).

TO KNOW

Devotions = a way of praying to and worshipping Jesus and the saints.

DEVOTIONS

Stations of the Cross

These are the fourteen images of Christ's journey to his Crucifixion. They are positioned in a church and people pray at each station, particularly on Good Friday.

Benediction

'Benediction' means 'blessing'. The Blessed Sacrament is adored in a gold monstrance (the Body of Christ). People pray and meditate to Christ in the bread of Eucharist. In Benediction the priest and people sing hymns of adoration, incense is used and the people are blessed. The Forty Hours is when people organised forty days of prayer to the Blessed Sacrament.

Rosary

Dedicated to Our Lady and prayed using Rosary beads. It celebrates the life of Jesus, His death and Resurrection through praying the 'Our Father' and ten 'Hail Mary's for each decade. Families recite the Rosary together during May, the month of Mary.

Stations

Stations were Masses held in family homes in parishes. The parish was split into areas, each dedicated to a neighbourhood house Mass. This was done at special times during the year.

Virgin Mary

Devotion to Our Lady was, and still is, very strong, especially after Knock was recognised as a Marian Shrine. Many counties had Grottos to Our Lady and during May people prayed to statues of Our Lady. Every Catholic church has a statue of Our Lady.

Sacred Heart

Adoration to the Sacred Heart took place in the church and at home. Many homes had a picture of the Sacred Heart with a light that was always switched on.

Over to you!

Q1. Name three reasons why Ireland was seen as a religious country in the past.

Q2. Why was Ireland called 'Catholic Ireland'?

Q3. Explain 'Devotion'.

Q4. What was Benediction?

Q5. Explain the Stations.

Q6. Write about Devotion to Our Lady.

Find the words in the Word Wheel.

BENEDICTIONAOUXTSACREDHEARTUORSKFAITHEEFCATHOLICUVXRELIGIONPUXDEVOTIONSUARSTATIONS

True / False?

- In the past Ireland was a Jewish country. **T / F**
- In the past many men joined the priesthood. **T / F**
- Devotions are pilgrimages. **T / F**
- The Stations was having a Mass in a house. **T / F**
- Stations of the Cross follow the route to Crucifixion. **T / F**
- Devotion to the Sacred Heart only took place in homes. **T / F**
- Benediction is learning to speak well. **T / F**

Unscramble the tiles

H T	THE	Y	TUA	N O	SI	TIO	F F
ODA	AIT						

EAR	DEV	SA	D H	TO	T	CRE	ON
OTI	THE						

More Questions ...

A. In your opinion, was it true to say Ireland was a religious country?

B. Can you say that about Ireland today?

C. Why did people involve themselves in Devotion?

D. Why was Devotion to Our Lady so important?

E. Is it still important today? Explain.

RESEARCH
JOURNAL IDEA

Check some history books and the internet and find out how Ireland has changed over the past century, especially in the area of religion. Interview a person who may have been involved in some or all of the Devotions listed above.

More signs of Catholic Ireland were ...

Sodalities

Sodalities were group meetings - men and woman met separately – held once a month to pray to the Sacred Heart of Jesus. The meetings usually took place in the church and finished with Benediction and the Rosary.

Retreats
(parish)

Parish retreat was when a visiting priest (usually a Missionary) would come and speak to the worshippers during the Mass over a set period of time.

For many Irish people religion and expressing their faith was a part of everyday living.

Attendance at the Sacraments was at 96 per cent.

CATHOLIC IRELAND

The seminaries were full of students for the priesthood.

The 1950s and 1960s 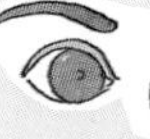 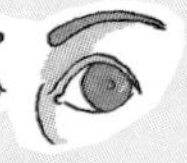 saw the beginning of change in Ireland

Moves to the city!

Access to TV!

Non-religious education!

Opportunities for women!

Towards the end of the twentieth century Ireland saw the move of people and families from the country to the city. People came looking for work and accommodation. Religious practices began to decline in country areas.

The accessibility of TV began to open doors to a whole wide world different from Catholic Ireland. An influx of new ideas, values and philosophies challenged the Irish viewer.

For many years the teaching of Ireland's children and young people was done by nuns, brothers and priests, but when vocations started to fall, religious influence began to decline.

Women began to take a more active role in the workplace and gain educational qualifications. Their role in passing on faith at home began to be eroded and to decline.

All these factors together caused changes in faith practice and development in Ireland towards the end of the twentieth century and the beginning of the twenty-first century.

Fall in Mass attendance!

Fall in numbers for Ordination!

Lack of interest of youth!

Decline of prayer in the home!

Feelings of non-relevance to people's lives!

Significant faith celebrations in Ireland

But the past century wasn't all about decline. There were moments of great celebration, too. Moments when Irish Catholicism seemed to grow and glow and was vibrant and revitalised.

For example ...

Eucharistic Congress – 1932

The **Eucharistic Congress** took place in Dublin between 21 and 26 June 1932. The purpose was to focus on the Blessed Sacrament, the Eucharist. Worshippers from all continents came to pray and celebrate together in Dublin.

Cardinal Lawri represented Pope Pius XI and was the guest of honour. The Congress took place over a week, with the highlight being a special Mass in the Phoenix Park and a Eucharistic procession to Dublin City Centre by 500,000 people. Benediction was celebrated there.

Visit of Pope John Paul II – 1979

John Paul II came to visit Ireland in September 1979. He was coming to mark the centenary of the Knock Shrine. Even at this time faith was still quite strong, with church attendance at 90 per cent. Every family and home made preparations for the visit: bunting was put up in gardens; pictures were put

in windows; prayers were said; and Devotions were made to Our Lady and the Sacred Heart. The Pope came for three days and over 2.5 million people went to see him during that time. Over one million people went to see him celebrate Mass in the Phoenix Park, Dublin.

Q1. When did change begin in relation to religion in Ireland?
Q2. What was part of everyday living for Irish people?
Q3. Name some of the influences that caused change in Ireland.
Q4. How did TV affect religion in Ireland?
Q5. What happened to change education?
Q6. Name some of the changes that occurred.
Q7. Name two significant faith celebrations in Ireland over the last 100 years.
Q8. When did John Paul II arrive in Ireland?

Fill in the blanks:

The 1950s and ______ saw the ______ of ______. For example, moves to the ______ access to ______, non-religious ______, opportunities for ______. These factors saw a ______ in faith ______ and development. Fall in ______ attendance, fall in numbers for ______, lack of ______ of ______. Decline of ______ in the home. Feeling of non- ______ to young people.

RESEARCH
JOURNAL IDEA

Find a person who was at the visit of the Pope in 1979. Ask them about the experience, the atmosphere and what they saw.

MOVES TO THE CITY	
ACCESS TO TV	
OPPORTUNITIES FOR WOMEN	
EDUCATION	

Where do each of these sentences belong on the chart?

- Government takes over some schools.
- Role in the home eroded.
- Opening up whole wide world.
- Looking for work and accommodation.
- Getting educational qualifications.
- No more nuns and brothers teaching.
- Influx of new ideas and values.
- County practices to decline.

Even with the excitement and joy caused by the Pope's visit in 1979, around this time faith in Ireland continued to decline.

EVS
(European Values Study)

Mass attendance down to 82 per cent in 1981.

ISR
(International Survey on Religion)

Mass attendance down to 72 per cent in 1991.

These statistics are for Mass attendance. Look at these.

EVS

'Belief in God' – 96 per cent in 1999
'Belief in Heaven' – 86 per cent in 1999
'Belief in sin' – 86 per cent in 1999

EVS

Important to have a religious ceremony for

BIRTH	MARRIAGE	DEATH	in 1999
91 per cent	93 per cent	96 per cent	

EVS

'Pray once a week' – 70 per cent in 1999

Looking at these figures, it would seem that personal spirituality is still present, but that what is declining is an overall attachment to the institution of the Church.

As well as surveys, if we look at two very revealing moments in Irish Catholic faith, what will we see?

1. The Relics of St Thérèse

The Relics of St Thérèse of Lisieux came to Ireland between 15 April and 1 July 2001. They were displayed at seventy-four different places around the country.

Despite negative media commentaries, it was reported that 3.5 million Irish people venerated the relics of this beloved saint from France.

2. Death of John Paul II

The death of Pope John Paul II was a devastating blow to Catholics the world over, as well as to members of the world's religious. He was seen as a man of true belief, peace, integrity, holiness and wisdom.

He died on 2 April 2005 after a long illness. Across Ireland, thousands of people attended commemorative Masses in their churches, signed Books of Condolences, prayed and lit candles. Thousands of pilgrims attended his funeral in Rome.

Is Catholic Ireland dead? You decide!

Qqs

Try these!

Q1. What was the percentage of Mass attendance in 1981?

Q2. What was it in 1991?

Q3. Give details of the EVS study of 1999.

Q4. How important were religious ceremonies for people in 1991?

Q5. Recently, which two events showed a rekindling of religious values in Ireland?

Q6. How many people visited the Relics of St Thérèse?

Q7. When did Pope John Paul II die?

Fill in the blanks:

EVS: European ______ Study.
ISR: International ______ on ______.
Mass ______ down to ______ per cent in 1981, down to ______ per cent in 1991.
Belief in ______ 96 per cent in 1999.
Belief in Heaven ______ in ______.
Importance of religious ceremony for death ______ in 1999.
Prayed ______ a week ______ in 1999.

To Do Create and draw up a pie chart of statistics to display the results of the EVS and ISR studies.

True / False?

- Mass attendance was down in 1991. **T / F**
- Belief in God was 96 per cent in 1999. **T / F**
- Importance of marriage was 100 per cent. **T / F**
- 70 per cent of people prayed in 1999. **T / F**
- St Thérèse's body was brought to Ireland. **T / F**
- John Paul II died in 2005. **T / F**
- St Thérèse was from Lisieux. **T / F**
- John Paul II was seen as a holy man. **T / F**

Q Write a brief word on the death of John Paul II – the ceremony, the place, the life of John Paul II.

Check!

Look up information about the visit of the Relics of St Therese and give as many details of the event as possible.

When we look at Ireland and faith today, we have to examine what are the influences on young people and their beliefs and practices. All young people carry with them a set of values, understandings, theories and philosophies that affect how a person sees his or her religion and his or her image of God.

Influences like

Home/Family!

The importance and practice of children in the home. Parents as faith role models! Religious opinions in the home. What religious values are transmitted?

Friends/Peers!

The values of the peer group. The view of religion in that group. Do they practise? Are they interested? How does a person belong to the group?

School/Teachers!

The values of the school. Is it a religious school? The values of the religious staff. What attitudes do they have? What happens in the classroom?

Parish/People!

The parish, the religious area that the young person grows up in. Is there a sense of belonging in a parish? What does that mean? Is there involvement in the liturgy? Is there a spiritual life or social life? Is there communication?

Other Activities!

There are moments outside any of the above, such as retreats, prayer groups, social and justice groups. What roles are presented? What is faith all about?

TO KNOW

Evangelisation = to spread the Good News contained in the Gospels.

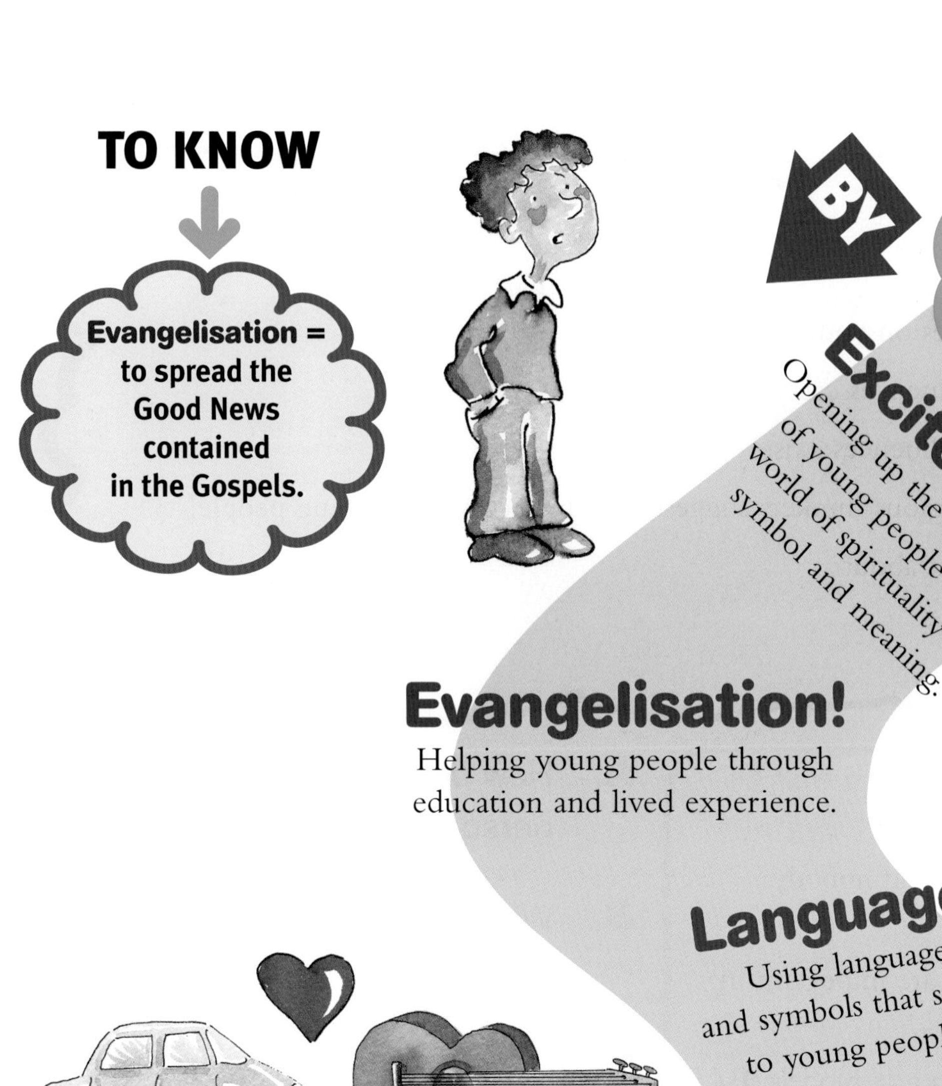

BY

Many religious thinkers have suggested ways to help young people and their faith.

Excitement!

Opening up the imagination of young people to the world of spirituality and symbol and meaning.

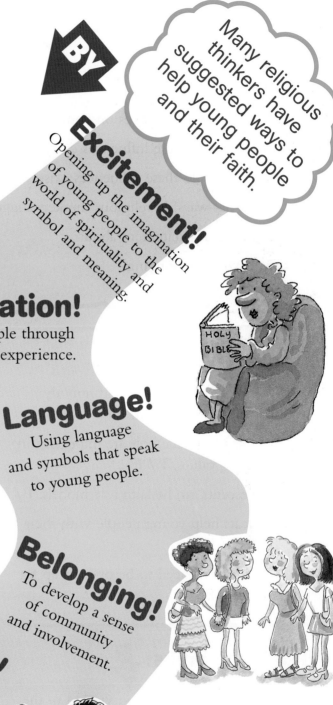

Evangelisation!

Helping young people through education and lived experience.

Language!

Using language and symbols that speak to young people.

Belonging!

To develop a sense of community and involvement.

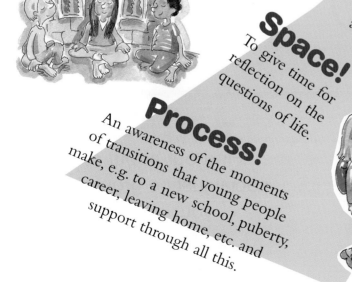

Space!

To give time for reflection on the questions of life.

Process!

An awareness of the moments of transitions that young people make, e.g. to a new school, puberty, career, leaving home, etc. and support through all this.

NB: The development of faith in young people is very special and very important and should be treated as such.

Qqs

Q1. Give two influences on young people's faith.

Q2. What do these influences carry with them?

Q3. Where do these influences exist?

Q4. What ways do religious thinkers suggest to help the faith of young people?

Q5. What is excitement about?

Q6. Explain 'belonging'.

True / False?

- My values are my own and nobody helped me with them. **T / F**
- Language and symbols are important in inspiring values. **T / F**
- Adolescents can be faith role models. **T / F**
- Retreats help young people with their faith. **T / F**
- Imaginations need to be opened up for faith. **T / F**

A. How does a parish influence a person's values?

B. What influences most affect your values?

C. How do your friends help you form your values?

D. What values can be found in your school motto/mission statement/school environment?

Fill in the blanks:

Home/______, how is religion viewed in the ______, is it ______? Friends/______ the group that a person is ______. What are its ______. ______/teachers, what are the ______ of the ______. Is it a ______ school?

Things to do!
Find out about a social justice group in your area.

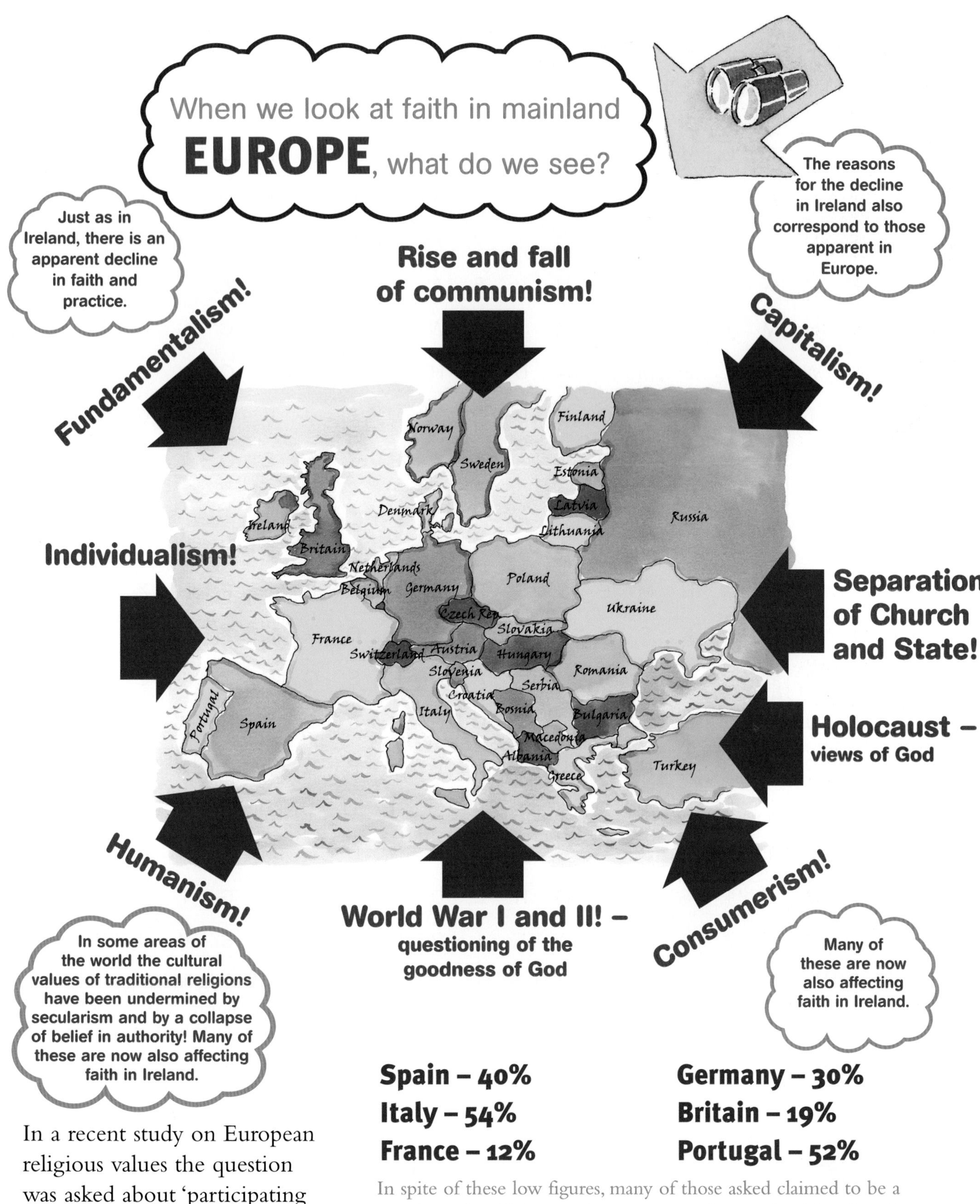
When we look at faith in mainland
EUROPE, what do we see?
Just as in Ireland, there is an apparent decline in faith and practice.
The reasons for the decline in Ireland also correspond to those apparent in Europe.
Rise and fall of communism!
Fundamentalism!
Capitalism!
Individualism!
Separation of Church and State!
Holocaust – views of God
Humanism!
World War I and II! – questioning of the goodness of God
Consumerism!
In some areas of the world the cultural values of traditional religions have been undermined by secularism and by a collapse of belief in authority! Many of these are now also affecting faith in Ireland.
Many of these are now also affecting faith in Ireland.
Norway
Sweden
Finland
Estonia
Latvia
Lithuania
Russia
Denmark
Ireland
Britain
Netherlands
Belgium
Germany
Poland
Czech Rep
Slovakia
Ukraine
France
Switzerland
Austria
Hungary
Romania
Slovenia
Croatia
Serbia
Bosnia
Bulgaria
Italy
Macedonia
Albania
Greece
Turkey
Portugal
Spain

In a recent study on European religious values the question was asked about 'participating in a religious service once a month'.

Spain – 40%
Italy – 54%
France – 12%
Germany – 30%
Britain – 19%
Portugal – 52%

In spite of these low figures, many of those asked claimed to be a member of a religion, so the percentage for membership of a religious organisation was very high.

WORDSEARCH

M	V	R	C	H	E	G	N	O	I	T	A	R	A	P	E	S	W	Y	E
L	S	U	C	U	U	Q	H	L	N	H	O	L	O	C	A	U	S	T	P
I	A	I	N	M	P	M	A	A	D	E	N	I	L	C	E	D	C	I	O
P	S	M	N	R	A	U	A	O	I	V	F	O	L	V	O	O	R	R	R
W	N	V	A	U	T	P	C	N	V	F	A	I	T	H	N	U	I	O	U
I	H	N	M	I	M	D	D	G	I	W	W	X	M	S	U	C	G	H	E
O	P	W	R	S	B	M	H	M	D	S	H	N	U	W	Y	Q	I	T	R
H	D	I	K	R	N	C	O	Y	U	W	M	M	Z	U	R	R	D	U	I
X	P	R	A	F	R	O	O	C	A	F	E	P	Y	W	E	D	L	A	S
S	Q	O	I	U	K	J	T	Q	L	R	B	G	V	L	I	L	Y	M	E
Q	Y	B	H	F	J	J	E	A	I	S	E	P	A	M	K	E	U	U	E
E	F	C	V	G	H	M	E	S	S	P	A	N	Q	P	S	P	H	Z	L
R	C	I	R	K	X	F	M	J	M	R	D	L	O	A	M	Z	O	J	Q
E	J	I	K	P	A	O	R	G	X	A	H	R	S	G	B	Z	I	E	H
S	T	U	V	L	P	T	H	O	G	C	H	R	U	S	U	R	K	E	O
A	T	Q	L	R	F	U	U	L	U	T	F	D	P	S	I	J	T	E	L
W	V	A	L	K	E	V	Q	E	E	I	V	T	O	U	U	Y	P	E	Q
S	P	L	T	E	H	S	M	V	C	C	P	N	D	E	M	Y	E	N	N
Q	W	J	I	E	S	K	S	Q	R	E	U	U	B	S	F	G	T	Z	P
S	Q	Q	D	Z	P	R	H	W	F	I	B	S	M	L	J	B	V	J	U

AUTHORITY	CHURCH	COMMUNISM
CONSUMERISM	DECLINE	EUROPE
FAITH	FALL	HOLOCAUST
HUMANISM	INDIVIDUALISM	IRELAND
PRACTICE	RISE	SEPARATION
SERVICE	SPIRITUAL	STATE

Q Name some of the reasons for decline of faith in Europe.

Give the monthly statistics for participating in religious services in some European countries.

From this there is a realisation that there are

Challenges to faith!

It is obvious that in the **twenty-first century** many challenges are posed to faith. Those challenges have developed over time and through history and they stem from the constant endeavour of people to know themselves, their world and their God better!

Travel back in time! As we said earlier, for centuries humanity had a view that God was behind everything: life, death, love, soul, sin, Heaven, Hell. By the seventeenth century, however, this perception had changed.

The Enlightenment! (also known as the Age of Reason)

This was the time of seeking answers!

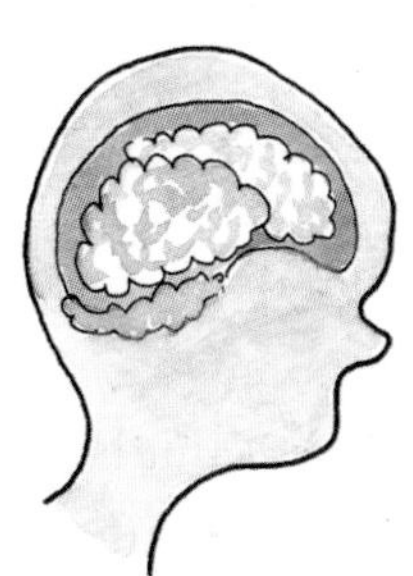

Looking for answers and explanations to everything!
This was the beginning of proof and evidence replacing religious belief in the pursuit of truth!

Up until the Enlightenment the universe was seen like this:

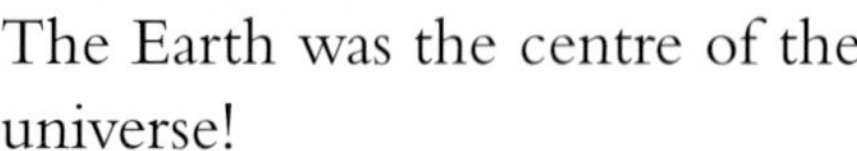

The Earth was the centre of the universe!
This idea was based on the thinking of an ancient **Greek philosopher** called **Aristotle**!
Originally, Christianity accepted this view!

During the late 1400s along came a Polish priest called **Copernicus**, who was also interested in **astronomy**. He put forward the idea that perhaps 'the Earth travelled around the sun'! He didn't say that this was fact because he was afraid of the reaction of the Catholic Church.

Another astronomer, named **Kepler**, studied the work of **Copernicus** and agreed with it and said it was fact! The Church was outraged!

Galileo

He continued the work of Copernicus and Kepler. He made his own telescope and looked to the stars. Galileo was certain to prove that the Earth and the other planets did indeed rotate around the sun. The Church leaders were not happy with this because religious belief and Bible accounts hold that the Earth is

the centre. The leaders became nervous that this finding might undermine their authority. They forced Galileo to take back all he had said. He did for a while, but then started his work again. The Church put him on trial for his ideas and he was sent home to Florence, Italy, where he died! But his theories continued to gain momentum.

… By this stage science **(science – knowledge)** was taking off. **Knowledge from science** is gained from …

- Observation of how things work!
- Conducting a series of experiments!
- Testing ideas from what is observed!
- Accepting or rejecting theories and ideas for good reason/knowledge!

AND ALONG CAME

Isaac Newton!

He was an English mathematician. Through his study and scientific research he explored the laws of gravity. Using those laws he proved that the Earth and the planets did indeed revolve around the sun. Some of the mysteries of the universe were now being solved by human reason – God was being taken out of the picture.

From this began conflict between the Church …

- God created everything!
- The Bible tells us about the creation of the universe!
- Every word in the Bible is fact!
- God knows everything!
- Humans created in God's image!

Vs

- The universe works because of scientific laws!
- Humanity evolved over time!
- Human reason and knowledge can give answers!

… and scientific discovery

Qqs

Q1. Give another name for the Age of Reason.

Q2. What was the Enlightenment?

Q3. Explain how the universe was seen pre-Enlightenment.

Q4. What was Copernicus interested in?

Q5. What were his ideas?

Q6. What did Kepler agree with?

Q7. What did Galileo prove?

Q8. Why were Church leaders not happy with these discoveries?

Q9. What did the Church make Galileo do?

Q10. How is knowledge acquired by science?

Match up correctly:

Enlightenment	Studies the work of Copernicus
Galileo	The Age of Reason
Aristotle	Between the Church and science
Kepler	Polish priest
Copernicus	Saw the Earth as the centre of the universe
Conflict	Proved the sun was the centre of the universe

Q In what areas did the Church and science come into conflict?

More questions ...

A. What did the Enlightenment mean in the history of humanity, do you think?

B. Why do you think the Church was so unhappy with the findings of scientific discovery?

C. How important were men like Galileo and Newton, do you think?

In time science came into conflict with Religion over the 'creation of the world'. For years in the western world the accepted Creation story was from the **Books of Genesis** in the Old Testament (Genesis 1 and 2).

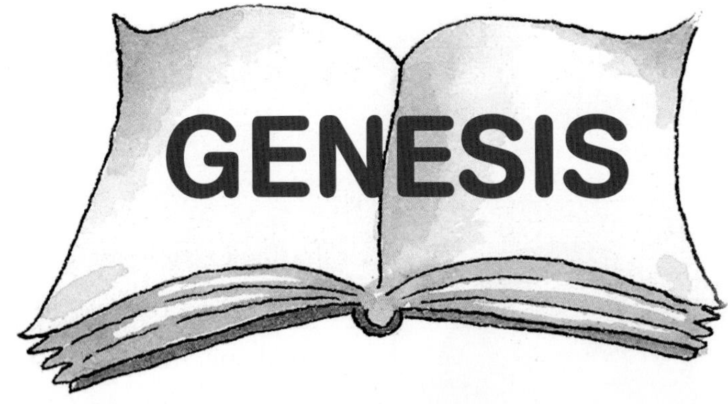

Let's have a look!

In the book of **Genesis** God creates the world in **6 days**.

Day 1 God created the Heavens and the Earth.
Day 2 God created the oceans and the sky.
Day 3 God created the land and plants.
Day 4 God created the sun, moon and stars.
Day 5 God created living creatures of the sea and sky.
Day 6 Humanity is created.
Day 7 God rests.

Many scientists were pushing for this explanation to be ignored while others said that science and religion can work together. What we must remember is that the writers of Genesis were inspired to write it because of their relationship with God. They weren't scientists. They wanted people to remember why the world was made and that;

- One loving and creative God created the world.
- The world and time had a beginning.
- It was created from God's design and plan.
- The world is good because God is good.
- We are created in God's image.
- We are loved by God.
- We are given unique abilities and have special abilities in this world.

The Genesis story was written, to show important points about us, the world and God and not to present a scientific study of the beginning of the world.

Many scientists began to investigate the world for themselves.

TO KNOW

Evolution = developed/ changed over centuries.

ONE SUCH SCIENTIST WAS

Charles Darwin

(1809–1882)

Charles Darwin was a scientist from Britain. He travelled the world collecting plant and animal specimens for scientific study. He travelled the world for twenty years. After studying his samples he published a book called ***On the Origin of Species*** (1859). This book explained **Evolution**!

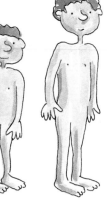

Evolution was the development and change of all life over millions of years.

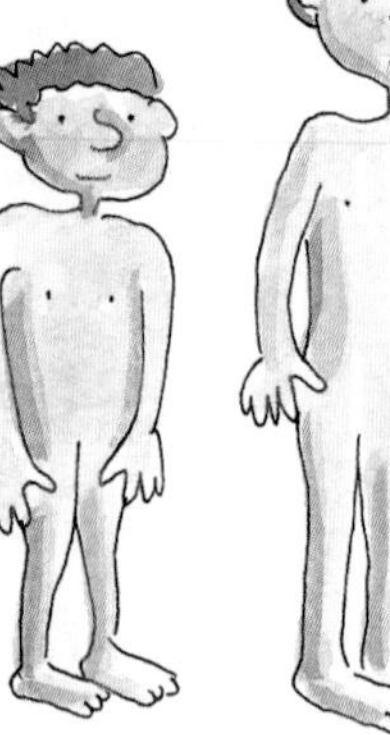

Central to Evolution, according to Darwin, was **Natural Selection** – this is the way in which plants and animals adapt to suit their environment. If they don't adapt, they die.

All this he applied to Humanity!

Darwin said he did not wish to shock those who were religious, but he did!

Do a bit!

Qqs

Q1. What did people believe was contained in the Book of Genesis?

Q2. How many days did it take to create the world according to Genesis?

Q3. What happened on Day 6 of the creation process?

Q4. Explain the word 'Evolution'.

Q5. What did Charles Darwin discover?

Q6. What did Genesis want people to remember?

Look up Genesis, Chapter 1. Read over the Creation process for yourself.

Complete each sentence:

On Day 3 God created …

On Day 7 God …

In the Book of Genesis we read the …

Charles travelled …

He collected …

He wrote …

Natural Selection was …

Evolution is …

Complete this chart in words and pictures in your copy.

Creation in Genesis …

Day 1 ....

Day 2 ....

Day 3 ....

Day 4 ....

Day 5 ....

Day 6 ....

Q Explain, in your opinion, why the Church might have been shocked at what Darwin discovered.

Art to do!

Draw picture of the seven-day creation of the world.

Draw a picture to describe Evolution.

… it was becoming clear that science was a challenge to religion and faith during the nineteenth century. Another challenge that occurred around this time was …

Communism!

Communism began with **Karl Marx** (1818–1883). He was a German philosopher. He looked at the world around him and saw that there were a few people who had lots of money and a lot of people who had very little money and spent most of their lives at work in factories. He wanted to balance things out. The aim of communism was to overthrow the wealthy and those in power and to give their money and land to the poor and lower classes, so that everyone had the same. Another aspect of communism was to get rid of religion because religion gave the poor and lower classes false hope of good things in the afterlife if they suffered now, on Earth!

Science and communism

were gradually eroding everything for which faith and religion had an answer!

God

began the world, but left it to fend for itself. He had nothing else to do with it!

Humans

had evolved to who they were, not created by the hand of God, or created in His image. The product of Natural Selection!

Heaven

The afterlife was seen as a 'carrot' for people to endure suffering in this life. Communism gave a non-religious meaning for life: make your own heaven and happiness through communism!

This led some people to think that happiness, contentment and fulfilment can be found in this world: nothing to do with faith, religion, or God.

Atheism

(A): without (Theism): God
An acceptance that there is no God; a person who doesn't believe in the existence of God.

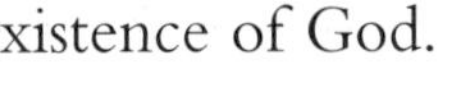

Agnosticism

Agnosticism (A): without (gnosus): knowledge
An acceptance that there is no way humans can be sure if God exists, or that it's not possible for us to know.

Humanism

An acceptance that there is no God and that people can be happy without God. **Secular humanists** are committed to making the world a better place for all people.

Materialism

An acceptance that to accumulate possessions brings meaning and status, especially money and possessions. In some cases there is no concern for others.

Fundamentalism

An acceptance that holy writings, beliefs and values are literally factual, leading to an unbending, blinkered view of religion and the world!

In our society today there is also an air of **apathy/indifference**! This can be seen in young people. The world of religion means nothing to them. They have no interest in participation in or connection with religion, and yet they may still be on a Spiritual Search!

Fill in the blanks:

Communism began with ______ ______ (1818–1883). He was a ______ philosopher. He looked at the ______ around him and saw that there were ______ who had ______ of money and ______ of people who had ______ money and spent most of their ______ at ______ in factories. He wanted to ______ things out. The aim of ______ was to overthrow the ______ and those in power and to give their ______ to the ______ and ______ classes. Part of communism was to get rid of ______ because religion gave the poor false ______ of good things in the ______life.

Give definitions for ...

- Atheism
- Agnosticism
- Humanism
- Communism

Q Analyse and describe why young people today might be indifferent/ apathetic towards religion and faith.

Q Are young people spiritual?

What views of the following did science and communism give us?

God: ______________________

Humans: ______________________

Heaven: ______________________

RESEARCH
JOURNAL IDEA

Do a survey of your class and home and ask people what category of belief they fit into from the earlier list.

A. Why was communism seen as anti-religion?

B. Marx once said that religion was the 'opium of the people': what did he mean?

C. Did communism give a positive view of religion: Why/Why not?

D. Why are some people agnostic, do you think?

E. Do you think materialism is a problem in our society today?

F. How do fundamentalist religious views affect the world today?

G. Which category of belief do you fit into, do you think?

When we look back at history we can see that religion was threatened and challenged by science and that science disregarded religion. In the twenty-first century there has been a move to reconcile and link the two together.

SCIENCE AND RELIGION

A RELATIONSHIP

'The Bible teaches us how to go to Heaven and not how the Heavens move.'
John Paul II

Religion can answer the WHY questions! Science can answer the HOW questions!

So, rather than religion and science being in conflict, or separated from each other, there is a positive move towards **interaction** between the two.

Scientists and religious thinkers are now working closer together in the search for 'Truth'.

There is a realisation that perhaps there are aspects of this world and beyond that can't be examined and solved by science!

Science and religion share in the search for Truth and the desire for the unity of all knowledge of the universe!

Science provides us with theories of the way the universe unfolded, enhancing and ratifying an understanding of the creative intelligence and coherence of God!

During the 1960s the Catholic Church saw how the beliefs and practices of the world were developing and examined all the world-views mentioned. The Pope and the Bishops, through inspiration from the Holy Spirit, decided to tackle many of the issues of the twentieth century.

Areas of discussion

Second Vatican Council

The Church
What the Church should be in the twenty-first century.

Revelation
The revelation of God to Humanity.

Liturgy
Changes in the ways of worship.

Ecumenism
Relationship with Protestant and Orthodox Christians.

Bishops
The role of Bishops in the twenty-first-century Church.

Religious life
The importance of religious life of Brothers and nuns around the world.

Laity
A greater role for the lay faithful.

Education
Religious education in the community.

Religious Freedom
The freedom to worship in all countries and situations.

Non-Christians
Interfaith dialogue with world religions!

Between 1962 and 1965, over the course of four sessions, 2,600 Bishops and Cardinals met in the Vatican in Rome. **It was begun by Pope John XXIII and later continued by Pope Paul VI.** The Bishops were joined by other world religious representatives. Over the four sessions, issues of importance to the world were debated, argued, discussed, prayed and meditated upon. These were issues that would be at the core of belief of all Catholics and religious people in the twentieth century and in the future.

NB Points to remember from the Second Vatican Council:

- more lay involvement in the worship rituals;
- laypeople involved in missionary work and education;
- the celebration of liturgy change to be worship-friendly;
- encouragement to study;
- Scripture, to have a deeper understanding and awareness of it;
- focus on Christ active in the world at all times. The Holy Spirit at work;
- communicating with a personal God;
- how to make the world a better place and the Kingdom of God.

Unscramble the tiles

TH	E H	S C I	N S W	Q S	E A	E N C	O W
E R S							

R E L	E N C	I G I	N D	E A	S C I	O N	O N

Match the word with its explanation

Non-Christians	Greater role for the faithful.
Religious life	Changes in the ways of worship.
Laity	Freedom to worship in all situations.
Liturgy	The role of nuns and Brothers.
Revelation	Dialogue with other religions.
Religious freedom	God revealed to humanity.

More questions ...

A. What did John Paul mean when he said the 'Bible teaches us how to go to Heaven'?

B. What is the 'Truth' that religion and science are searching for, do you think?

C. Overall, is it more beneficial for science and religion to work together?

D. How did Vatican II try to look at and answer the challenges of the twentieth and twenty-first century?

E. What specific changes did Vatican II make?

Qqs

1. How did science threaten religion?
2. What did Pope John Paul II say about the Bible?
3. What questions did religion answer?
4. What questions did science answer?
5. What do science and religion share?
6. What does science provide us with?
7. What did the Catholic Church do in the 1960s?
8. What areas of discussion did the Vatican Council have?

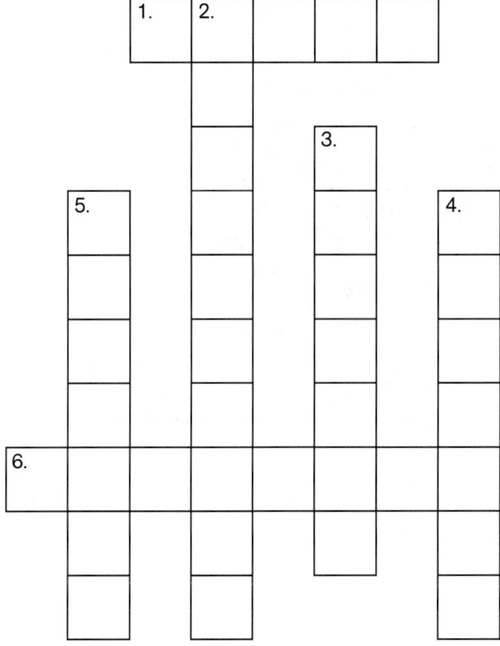

Across

1. Together searching for this.
6. Science and ...

Down

2. God revealing himself.
3. Called by the Vatican.
4. Teaches us how to go to Heaven.
5. Teaches us how the heavens move.

As a class we will take time to pray and worship together.

Light a candle ...
Listen to some music ...

To Think and Pray

As a person I will bring myself closer to God through prayer and worship.

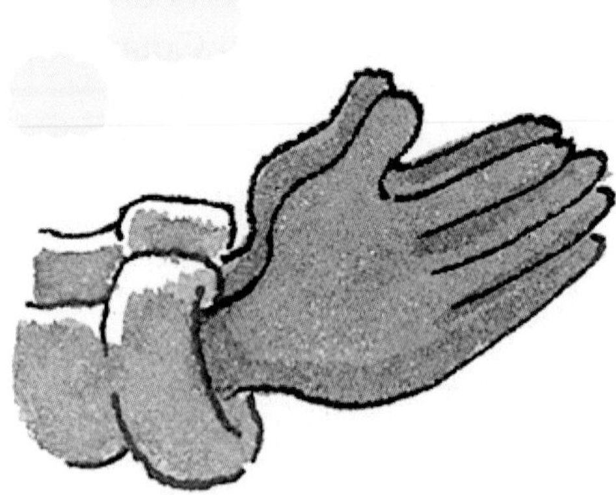

'In your presence'

- I sit and wait. Waiting is patience and trust, love and wonder. I join others, your community, your 'body'.
- I pray and lift my thoughts to Heaven. I have made the bond, made religion.
- I worship and say thanks to you for everything!
- I pray and worship.

'We love this place, O God, this Holy Ground where we are fed and you are found.'

(from the hymn, 'The Holy Ground')

Let us pray ...

- That our prayers will be sincere and from the heart. **Amen**.
- That we never lose sense of the mystery of life or God. **Amen**.
- That with God's help we will see His work in our world. **Amen**.
- That we will take time to be with God in worship and prayer. **Amen**.

Morality – 'Knowing and doing what is right'

- What is Morality?
- Moral Decisions
- My Values
- Sources of our Morality
- Codes of Practice of Morality
- Tradition and Authority
- Stages of Moral Development
- Conscience and Morality
- Religious Morality
- A Christian Moral View
- Morality and Law
- To Think and Pray

WHAT IS MORALITY?

TO KNOW

Immoral = something non-moral. Very wrong!
Amoral = having no moral principles. Morality isn't of concern to an amoral person!

Knowing what is right – 'Morality'!

TO KNOW

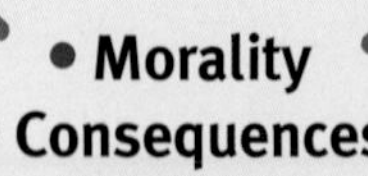

- Morality
- Consequences
- Influence
- Choice

Stop and think for a moment about your daily routine. During the day you make lots of decisions and choices!

Clothes to wear? Hairstyle? How much to bring? What to eat? What to say? etc ...

These choices and decisions seem insignificant: we make them in a moment's thought!

There are, however, decisions and choices we make in relation to people and to the world around us. These are

Moral Decisions!

Morality is a set of beliefs that offers guidance about the rightness or wrongness of human actions.

In our daily routines our morality comes into action when we have to decide the **right and good thing to do** in any given situation!

Morality is:

- Knowing right from wrong!

- Knowing what is good and what is bad!
- Doing right rather than wrong!

Every person around the world is moral: they make daily judgments about the right and good thing to do!

FOR EXAMPLE

- I choose to be honest.

- I choose to pay the correct fare on the bus.

- I choose not to buy counterfeit DVDs.

- I choose to help a blind person across the road.

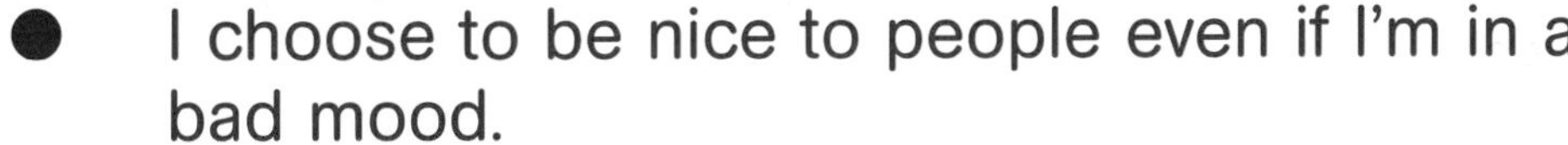

- I choose to be nice to people even if I'm in a bad mood.

- I choose to say sorry when I am wrong.

- I choose to stand up for the needy in my community.
- I choose to assist the Gardaí in their keeping of the peace.

Q1. Name some of the decisions you make everyday.
Q2. What is 'Morality'?
Q3. What are Moral Decisions?
Q4. Give examples of Moral Decisions.
Q5. What judgments do people have to make?

Fill in the blanks:

In my ______ routine I make ______ like: what ______ to wear, how to style my ______. How much ______ to bring with me. What to ______ to people. There are ______ choices I make in relation to the ______ and the ______ around me. These are ______ decisions. Morality is a ______ of ______ which offer ______ about the rightness or ______ of human actions.

True / False?

- Everyday we make decisions. **T / F**
- Choices in relation to people and the world are moral. **T / F**
- Morality is a book of rules. **T / F**
- Morality is a set of beliefs. **T / F**
- Moral beliefs offer guidance on right and wrong. **T / F**
- 'I choose to be honest' is a Moral choice. **T / F**
- 'I choose to stay in bed' is a Moral choice. **T / F**

More questions to do ...

A. Name some Moral Decisions you have made recently.
B. Have you made some right Moral Decisions or some wrong ones?
C. Explain the difference between Moral Decisions and normal daily decisions and choices.
D. How does your Morality tell you what is right and what is wrong?

Moral Decisions

These are just some of the important Moral Decisions we have to make, but of course there are very many more.

The Moral Decisions we make affect us!

They also affect the people and the world around us.

Therefore, as humans, we are living in a community and interacting with people on a daily basis.

Morality is about how we should behave towards one another.

All the choices you make, all the **Moral Decisions**, have **consequences** for your friends, family, neighbourhood and world.

Consequences are the events that happen because of a decision you have made. These can be positive consequences or negative consequences.

EXAMINE THESE

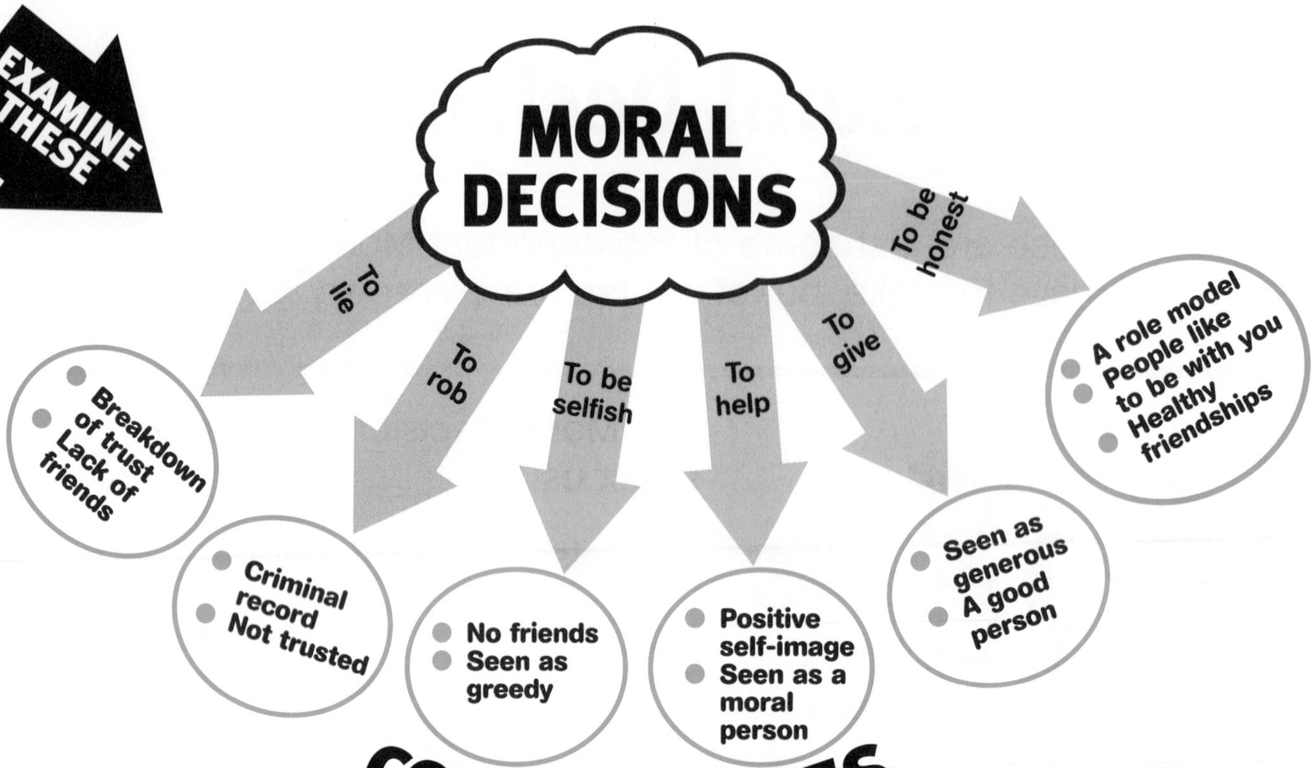

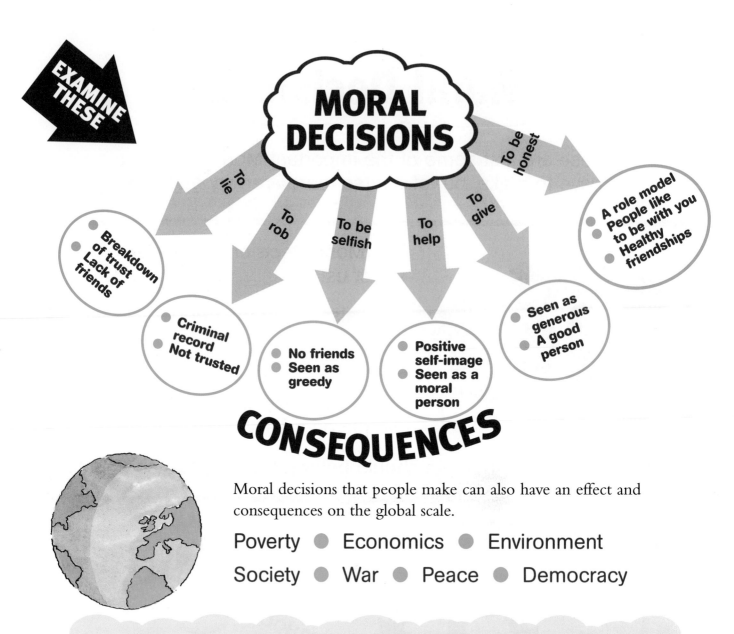

MORAL DECISIONS

- To lie
  - Breakdown of trust
  - Lack of friends
- To rob
  - Criminal record
  - Not trusted
- To be selfish
  - No friends
  - Seen as greedy
- To help
  - Positive self-image
  - Seen as a moral person
- To give
  - Seen as generous
  - A good person
- To be honest
  - A role model
  - People like to be with you
  - Healthy friendships

CONSEQUENCES

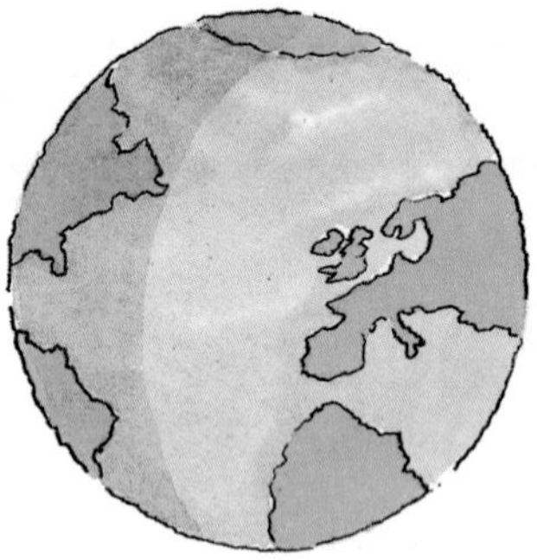

Moral decisions that people make can also have an effect and consequences on the global scale.

Poverty ● Economics ● Environment

Society ● War ● Peace ● Democracy

People in positions of power and governments have to examine constantly whether they are making the right Moral Decisions.

When faced with a Moral Decision:

The right choice strengthens and increases positive relationships.

The wrong choice breaks down relationships and has negative consequences.

Therefore we can say … 

There are • **Interpersonal Relationships.**

• **Communal Relationships.**

• **Global Relationships.**

All the Moral Decisions that are made and their consequences affect these three areas of people's lives.

We don't exist on our own in the world, everything we do and say has an effect on everything and everybody around us.
And the opposite of this is also true.

People around us, our society, the world have influences on us.

Complete these sentences

- Moral Decisions we make …
- They also affect the …
- As humans we are living …
- Morality is about how we …
- What I do affects my …
- All Moral Decisions have …
- Consequences are the events that …

Unscramble the tiles to reveal a message

AL	T T	DEC	US	ARO	AF	ISI	LD
ONS	FEC	UND	MOR	WOR	HE		

ONS	NCE	O O	DEC	UR	S T	RE	ARE
NSE	ISI	QUE	THE	CO			

Complete this Consequences Chart

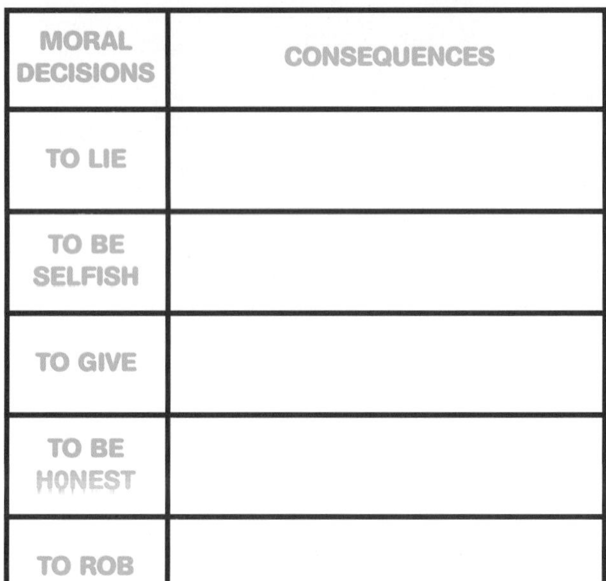

MORAL DECISIONS	CONSEQUENCES
TO LIE	
TO BE SELFISH	
TO GIVE	
TO BE HONEST	
TO ROB	

Qqs

Q1. Who and what do our Moral Decisions affect?

Q2. What areas of life do our decisions affect?

Q3. What are consequences?

Q4. What are the consequences of lying?

Q5. What are the consequences of being honest?

Q6. What are the consequences on a global scale?

Q7. What happens when we make the right decisions?

Q8. Name the three types of human relationship.

A. Consequences on a global scale affect which areas?

B. Can you name some consequences of your choices and decisions?

C. How do your choices affect people around you?

D. Name some interpersonal, communal and global relationships.

Our **VALUES**, in particular, are influenced by outside sources.

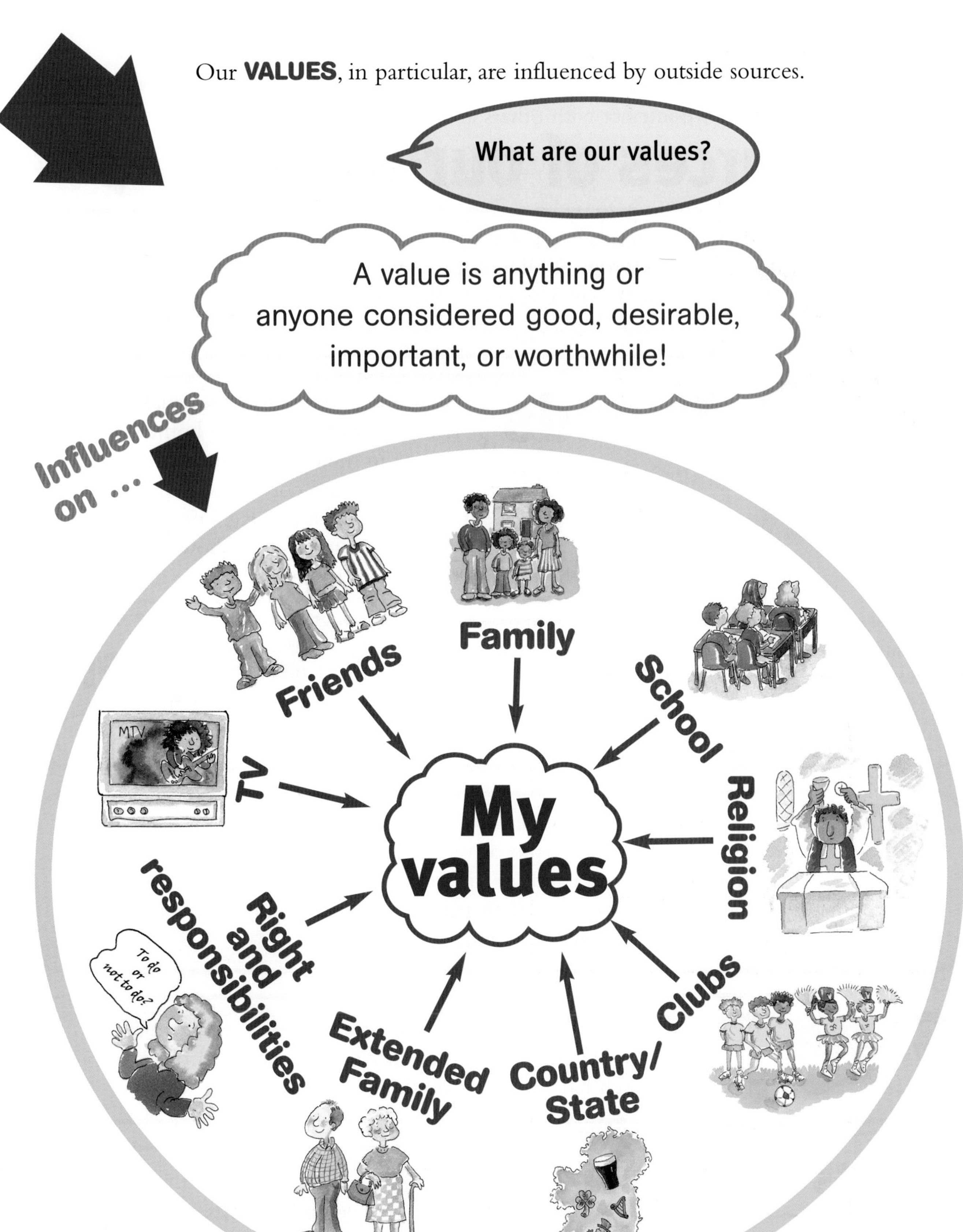

These influences, on our **VALUES** (all that we see is good and worthwhile) ultimately affect our **MORALITY** (how we interact with others and the world) and are the

Sources of our Morality

Family

At home, it is parents who first pass on the message of right and wrong. Children learn about sharing, playing, manners, honesty, etc. The family and home play a vital role in establishing a person's moral outlook.

Friends

As young people grow they make friends outside the family home – in school, in their areas. When this happens they come into contact with people who may have different values about things, e.g. honesty, TV programmes, what they are allowed to do. This shows the young person that there are different ways to behave and be moral.

Religion

Many young people are influenced by the religion in which they are brought up. This presents to them a moral vision that they take on board and from which they tend to act. Their school may be religious, or religious education will affect their moral vision.

TV

For young people, and indeed for everyone, television has presented us with a whole new spectrum of values. Young people watch programmes from across the world and see different values, some of which may come into conflict with their own and those of their parents. Television and the media have a strong influence on young people's moral vision.

State

The society a young person lives in also influences their moral vision. Each State has guidelines on what is considered right and wrong, which has an impact on the lives of all citizens.

Rights and Responsibilities

Across the world rights and responsibilities are laid down for all people. There is a certain way that we ought to interact with each other, based on a positive moral vision, e.g. the United Nations Declaration on Human Rights.

source is **'The Sermon on the Mount**
contained in this sermon by Jesus. In it h
spirit, gentle, mournful, thirsting for righ
those persecuted for rightiousness will receive in
understanding of the gifts of happiness, grace and love that all followers of Jesus will receive. Christian Morality is based around an understanding that to follow Jesus is to be given the gifts of **Happiness**, **Grace** and **Love**. The ultimate counsel of Jesus was to love your neighbour as yourself (Matt 7:12). The words and actions of Jesus are sources of morality for Christians.

ISLAM has a similar command, 'No one of you is a believer until he desires for his brother that which he desires for himself' (Sunnah).

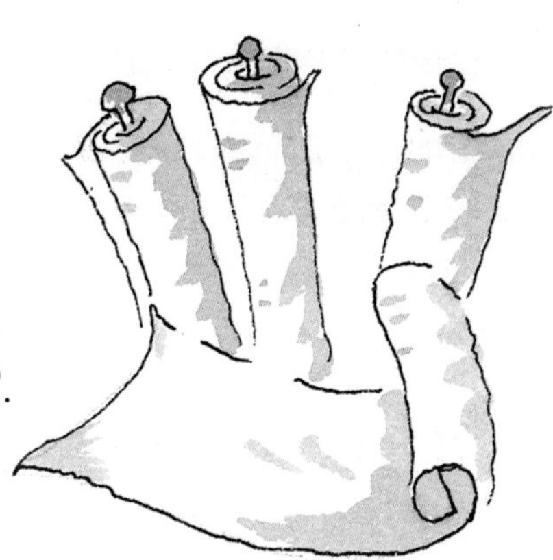

JUDAISM says 'What is harmful to you, do not to your fellow man' (Shabbah, 3rd). These are called the **'Golden Rules'**.

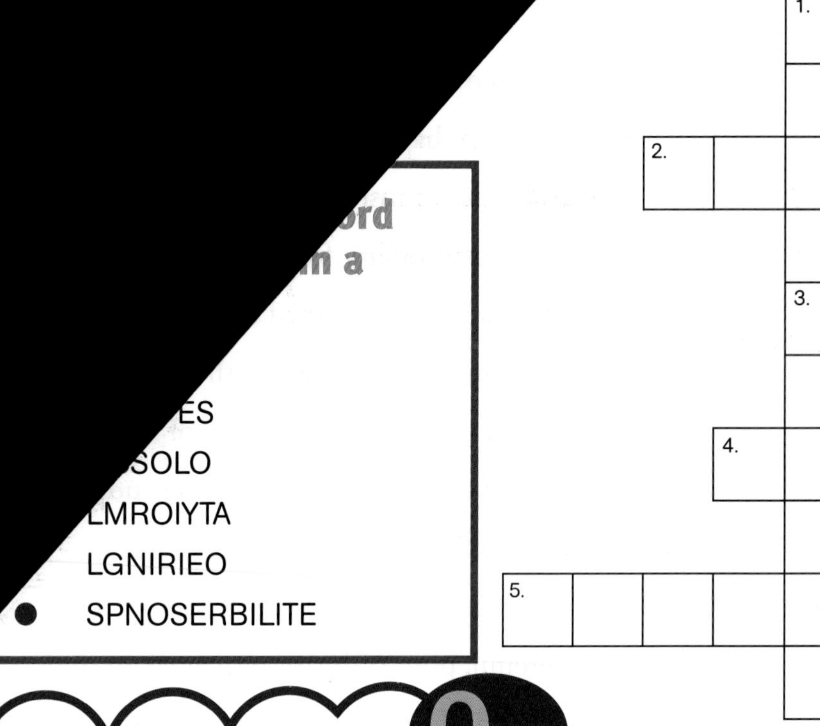

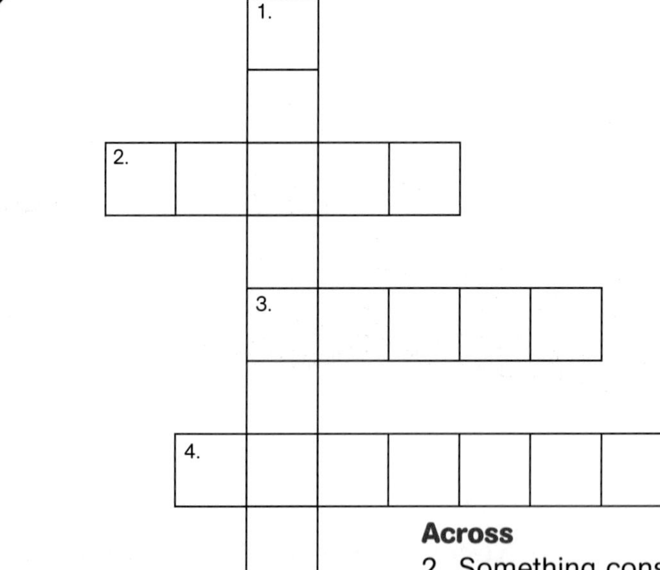

Across
2. Something considered worthwhile.
3. The number in the Beatitudes.
4. Influences my values.
5. A source of morality.

Down
1. Treat others as you want to be treated.

Qqs

Q1. What is a value?
Q2. Name four areas of influence on our values.
Q3. Name four sources of our morality.
Q4. How are families a source of morality?
Q5. How are friends a source of morality?
Q6. What guidelines do religions provide about a moral life?
Q7. What are the Beatitudes?

RESEARCH
JOURNAL IDEA

Ask members of your class and family to indicate what their values are, what is worthwhile in their lives.

More questions ...

A. Can you think of any other influences on your morality?
B. How is Jesus a source of morality?
C. In your opinion, how do your friends influence your morality?
D. In your opinion, how does TV influence your morality?
E. What do the religions' Golden Rule have in common? Explain.

Correct each sentence

- A value is anything considered good/bad, desirable/undesirable, worthwhile/worthless!
- Our values/opinions are influenced by outside/upstairs sources!
- Family/aeroplanes are sources of morality!
- Religion is a source of /ignores our morality!
- Friends influence/don't influence our morality!
- All religions/governments have the Golden/Yellow Rule!

In every society across the world there are

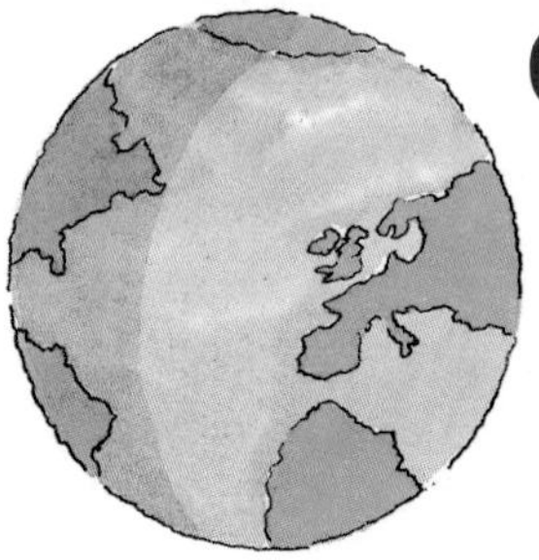

Codes of practice of morality!

Formal and Informal

TO KNOW

Code = a collection of rules and laws and guidelines.

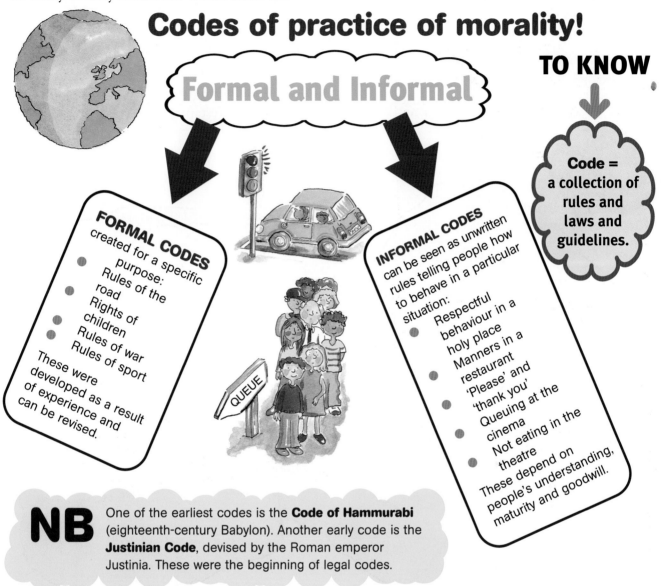

FORMAL CODES
created for a specific purpose:

- Rules of the road
- Rights of children
- Rules of war
- Rules of sport

These were developed as a result of experience and can be revised.

INFORMAL CODES
can be seen as unwritten rules telling people how to behave in a particular situation:

- Respectful behaviour in a holy place
- Manners in a restaurant
- 'Please' and 'thank you'
- Queuing at the cinema
- Not eating in the theatre

These depend on people's understanding, maturity and goodwill.

QUEUE

NB One of the earliest codes is the **Code of Hammurabi** (eighteenth-century Babylon). Another early code is the **Justinian Code**, devised by the Roman emperor Justinia. These were the beginning of legal codes.

Most societies across the world that are religious have **religious codes** of practice of morality!

Over the centuries religious people have accepted one or other of the world religions as a guide in developing their morality, their **moral vision**.

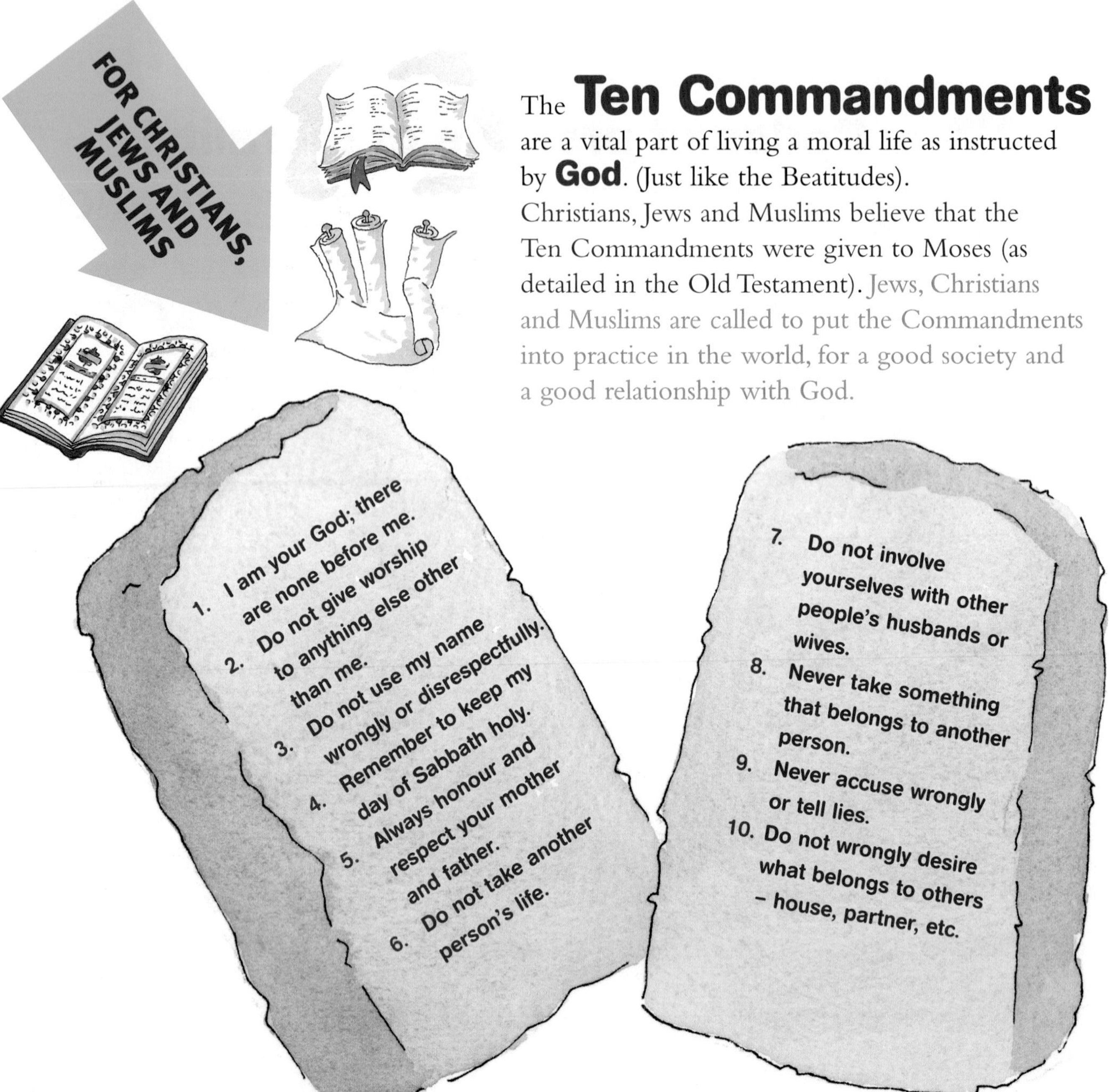

FOR CHRISTIANS, JEWS AND MUSLIMS
1. I am your God; there are none before me.
2. Do not give worship to anything else other than me.
3. Do not use my name wrongly or disrespectfully.
4. Remember to keep my day of Sabbath holy.
5. Always honour and respect your mother and father.
6. Do not take another person's life.
7. Do not involve yourselves with other people's husbands or wives.
8. Never take something that belongs to another person.
9. Never accuse wrongly or tell lies.
10. Do not wrongly desire what belongs to others – house, partner, etc.

The **Ten Commandments** are a vital part of living a moral life as instructed by **God**. (Just like the Beatitudes). Christians, Jews and Muslims believe that the Ten Commandments were given to Moses (as detailed in the Old Testament). Jews, Christians and Muslims are called to put the Commandments into practice in the world, for a good society and a good relationship with God.

- The Ten Commandments are a code with a **moral vision** ... dealing with the world and people in a good way!
- They detail how we can keep God a priority in our lives!
- They tell us to love God and love those around us!
- They tell how to live with others in our community and world!
- They describe how certain morally bad things can interfere with our relationships with each other and with God!

Find the words and use each one in a sentence about this topic.

COMMANDMENTSATXYGODANSFCODESWUDDTENSTIYMORALITYXUTRFORMALOEAFGLNFORMALGHUPRULESTUPRELIGION

Q Explain the difference between a formal and informal code.

Q Name some formal codes and explain their purpose.
Name some informal codes and explain their purpose.

Art to do

Draw a large poster detailing the Ten Commandments. Explain how they are a code for living a good life. Draw illustrations around it.

Qqs

1. What is the meaning of 'Code'?
2. Name one of the earliest Codes in existence.
3. Where does the religious moral code come from?
4. Who views the Ten Commandments as important?
5. Pick five of the Commandments and explain how they relate to our lives today.
6. What do they tell us about our relationship with God?

The Ten Commandments Fill in the blanks:

I am your ______ there are none before ______. Do not give ______ to anything else other than ______. Do not use my ______ wrongly or ______. Remember to keep my day of ______ holy. Always ______ and ______ your father and mother. Do not ______ another person's ______. Do not ______ yourself with other people's ______ and ______. Never take ______ that belongs to ______ person. Never ______ wrongly or tell ______. Do not wrongly ______ what belongs to ______ person.

All the codes of the world religions have a **moral vision**, that is 'sets of beliefs that influence people's moral development and actions'.

So far, we've seen that the Holy Scriptures of the world religions contain moral guidelines …

Moral guidelines are also given by the

Tradition and authority of the world religions

Tradition

In a religious community, faith is handed down from one generation to the next. This tradition of faith is made up of doctrines, beliefs and customs that have been preserved and continue to be respected because of their importance.

Leadership/Authority

In the world religions, the leaders are seen as having a special responsibility: they are seen as the caretakers of all that the religion sees as important. They guide the believers in proper ways of worship and prayer. They present and interpret the code of moral practice and history contained in the Holy Scriptures for the worshippers.

Wordsearch

C	0	M	M	I	T	M	E	N	T
L	T	Y	G	Q	W	L	H	U	T
Y	E	Y	U	M	S	J	Y	R	S
T	I	A	I	E	C	N	A	U	E
I	C	B	D	E	P	D	W	K	C
R	N	O	E	E	I	J	L	V	I
O	C	K	L	T	R	M	F	N	T
H	R	E	I	Y	E	S	N	C	C
T	V	O	N	X	N	A	H	M	A
U	N	R	E	C	Y	F	O	I	R
A	Q	Z	S	K	Y	P	A	S	P

COMMITMENT
AUTHORITY
LEADERSHIP
CODES
PRACTICES
GUIDELINES
TRADITION

Q1. What is a moral vision?

Q2. What do the Holy Scriptures of world religions contain?

Q3. Who else gives moral guidelines?

Q4. What does 'Tradition' mean?

Q5. Explain leadership in the world religions.

Q

Who is the leader of the Catholic Church? Who/what has responsibility for teaching in the Catholic Church?

Match up the following!

Moral guidelines	**Doctrines, beliefs, customs, belonging to a religion.**
Moral vision	**Leadership in the world religions.**
Tradition	**Given by tradition and authority.**
Authority	**Part of tradition.**
Doctrines	**Set of beliefs that influence our moral development.**
Interpret	**Part of the leadership job.**

The success of any community (religious or not) depends on good leadership. The factors which make a good leader are:

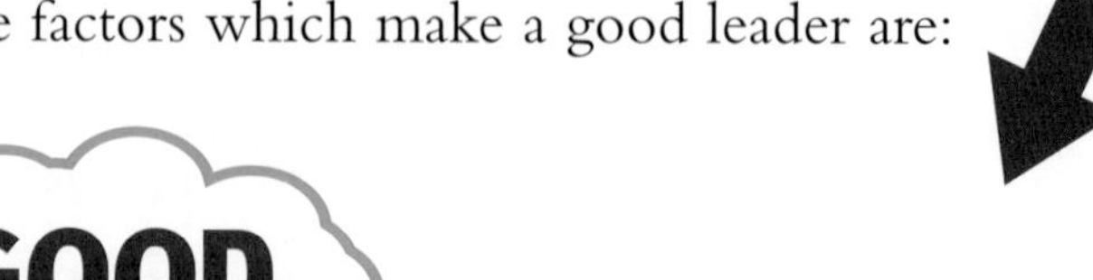

Competence
Being able to do the job well.

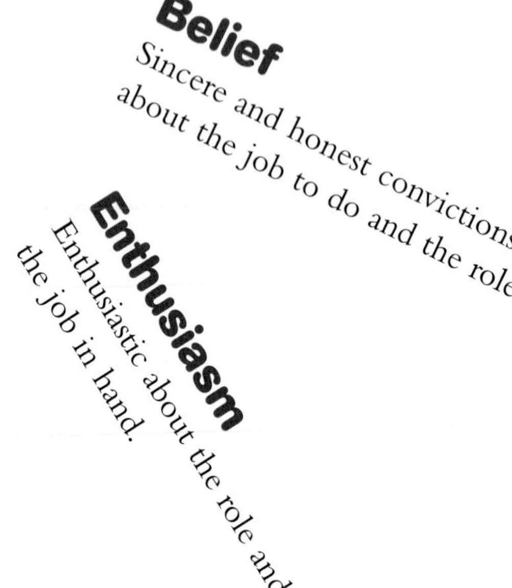

Belief
Sincere and honest convictions about the job to do and the role.

Relationship
A positive relationship between the leader and the people.

Acceptance
The people accept the authority of the leader.

Intentions
Positive desires and intentions of the leader for the group.

Enthusiasm
Enthusiastic about the role and the job in hand.

Every leader must:

- Think clearly about the job and the people they deal with.
- Make decisions for the good of the whole group.
- Have regular contact and consultations with the group.
- Examine the past, be in the present and look to the future.

Two styles of leadership are ...

1. Democracy (People's rule)

All the people agree on the rules and laws that are being created for the good of all.

2. Sole rule

One person is in charge and has all the authority. This works well when the needs of the community are centre-stage and a positive vision of the community is created. However, it doesn't work when the individual becomes power hungry, e.g. Hitler, Stalin, Mussolini. When that happens, it becomes a dictatorship.

As we said, leadership in the world's religions is there to …

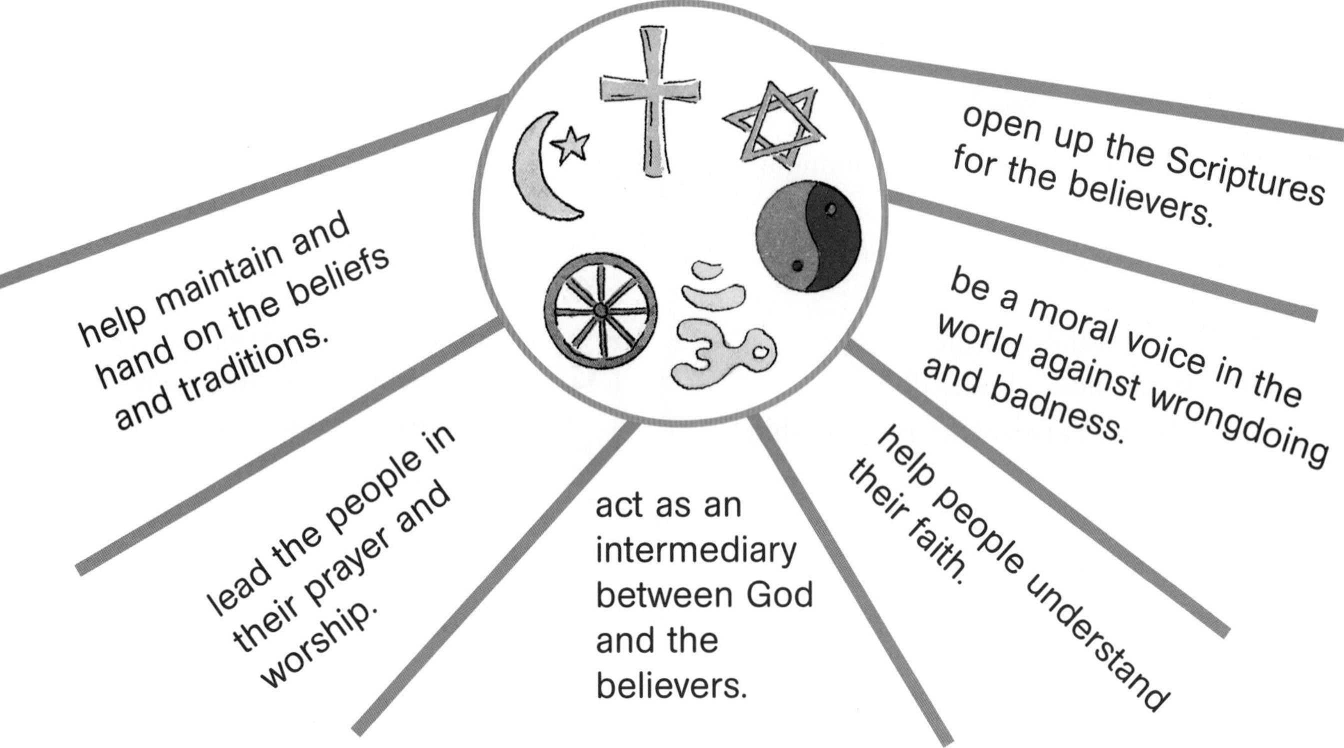
help maintain and hand on the beliefs and traditions.
lead the people in their prayer and worship.
act as an intermediary between God and the believers.
help people understand their faith.
be a moral voice in the world against wrongdoing and badness.
open up the Scriptures for the believers.

In Catholicism the ***'Magisterium'*** is the **teaching authority**. It is made up of the Pope and the Bishops who gather in the Vatican in Rome.

The *Magisterium* has the authority and responsibility to guide the Church's traditions, beliefs and **moral values**.

Over the centuries the Pope and Bishops, as well as holy men and women, have been witnesses to Gospel values in the world. They have spoken and written words of **wisdom** which have influenced the **morality** of the world's Catholics and Christians.

OVER TO YOU

Q1. What does a successful community depend on?

Q2. Give six characteristics of a good leader.

Q3. Explain three of them.

Q4. What must a leader do?

Q5. Name the two styles of leadership mentioned.

Q6. Explain the democratic style of leadership.

Q7. How important is leadership in the world religions? Explain.

Q8. What does the *Magisterium* have the authority to do?

Think and do!

A. If you were a leader, e.g. school principal, how would you make yourself a good leader? (Remember the qualities and what a leader must do.)

B. If you were An Taoiseach, how would you make yourself a good leader?

C. If you were the Pope, how would you make yourself a good leader?

D. If you were Secretary General of the United Nations, how would you make yourself a good leader?

Q What is the difference between democratic rule and sole rule?

Q How important is the '*Magisterium*', do you think? Is it necessary for Catholics, do you think?

Complete this table

Qualities of a good leader are ...	Explain each ...
Intentions	
Enthusiasm	
Relationship	
Competence	
Acceptance	
Beliefs	

It is my role to ...

help maintain and ...

lead the people in ...

act as an ...

help people under ...

be a moral voice in ...

open up the ...

As we discussed earlier, an individual's faith develops over time, as he/she grows up, or else it can cease to develop. The same can be said of **Morality**.

As we grow, from the moment we are born, we develop:

- **Physically**
- **Socially**
- **Psychologically**
- **Intellectually**

To grow in morality is to develop the ability to distinguish between **right and wrong**/**good and evil**.

STAGES OF MORAL DEVELOPMENT

Infant

Small child

Pre-teens

Teenager/ young adult

Mature adult

Small child

Children seek approval and avoid disapproval. They seek praise and do the 'right thing' for a reward. They may not necessarily know the reasons why something is right or wrong. Roles are black and white, and always from an external source.

Infant

Infants and children look to their parents for protection, guidance, love and approval. Infants are self-centred and their behaviour is determined by immediate gratification. They understand approval and disapproval.

Pre-teens

Beginning to see the point of rules. The use of reason begins. Beginning to see rules as good for them personally and to assimilate them into society. They understand choices as right or wrong.

Teenager/young adult

Development of the idea of consequences. The teenager continues to use reason to decide the right or wrong thing to do. Friends and peers influence the decision-making process and sometimes they will rebel against authority figures.

Maturity

Reaches a level of moral maturity in adulthood. Choices made are based on personal convictions. Many ideas and choices have to be mulled over and debated before a decision is made. Behaviour is dictated by a conviction that it is the right thing to do. Rights and responsibilities come into play and influence decisions. Promotion of goodness is seen as important. Reflection on choices is difficult in certain situations.

Infant	Small child	Pre-teen	Teenager/ Young adult

Put these descriptions into the correct box

- The stage of moral development
- Self-centred
- Development of idea of consequences
- Look to parents for protection
- Friends and peers influence decisions
- The use of reason
- Beginning to see the point of rules
- May not know something is right or wrong
- Behaviour determined by immediate gratification
- Rebel against authority figures
- Rules are black and white
- Avoid disapproval

Qqs

Q1. From the moment we are born what do we develop?
Q2. What does it mean 'to grow in morality'?
Q3. What are the stages of moral development?
Q4. How important are parents for infants?
Q5. When does the use of reason begin?
Q6. When do personal convictions come into play?

Q What are the characteristics of a morally mature person?

Q How important are personal convictions, rights and responsibilities and mulling over for a morally mature person when making a decision?

As in any developmental process, some people get stuck. In moral development there are people who stay at a **morally immature level**.

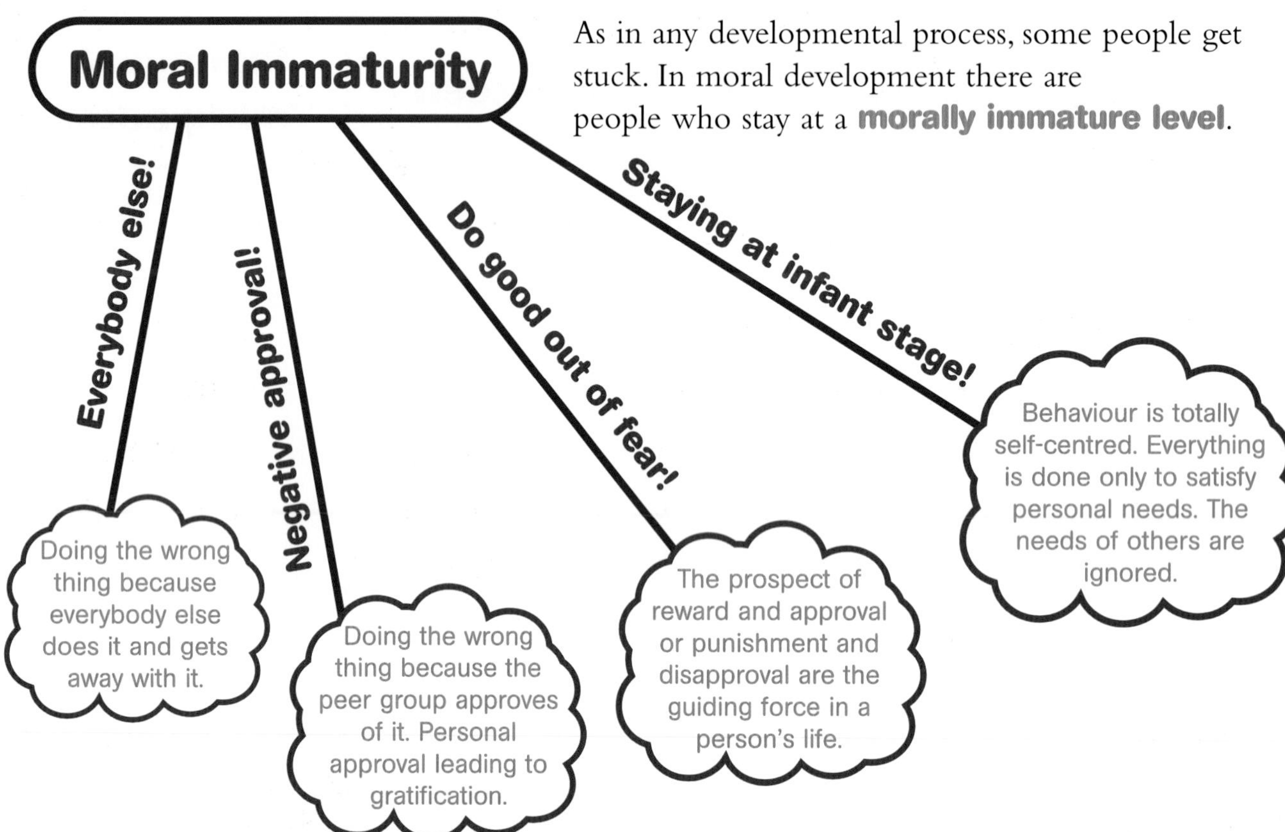

Moral Immaturity
Everybody else!
Doing the wrong thing because everybody else does it and gets away with it.
Negative approval!
Doing the wrong thing because the peer group approves of it. Personal approval leading to gratification.
Do good out of fear!
The prospect of reward and approval or punishment and disapproval are the guiding force in a person's life.
Staying at infant stage!
Behaviour is totally self-centred. Everything is done only to satisfy personal needs. The needs of others are ignored.

Conscience and morality!

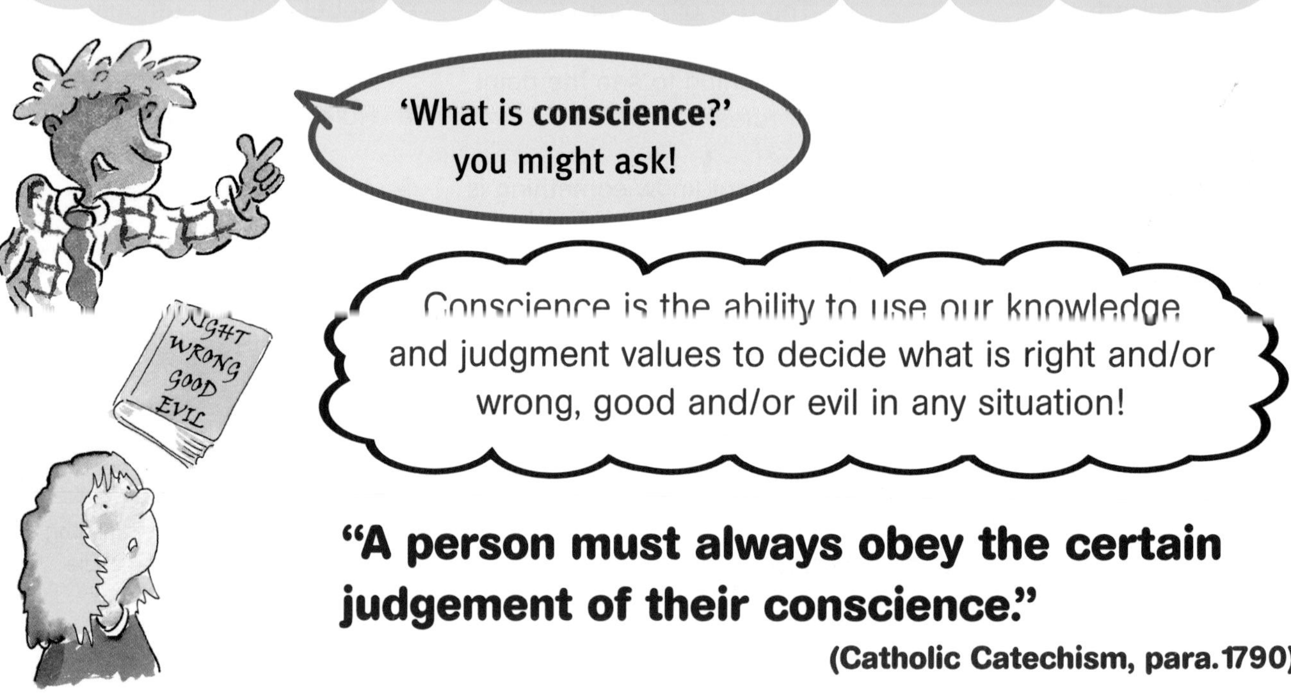

Conscience is the ability to use our knowledge and judgment values to decide what is right and/or wrong, good and/or evil in any situation!

"A person must always obey the certain judgement of their conscience."

(Catholic Catechism, para. 1790)

Your conscience is that little voice in your head, telling you what is right and what is wrong.

Many of the world's religions place great emphasis on the role of our conscience in our lives. They also point to the importance of family and parents in helping the young person to develop a healthy and informed conscience. The formation of conscience takes place as moral growth occurs.

Doing good deeds!

Reading up on moral issues!

Praying!

...can help a person develop their conscience!

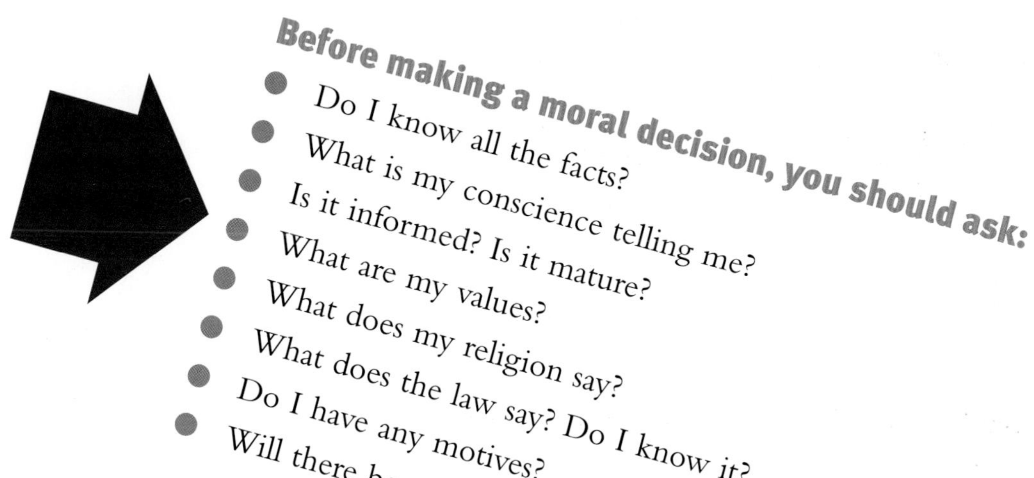

Before making a moral decision, you should ask:
Do I know all the facts?
What is my conscience telling me?
Is it informed? Is it mature?
What are my values?
What does my religion say?
What does the law say? Do I know it?
Do I have any motives?
Will there be any consequences to my decision?

'Within our conscience God calls us to love and do what is good and avoid evil.
In our conscience, God's voice echoes.' (The Church in the Modern World Vatican II)

Let's try some of these!

Explain each of these

- Moral immaturity ____________
- Everybody else ____________
- Negative approval ____________
- Do good out of fear ____________
- At infant stage ____________

Qqs

Q1. Name four ways a person can be morally immature.

Q2. What does 'moral immaturity' mean?

Q3. What is conscience?

Q4. What does the **Catholic Catechism** say about conscience?

Q5. How important is family when it comes to developing a healthy conscience?

Q6. Name four things you should do before making a moral decision.

1. What does 'informed conscience' mean?
2. How do you inform your conscience?
3. Why is praying important, do you think?

Describe how you would make these decisions ...

- Voting for a new government.
- Allowing abortion in Ireland.
- Walking out without paying.
- Going to get drunk.
- Going to take drugs.
- Giving the Gardaí information about a crime.
- Getting revenge.

Find and then use each word in a sentence appropriate to this section:

KNOWLEDGEATHFACTS MORALITYUTSCONSCIENCEUSATINFORMEDRPTINFORMEDSAPRAYUTSJUDGEMENTSW

RELIGIOUS MORALITY

Is about doing what is right and good in God's eyes so that our relationships grow and the 'Kingdom of God' is made real.

It is only right that the world religions should have a say about morality. All religions emphasise the fact that God calls us to do good to each other and the world **(Golden Rule)**, as do the Beatitudes and the 10 Commandments.

It is based around

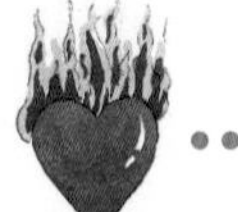

... love of God!

... love of neighbour!

Searching for Truth

Giving to those who are needy

All life is sacred

Social and sexual morality

Stewardship of the Earth

Sin and forgiveness

... are some of the areas that religious morality deals with across the world.

A Christian Moral View

A **moral view** for a Christian person is seeing the world through the eyes of Christ.

A **moral life** is living a life according to Gospel values and Jesus' example.

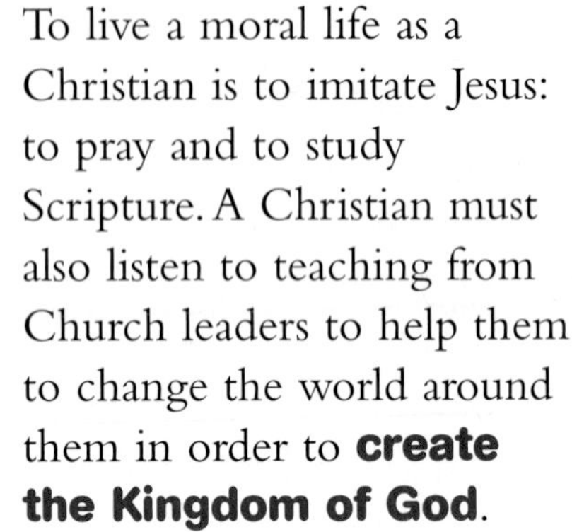

To live a moral life as a Christian is to imitate Jesus: to pray and to study Scripture. A Christian must also listen to teaching from Church leaders to help them to change the world around them in order to **create the Kingdom of God**.

Jesus taught …

Love your enemies

Care for the poor

Welcome the stranger

Justice for all

Being moral means doing good in the way that Jesus did!

NB Christianity teaches that to live a life according to these **virtues** is to live a life for Christ.

CARDINAL VIRTUES

Prudence (common sense)

Temperance (control desires)

Justice (do the right thing)

Fortitude (courage in the face of evil)

THEOLOGICAL VIRTUES

Faith (believe in God)

Hope (trust in Jesus' promises)

Love (love as God loves)

SEVEN DEADLY SINS

Pride (full of our own importance)

Greed (looking for more)

Envy (jealous of others)

Anger (built-up resentment and hurts)

Lust (sexual pleasure/desires)

Gluttony (excessive eating and drinking)

Sloth (laziness)

Through prayer,  action  and the Holy Spirit 
Christians answer the call of Jesus to …

'Love one another as I have loved you.'

(John 13:31)

The Catholic Church, as with all Christian Churches, offers moral vision to all believers. The Church, founded by Christ and guided by the Holy Spirit, sees that it has a moral obligation to tackle real life in the twenty-first century.

Life/Environment/Reconciliation

Abortion

All people are made in the image of God.

'You shall not kill the unborn by abortion nor cause the newborn child to perish.' (Didache)

Life begins at the moment of conception. The tiny life has rights and is a person. Abortion is to deny the 'right to life'. Human life is sacred – a gift from God.

Stewardship

All Catholics are called to be stewards of the Earth. The Book of Genesis says that the Earth was given into the care of humanity. Up to recently, humans destroyed many natural, beautiful areas of the world. Today we are coming to the realisation that we should care for the Earth. The Catholic Church promotes this and emphasises the world and humans as God's creation (Genesis 1:28)

Sin and Reconciliation

Sin is doing wrong and going against Christian values. Sin affects a person's relationship with others and with God.
To sin is to reject God's will for the world, as revealed through Jesus.
But for Christians there is a way to return to God: **Reconciliation**. Reconciliation is a Sacrament of the Catholic Church. Through it we feel sincerely sorry for our sins, take a penance and receive God's forgiveness and love. We promise not to sin again.

The principles of Christian morality are based on all that Jesus said and did. From the Gospels Christian morality, a moral vision begins and through Christian morality it is lived.

'Morality in Action'. In Christianity there are important areas of Morality in Action.

Dignity of the Human Person

Human life is sacred and this is the basis of all Christian social thinking. The dignity of the human person is the starting point for a Moral vision for society. The person is made in the image of God. The person is the clearest reflection of God among us. From this Moral Vision Christianity is against Abortion and Euthanasia.

'Human life begins at conception' Gaudiem et specs

Justice for all people

Justice is treating all people fairly. Christianity bases its Justice Morality on the words and actions of Jesus, especially the idea that we love each other. Christianity believes that all people should be treated justly because they are created in God's image. The Christian view of justice is that all people have a God-given dignity that must be respected. Human rights are very much part of the Christian view of justice. Christians have a duty to act justly and help others.

Stewardship

As mentioned earlier Christianity sees Stewardship as a part of the Moral Actions of the Church. We are to look after the Earth for God because it was given to us ('look after it and guard it' Genesis 2:15).

Complete these sentences

Jesus taught

Love ______________________

Care ______________________

Justice ______________________

Compassion ______________________

Art to do!

When you have completed the sentences above, draw a big picture of these teachings of Jesus and include your sentences with each image.

Match the word and explanations:

Temperance	Love as God loves
Fortitude	Looking for more
Love	Sexual pleasure/desires
Faith	Controlling desires
Greed	Laziness
Lust	Trust in Jesus' promises
Sloth	Belief in God
Hope	Courage in the face of evil
Prudence	Common Sense

Being Moral means doing good in the way that Jesus did!

COPY AND COLOUR

Qqs

Q1. What is a moral view for a Christian?
Q2. What is a moral life for a Christian?
Q3. What does it mean to live a moral life as a Christian?
Q4. What does 'Being moral' mean?
Q5. What are the Cardinal Virtues?
Q6. What are the Theological Virtues?
Q7. How do they help a person live a life for Christ?
Q8. Why is life sacred?

More Questions ...

A. How do prayer, action and the Holy Spirit help us to lead a moral life?
B. What is the 'call of Jesus'? What does it mean?
C. Name some moral issues that the Catholic Church teaches.
D. Why is the Catholic Church against abortion?
E. What does the Church say about 'stewardship'?
F. Explain 'Sin and Reconciliation' in your words.
G. Explain Christian justice.

Members of the world religions are called upon to reflect on the moral guidelines that the religion sets down and to have an informed conscience about moral religious issues.

Moral Issues

Euthanasia

is intentionally bringing about the death of a person who is suffering from a terminal illness.

Like Christianity, Islam is opposed to Euthanasia, for all life comes from God.

'To Allah belongs the Kingdom of the Heavens and the earth. He created what he pleases.' (Sunnah 4:29)

'Destroy not yourselves. Surely Allah is ever merciful to you.' (Sunnah 4:29)

In Islam, those who are suffering are to ask for help ...

'O ye who believe, seek help with patient perseverance and prayer, surely Allah is with those who patiently persevere.' (Sunnah 2:15)

Muslims are called to follow the words of Allah in the Koran in their lives, especially in their morality.

Try these

Q1. What do religions emphasise about morality?
Q2. What is religious morality about?
Q3. Religious morality is based around …?
Q4. What areas does religious morality concern?
Q5. Name a moral issue that religions tackle.

Art to do!

Draw a poster and on it put all the areas with which religious morality is concerned.

More questions …

A. Why do religions have a great interest in morality?

B. Through religious morality, how does a relationship with God grow?

C. Why does Islam oppose euthanasia?

D. Why might someone want euthanasia?

E. What does Islam say about suffering?

F. In your view, how important is it for religions to have a say about moral issues?

Fill in the blanks:

It is only right that the world ______ should have a say about ______. All ______ emphasise the _____ that God calls us to do ______ to each other and the ______, to see ______ and ______ it is this ______. Religions ______ is about doing what is ______ and good in ______ eyes so that our ______ grow and the ______ of God is made ______.

True / False?

- Religious morality is concerned with life. **T / F**
- Religious morality is based on love of neighbour. **T / F**
- All religions emphasise that God calls us to ignore people. **T / F**
- Euthanasia is not a moral issue. **T / F**
- Islam is opposed to euthanasia. **T / F**
- Euthanasia is about helping people live. **T / F**

TO KNOW

There are two types of euthanasia:

Voluntary euthanasia = when the person concerned asks someone else to help them die.

Involuntary euthanasia = when the person concerned is no longer able to make the decision for themselves and his or her family or medical experts take the decision on their behalf.

Like Christianity, Judaism teaches that all life comes from God:

> 'Then God said, "Let us make man in our image, in our likeness, and let them rule over the fish of the sea and the birds of the air, over the livestock, over all the earth, and over all the creatures that move along the ground."
>
> So God created man in his own image, in the image of God he created him; male and female he created them. God blessed them and said to them, "Be fruitful and increase in number; fill the earth and subdue it. Rule over the fish of the sea and the birds of the air and over every living creature that moves on the ground."'
>
> **Genesis 1:26-28**

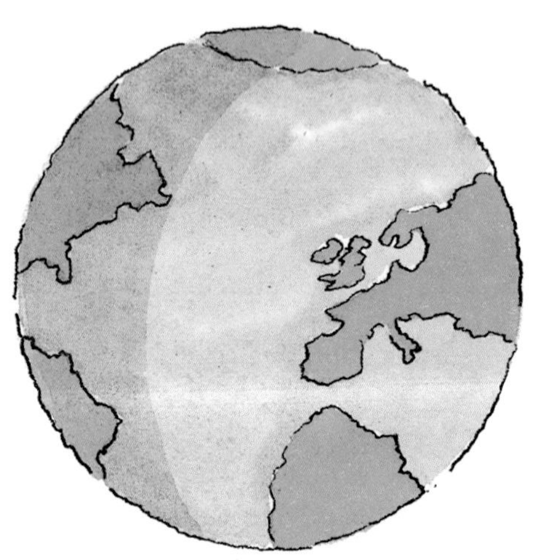

Jews believe that since God created all life, only God is permitted to decide when a person should die. Euthanasia and suicide are therefore against the teachings of the Jewish Holy Scripture.

All Jews are called to live a life according to the moral values set down in the Holy Scripture and in their religious tradition.

Another religious moral issue that the world religions must deal with is **ABORTION**.

This is the artificial ending of the life of an embryo or foetus in the womb.

In **ISLAM** it is opposed because the Koran says:

'Kill not your offspring for fear of poverty, it is we who provide for them and for you. Surely killing them is a great sin.' (Sunnah 17:32)

NB
Some Muslim groups believe that during the first four months of pregnancy the woman has more rights than the foetus.

In **Judaism** abortion is not allowed because it interferes with a potential life. However, it may be permitted where the life of the mother is at risk.

All world religions emphasise **stewardship of the Earth**.

This means respecting and caring for this world.

Islam focuses on the belief that Allah created all things and that we should respect and take care of the creation.

For Jews, the Old Testament tells about the creation of the world from God's love and infinite knowledge. We are called to be stewards of His creation.

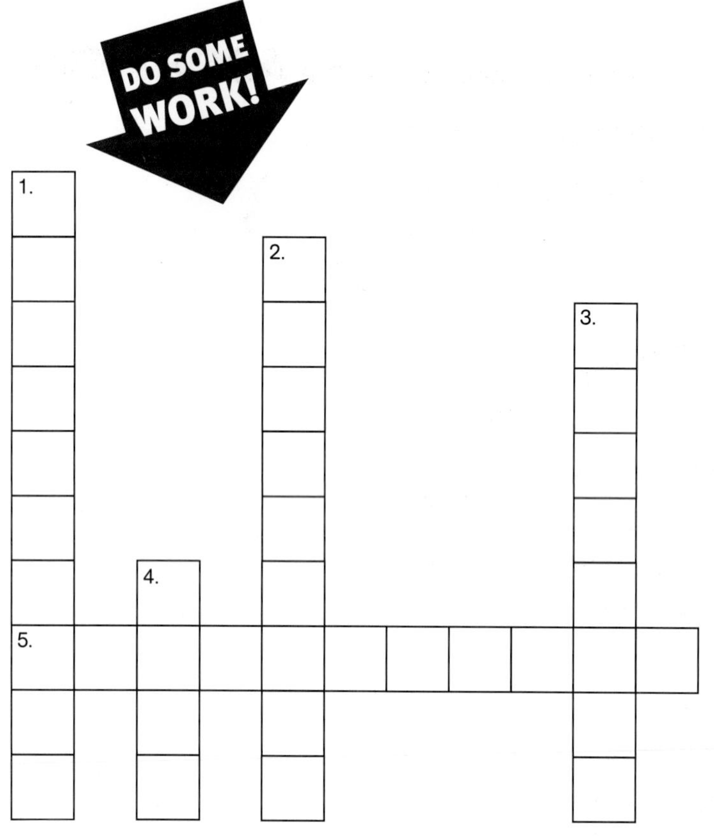

Use each word in a sentence appropriate to this section:

ABORTIONSTEWARDSHIPSTAFKORANUTEUTHANASIAPXUJUDAISMPOOUVOLUNTARYSNNISLAMREE

Name some other moral issues that the world religions have a view about.

Across

5. To look after the Earth.

Down

1. Intentionally ending a life of a sick person.
2. One type of euthanasia.
3. Another religious moral issue.
4. They believe all life comes from God.

Q1. What does Judaism teach about euthanasia?

Q2. What is written in the Old Testament?

Q3. Name the two types of euthanasia.

Q4. What does 'voluntary euthanasia' mean?

Q5. Name another moral issue that religious are concerned with.

Q6. Explain 'abortion'.

Q7. What does the Koran say about abortion?

Q8. Explain 'stewardship of the Earth'.

Complete these sentences

- Judaism teaches that all life …
- Jews believe that only God is permitted …
- Two types of euthanasia are …
- All Jews are called to live a life …
- Abortion is …
- Islam says, 'Kill not your …
- In Judaism abortion is not allowed because …
- Stewardship of the Earth is …
- The Old Testament tells us about the …

More questions

A. Why do religions have a view about abortion?

B. How important is the Old Testament extract in relation to euthanasia and abortion?

C. In your view, what is 'stewardship of the Earth'?

D. How are you a 'steward of the Earth'?

E. How can you play your part in 'stewardship of the Earth'?

F. In your moral view, is abortion right or wrong? Debate and explain.

As we are all moral people we should take a look at how our morality, religious morality and the laws of the land interact.

Human rights are the rights of all people across the world. In 1998 the **United Nations** issued **The Declaration of Human Rights**. All countries are to obey these rules.

For some people the State has the final say in what is right or wrong.

'State' is the word used to describe a country that has a government.

The government makes laws that maintain the peace and order of the State for all people.

The law is the set of rules laid out by State authorities and which people must obey.

The Irish Constitution details all the laws of the Irish State.

For Christians there is a higher authority that tells us what is right and wrong. That **higher authority** is **God**.

It is important to distinguish between **'Law' and 'Morality'** – some laws may not always be morally right, **e.g. military conscription, apartheid**.

Most people obey the laws of their State. However, there are times when the law and **personal morality** can come into conflict.

People have a personal, mature morality that goes deeper than the laws of the State. Choices made are made from values and religious convictions, which shape a person's actions, sometimes irrespective of the law of the State.

If a person believes that a law is immoral, they can walk away from it, if they wish.

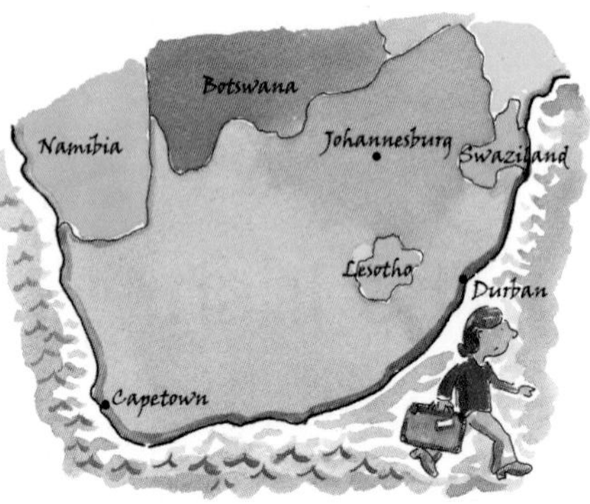

Others may have no choice but to deal with it and thereby come into conflict with the State, **e.g. apartheid in South Africa**.

Christians believe that people should respect and obey the laws of the land. But they should also ask if the law is morally right. If it is not, according to their religious beliefs, then morality must prevail and the person must obey the law of God.

'God's law continues to bind, no matter what the State law says.'

(CCC 1951)

Three theories about the relationship between law and religious morality

1. Religious fundamentalism

This refers to the notion that the laws of the State are completely based on religious laws and morality. Usually there is a complete intolerance of any other view or opinion.

2. Pluralism

This means that all groups within the State have a right to carry out their religious and cultural practices. Separation of Church and State is central to pluralism, therefore religious laws are separate from the law of the land.

3. Libertarianism

This means that neither religion nor government should place restrictions on how people act and think. The rights of the individual are central to this.

As a religious person you have a relationship with God. As a citizen you have obligations to your country. Getting the balance right leads to an informed conscience and a mature morality. A mature morality leads to a better relationship with God and with the world around you.

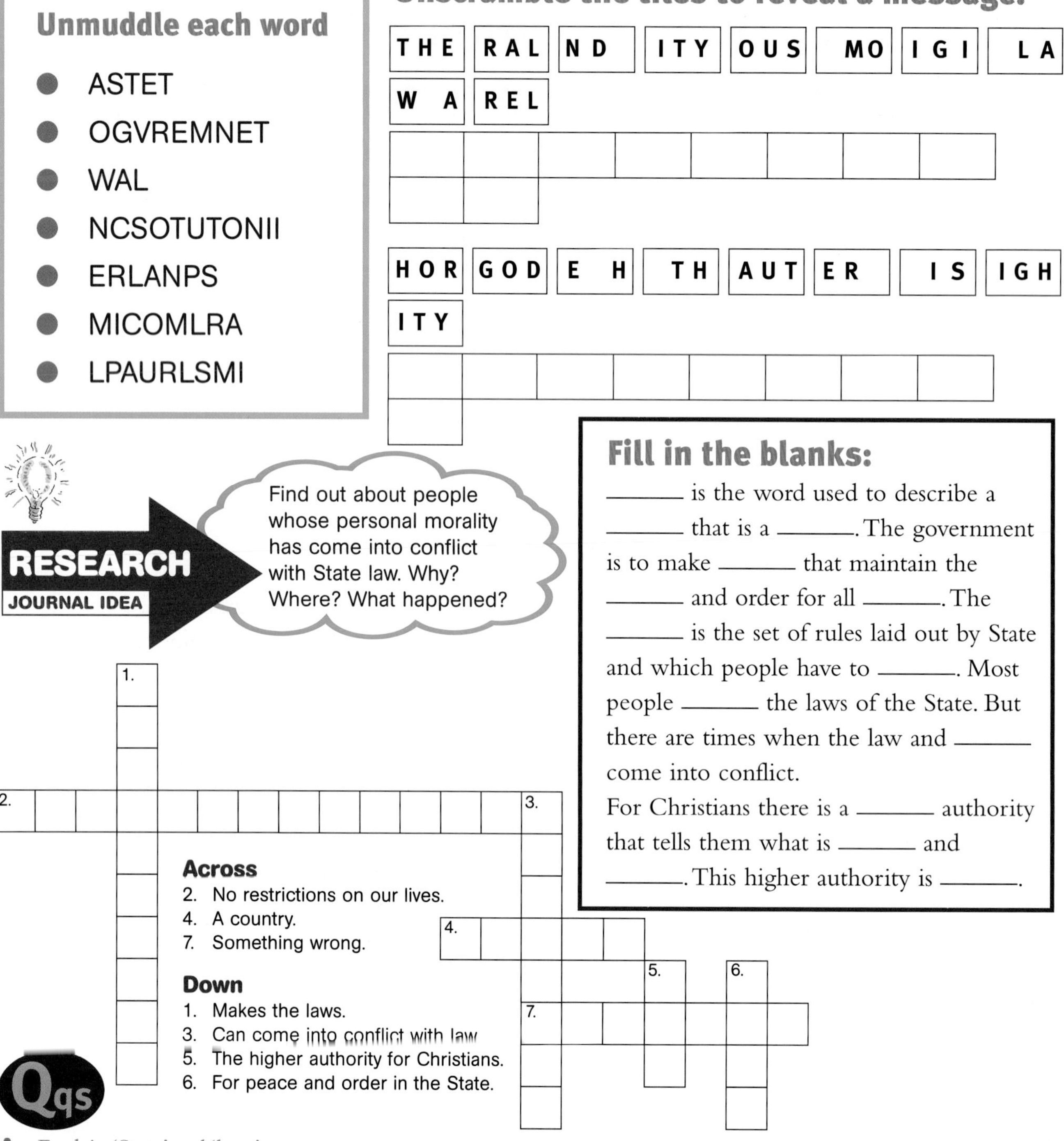

Unmuddle each word
ASTET
OGVREMNET
WAL
NCSOTUTONII
ERLANPS
MICOMLRA
LPAURLSMI
Unscramble the tiles to reveal a message:
THE
RAL
ND
ITY
OUS
MO
IGI
LA
W A
REL
HOR
GOD
E H
TH
AUT
ER
IS
IGH
ITY
Fill in the blanks:
______ is the word used to describe a ______ that is a ______. The government is to make ______ that maintain the ______ and order for all ______. The ______ is the set of rules laid out by State and which people have to ______. Most people ______ the laws of the State. But there are times when the law and ______ come into conflict.
For Christians there is a ______ authority that tells them what is ______ and ______. This higher authority is ______.
RESEARCH
JOURNAL IDEA
Find out about people whose personal morality has come into conflict with State law. Why? Where? What happened?
1.
2.
3.
4.
5.
6.
7.
Across
2. No restrictions on our lives.
4. A country.
7. Something wrong.
Down
1. Makes the laws.
3. Can come into conflict with law
5. The higher authority for Christians.
6. For peace and order in the State.

Qqs

A. Explain 'State' and 'laws'.
B. Where can we read about Irish laws?
C. Who is the 'higher authority' for Christians?
D. How can you distinguish between 'law' and 'morality'?
E. When might the law and personal morality come into conflict?
F. What can a person do with an immoral State law?
G. What does the Catholic Church say about God's law and State law?
H. Name and explain the three theories about the relationship between law and religious morality.

To Think and Pray

I pray for ...

- Strength to continue my faith journey.
- Hope to see a vision of the future.
- Love to give and receive in return.
- Faith to grow in my relationship with God.
- Courage to face the challenges of this world.
- Grace to see God in the world and my neighbours.
- Peace so that all may have time for God.
- Justice so that all will stand up for what is morally right.
- **I pray for you: that you will see God!**

'Thy word is a lamp unto my feet and a light unto my path.'

Scripture reflection:
The Beatitudes (Matthew 5:1-12).

Reflect ...

I come to it at last, the time to decide. Do I help create a world that God wants? Do I look to my neighbour and reach out to help? When do I love? How have I sinned? How moral am I? Do I imitate the holy men and women of this world? Today I will try, today I will be a light to people's path. Today I will reconcile. Today I reach to the heavens and see God at my side. Today!